A Field Guide to the Classroom Library D

A Field Guide to the Classroom Library D

Lucy Calkins

and

*The Teachers College
Reading and Writing
Project Community*

HEINEMANN
Portsmouth, NH

Heinemann
A division of Reed Elsevier Inc.
361 Hanover Street
Portsmouth, NH 03801–3912
www.heinemann.com

Offices and agents throughout the world

Library of Congress Cataloging-in-Publication Data
Calkins, Lucy McCormick.
    A field guide to the classroom library / Lucy Calkins and the Teachers College Reading and Writing Project community.
        v. cm.
    Includes bibliographical references and index.
    Contents: [v. 4] Library D : grades 2–3
    ISBN 0-325-00498-6
    1. Reading (Elementary)—Handbooks, manuals, etc.   2. Children—Books and reading—Handbooks, manuals, etc.   3. Children's literature—Study and teaching (Elementary)—Handbooks, manuals, etc.   4. Classroom libraries—Handbooks, manuals, etc.   I. Teachers College Reading and Writing Project (Columbia University).   II. Title.

LB1573 .C183 2002
372.4—dc21   2002038767

Editor: Kate Montgomery
Production: Abigail M. Heim
Interior design: Catherine Hawkes, Cat & Mouse
Cover design: Jenny Jensen Greenleaf Graphic Design & Illustration
Manufacturing: Louise Richardson

Printed in the United States of America on acid-free paper

06   05   04   03   VP   4   5

This field guide is dedicated to

Kathleen Tolan

The Field Guides to the Classroom Library *project is a philanthropic effort. According to the wishes of the scores of contributors, all royalties from the sale of these field guides will be given back entirely to the project in the continued effort to put powerful, beautiful, and thoughtfully chosen literature into the hands of children.*

Contents

Acknowledgments

The entire Teachers College Reading and Writing Project community has joined together in the spirit of a barn-raising to contribute to this gigantic effort to put the best of children's literature into the hands of children.

There are hundreds of people to thank. In these pages, I will only be able to give special thanks to a few of the many who made this work possible.

First, we thank Alan and Gail Levenstein who sponsored this effort with a generous personal gift and who helped us remember and hold tight to our mission. We are grateful to Annemarie Powers who worked tirelessly, launching the entire effort in all its many dimensions. Annemarie's passionate love of good literature shines throughout this project.

Kate Montgomery, now an editor at Heinemann and a long-time friend and coauthor, joined me in writing and revising literally hundreds of the field guides. Kate's deep social consciousness, knowledge of reading, and her commitment to children are evident throughout the work. How lucky we were that she became a full-time editor at Heinemann just when this project reached there, and was, therefore, able to guide the project's final stages.

Tasha Kalista coordinated the effort, bringing grace, humor, and an attention to detail to the project. She's been our home base, helping us all stay on track. Tasha has made sure loose ends were tied up, leads pursued, inquiries conducted, and she's woven a graceful tapestry out of all the thousands of books, guides, and people.

Each library is dedicated to a brilliant, passionate educator who took that particular library and the entire effort under her wing. We are thankful to Lynn Holcomb whose deep understanding of early reading informed our work; to Mary Ann Colbert who gave generously of her wisdom of reading recovery and primary texts; to Kathleen Tolan who championed the little chapter books and made us see them with new eyes; to Gaby Layden for her expertise in the area of nonfiction reading; to Isoke Nia for passionate contributions to our upper grade libraries; and to Kathy Doyle who knows books better than anyone we know.

We thank Pam Allyn for her dedication to this effort, Laurie Pessah for working behind the scenes with me, and Beth Neville for keeping the Project on course when this undertaking threatened to swamp us.

Finally, we are grateful to Mayor Guiliani for putting these libraries into every New York City school. To Judith Rizzo, Deputy Chancellor of Instruction, Adele Schroeter, Director of Office of Research, Development and Dissemination, Peter Heaney, Executive Director of the Division of Instructional Support, and William P. Casey, Chief Executive for Instructional Innovation, we also offer our heartfelt thanks for contributing their wisdom, integrity, and precious time to making this miracle happen.

Contributors

Christina Adams
Lisa Ali Chetram
Pam Allyn
Francine Almash
Janet Angelillo
Liz Arfin
Anna Arrigo
Laura Ascenzi-Moreno
Maureen Bilewich
Melissa Biondi
Pat Bleichman
Christine Bluestein
Ellen Braunstein
Dina Bruno
Theresa Burns
Lucy Calkins
Adele Cammarata
Joanne Capozzoli
Laura Cappadona
Justin Charlebois
Linda Chen
Mary Chiarella
Danielle Cione
Erica Cohen
Mary Ann Colbert
Kerri Conlon
Denise Corichi
Danielle Corrao
Sue Dalba
Linda Darro
Mildred De Stefano
Marisa DeChiara
Erica Denman
Claudia Diamond
Renee Dinnerstein
Kathy Doyle
Lizz Errico
Rosemarie Fabbricante
Gabriel Feldberg
Holly Fisher

Sofia Forgione
Judy Friedman
Elizabeth Fuchs
Jerilyn Ganz
Allison Gentile
Linda Gerstman
Jessica Goff
Iris Goldstein-
    Jackman
Ivy Green
Cathy Grimes
David Hackenburg
Amanda Hartman
Grace Heske
Caren Hinckley
Lynn Holcomb
Michelle Hornof
Anne Illardi
Maria Interlandi
Erin Jackman
Debbie Jaffe
Helen Jurios
Kim Kaiser
Tasha Kalista
Beth Kanner
Michele Kaye
Laurie Kemme
Hue Kha
Tara Krebs
Joan Kuntz Verdino
Kathleen Kurtz
Lamson Lam
Gaby Layden
Karen Liebowitz
Adele Long
Cynthia Lopez
Natalie Louis
Eileen Lynch
Theresa Maldarelli
Lucille Malka

Corinne Maracina
Jennifer Marmo
Paula Marron
Marjorie Martinelli
Esther Martinez
Debbie Matz
Teresa Maura
Leah Mermelstein
Melissa Miller
Kate Montgomery
Jessica Moss
Janice Motloenya
Marie Naples
Marcia Nass
Beth Neville
Silvana Ng
Isoke Nia
Jennie Nolan
    Buonocore
Lynn Norton Manna
Beth Nuremberg
Sharon Nurse
Liz O'Connell
Jacqueline O'Connor
Joanne Onolfi
Suzann Pallai
Shefali Parekh
Karen Perepeluk
Laurie Pessah
Jayne Piccola
Laura Polos
Annemarie Powers
Bethany Pray
Carol Puglisi
Alice Ressner
Marcy Rhatigan
Khrishmati Ridgeway
Lisa Ripperger
Barbara Rosenblum
Jennifer Ruggiero

Liz Rusch
Jennifer Ryan
Karen Salzberg
Elizabeth Sandoval
Carmen Santiago
Karen Scher
Adele Schroeter
Shanna Schwartz
India Scott
Marci Seidman
Rosie Silberman
Jessica Silver
Miles Skorpen
Joann Smith
Chandra Smith
Helene Sokol
Gail Wesson Spivey
Barbara Stavetski
Barbara Stavridis
Jean Stehle
Kathleen Stevens
Emma Suarez Baez
Michelle Sufrin
Jane Sullivan
Evelyn Summer
Eileen Tabasko
Patricia Tanzosh
Lyon Terry
Kathleen Tolan
Christine Topf
Joseph Turzo
Cheryl Tyler
Emily Veronese
Anne Marie Vira
Marilyn Walker
Gillan White
Alison Wolensky
Michelle Wolf
Eileen Wolfring

Introduction: What Is This Field Guide?

Lucy Calkins

When I was pregnant with my first-born son, the Teachers College Reading and Writing Project community organized a giant baby shower for me. Each person came with a carefully chosen book, inscribed with a message for baby Miles. Since then, we have commemorated birthdays, engagements, graduations, and good-byes by searching the world for exactly the right poem or picture book, novel or essay, and writing a letter to accompany it. Inside the letter, it says "This is why I chose this piece of literature precisely for you." In this same way, the book lists and the written guides that accompany them in this field guide have become our gift to you, the teachers of our nation's children. We have chosen, from all the books we have ever read, exactly the ones we think could start best in your classroom, and with these books, we have written notes that explain exactly why and how we think these texts will be so powerful in your children's hands.

The book lists and guides in this field guide are the Teachers College Reading and Writing Project's literacy gift to New York City and to the nation. When, two years ago, patrons Alan and Gail Levenstein came to us asking if there was one thing, above all others, which could further our work with teachers and children, we knew our answer in a heartbeat. We couldn't imagine anything more important than giving children the opportunity to trade, collect, talk over, and live by books. We want children to carry poems in their backpacks, to cry with Jess when he finds out that his friend Leslie has drowned, to explore tropical seas from the deck of a ship, to wonder at the life teeming in a drop of water. We want our children's heroes to include the wise and loving spider Charlotte, spinning her web to save the life of Wilbur, and the brave Atticus Finch.

We told the Levensteins that for teachers, as well as for children, there could be no finer gift than the gift of books for their students. We want teachers to be able to read magnificent stories aloud as the prelude to each school day, and to know the joy of putting exactly the right book in the hands of a child and adding, with a wink, "When you finish this book, there are more like it." We want teachers to create libraries with categories of books that peak their students' interests and match their children's passions, with one shelf for Light Sports Books and another shelf for Cousins of the Harry Potter books, one for Books That Make You Cry and another for You'll-Never-Believe-This Books. With this kind of a library, how much easier it becomes to teach children to read, to teach them what they need to become powerful, knowledgeable, literate people!

Even as we embarked on the effort to design magnificent classroom libraries, we knew that the best classroom library would always be the one assembled by a knowledgeable classroom teacher with his or her own students in mind. But, in so many cities, twenty new teachers may arrive in a school in a single year, having had no opportunity to learn about children's books at all. Even though some teachers have studied children's books, they may not be the ones given the opportunity to purchase books. Or, too often, there is no time to make book selections carefully—funds are discovered ten minutes before they must be spent or be taken from the budget. For these situations, we knew it would be enormously helpful to have lists and arrangements of recommended books for classroom libraries. Even without these worries, we all know the value of receiving book recommendations from friends. And so, our commitment to the project grew.

Our plan became this: We'd rally the entire Project community around a gigantic, two-year-long effort to design state-of-the-art classroom libraries and guides, exactly tailored to the classrooms we know so well. Simultaneously, we'd begin working with political, educational, and philanthropic leaders in hopes that individuals or corporations might adopt a school (or a corridor of classrooms) and create in these schools and classrooms the libraries of our dreams. Sharing our enthusiasm, colleagues at the New York City Board of Education proposed that idea to the mayor. Two years later, that dream has come true—In his January 2001 state of the city address, Mayor Giuliani promised $31.5 million of support to put a lending library in every New York City classroom, kindergarten through eighth grade.

Hearing this pronouncement, educational leaders from around the city joined with us in our philanthropic effort. People from the New York City Board of Education reviewed the lists and added suggestions and revisions. The Robin Hood Foundation, which had already been involved in a parallel effort to develop *school* libraries, contributed their knowledge. Readers from the Teachers Union and from the Office of Multicultural Education and of Early Childhood Education and of Literacy Education all joined in, coordinated by Peter Heaney, Executive Director of the Division of Instructional Support, and Adele Schroeter, Director of the Office of Research, Development and Dissemination. The book selections for the classroom libraries became even more carefully honed, and the written guides became richer still.

Over the past few months, boxes upon boxes of books have arrived across New York City, and in every classroom, children are pulling close to watch, big-eyed, as one exquisite, carefully chosen book after another is brought from the box and set on the shelf. Each teacher will receive between three and four hundred books. With most of these books, there will be a carefully crafted guide which says, "We chose this book because . . ." and "On page . . ." and "You'll notice that . . ." and "If you like this book, these are some others like it. . . . " I cannot promise that in every town and city across the nation the effort to put literature in the hands of students and guidance in the hands of their teachers will proceed so smoothly. But I'm hoping these book lists and these ready-made libraries bearing a stamp of approval will catch the eye of funders, of generous patrons, and of foresighted school leaders. And, every penny that comes to the authors from the sale of these field guides will go directly back into this project, directly back into our efforts to get more books into children's hands.

In the meantime, we needn't be idle. We'll comb through the book sales at libraries, and we'll write requests to publishers and companies. In a letter home to our children's parents, we might say, "Instead of sending in cupcakes to honor your child's birthday, I'm hoping you'll send a book. Enclosed is a list of suggestions." We can and will get books into our children's hands, by hook or by crook. And we can and will get the professional support we need for our reading instruction—our vitality and effectiveness as educators depend on it.

About the Books

When hundreds of teachers pool their knowledge of children's books as we have here, the resulting libraries are far richer than anything any one of us could have imagined on our own. We're proud as peacocks of these selections and of the accompanying literary insights and teaching ideas, and can't wait to share them both with teachers and children across the country. Here is a window into some of the crafting that has gone into the book selections:

- We suggest author studies in which the texts that students will study approximately match those they'll write and will inform their own work as authors.

- In upper-grade libraries, we include books that are relatively easy to read, but we have tried to ensure that they contain issues of concern to older children as well.

- We include books that might inform other books in the same library. For example, one library contains three books about dust storms, another contains a variety of books on spiders.

- We know that comprehension and interpretive thinking must be a part of reading from the very beginning, so we include easy to read books that can support thoughtful responses.

- We try to match character ages with student ages, approximately. For example, we have put the book in which Ramona is five in the library we anticipate will be for kindergartners, and put fourth-grade Ramona in the library we anticipate will be for fourth graders.

- We include complementary stories together when possible. For example, Ringgold's *Tar Beach* and Dorros' *Abuela* appear in the same library, anticipating that readers will recognize these as parallel stories in which the narrator has an imagined trip.

- We have never assumed that books in a series are all of the same level. For example, we have determined that some of the *Frog and Toad* books are more challenging, and this is indicated in our libraries.

- We understand that books in a series cannot always be easily read out of sequence. Because we know the *Magic Treehouse* series is best read in a particular sequence, for example, we have been careful with regard to the books we select out of that series.

- We selected our libraries to reflect multicultural values and bring forth characters of many different backgrounds and lives.

■ We try to steer clear of books that will not meet with general public approval. We do not believe in censorship, but we do believe that books purchased en masse should not bring storms of criticism upon the unsuspecting teacher.

At the same time that we are proud of the work we've done, we also know that there are countless magnificent books we have omitted and countless helpful and obvious teaching moves we have missed. We are certain that there are authors' names we have inadvertently misspelled, opinions expressed with which we don't all agree, levels assigned that perhaps should be different, and so on. We consider this work to be a letter to a friend and a work in progress, and we are rushing it to you, eager for a response. We are hoping that when you come across areas that need more attention, when you get a bright idea about a guide or booklist, that you will write back to us. We have tried to make this as easy as possible for you to do—just go to our website and contact us!

Choosing the Library for Your Class

We have created seven libraries for kindergarten through sixth grade classrooms. The libraries are each assigned a letter name (A–G) rather than a grade-level in recognition of the fact that the teacher of one class of fourth graders might find that Library D is suited to her students, and another fourth grade teacher might opt for Library E or Library F.

In order to determine which classroom library is most appropriate for a particular class in a particular school, teachers need to determine the approximate reading levels of their students in November, after the teachers have had some time to assess their students as readers. Teachers can compare the book the middle-of-the-class reader tends to be reading with the books we note for each level, and choose the library that corresponds to that average text level. More detail follows this general description. In shorthand, however, the following equivalencies apply:

Library **A** is usually Kindergarten
Library **B** is usually K or 1st grade
Library **C** is usually 1st or 2nd grade
Library **D** is usually 2nd or 3rd grade
Library **E** is usually 3rd or 4th grade
Library **F** is usually 4th or 5th grade
Library **G** is usually 5th or 6th grade

The system of saying, "If in November, your children are reading books like these," usually doesn't work for kindergarten children. Instead, we say Library A is suitable if, in November, the average student cannot yet do a rich, story-like, emergent (or pretend) reading of a familiar storybook, nor can this child write using enough initial and final consonants that an adult can "read" the child's writing.

It is important to note that all of the books in any given library are not at the same level of difficulty. Instead, we have created a mix of levels that tend to represent the mixed levels of ability of readers in the classes we have studied. The composition of the libraries, by level, is described on pages xlvii–lvi.

Once you have chosen the library that best corresponds to the average level of your students as readers, you will need to decide which components of the library best suit your curriculum. Each library is divided into components—a core and some modules. The core is the group of books in the library we regard as essential. Each library also contains six modules, each representing a category of books. For example, in each library there is a module of nonfiction books, and in the upper-grade libraries there are modules containing five copies each of ten books we recommend for book clubs. Each module contains approximately fifty titles. The exact quantity from module to module varies slightly because we have tried to keep the cost of each module approximately equal. This means, for example, that the nonfiction module that contains more hardcover books has fewer books overall.

There are a variety of ways to assemble a library. Some teachers will want to purchase the entire library—the core plus the six modules. Sometimes, teachers on the same grade level in a school each purchase the same core but different modules, so a greater variety of books will be available across the hall for their students. In New York City, teachers automatically received the core of their library of choice, 150 books, and then could choose three of the six possible modules.

The Contents of Each Library

Researchers generally agree that a classroom should contain at least twenty books per child. Obviously, the number of books needs to be far greater than this in kindergarten and first grade classrooms, because books for beginning readers often contain fewer than 100 words and can generally only sustain a child's reading for a short while. We would have liked to recommend libraries of 750 titles but decided to select a smaller number of books, trusting that each teacher will have other books of his or her choice to supplement our recommendations.

Because we predict that every teacher will receive or buy the core of a library and only some teachers will receive any particular module, we tried to fill the core of the libraries with great books we couldn't imagine teaching, or living, without. Because we know children will borrow and swap books between classrooms, it is rare for books to be in the core of more than one library, even though some great books could easily belong there.

Usually, these classroom libraries include enough books from a particularly wonderful series to turn that series into a class rage, but the libraries frequently do not contain all the books in a series. Often, more books in the series are included in Modules One and Two, which always contain more books for independent reading, divided into the same levels as those in the core. Our expectation is that once readers have become engrossed in a series, teachers or parents can help them track down sequels in the school or public library.

Within the core of a library, we include about a dozen books of various genres that could be perfect for the teacher to read aloud to the class. These are all tried-and-true read aloud books; each title on the read-aloud list is one that countless teachers have found will create rapt listeners and generate rich conversation.

In every library we have included nonfiction books. They were not chosen to support particular social studies or science units; that would be a different and admirable goal. Instead, our team members have searched for nonfiction texts that captivate readers, and we imagine them being read within the reading workshop. The nonfiction books were chosen either because their topics are generally high-interest ones for children (animals, yo-yo tricks, faraway lands, disgusting animals), or because they represent the best of their genre.

Each library contains about fifteen books that could be splendid mentor texts for young writers. That is, they contain writing that students could emulate and learn from easily since it is somewhat like the writing they are generally able to create themselves.

In each core library, an assortment of other categories is included. These differ somewhat from one library to another. Libraries D and E, for example, contain many early chapter books, but since it is also crucial for children at this level to read the richest picture books imaginable, the core contains a score of carefully chosen picture books. Some cores also contain a set of books perfect for an author study. The categories are indicated on the book lists themselves, and under "Teaching Uses" in the guides.

The vast majority of books in each library are single copies, chosen in hopes that they will be passed eagerly from one reader to another. The challenge was not to find the number of books representing a particular level, but instead to select irresistible books. The chosen books have been field tested in dozens of New York City classrooms, and they've emerged as favorites for teachers and children alike.

The few books that have been selected in duplicate are ones we regard as particularly worthwhile to talk over with a partner. We would have loved to suggest duplicate copies be available for half the books in each library—if libraries had more duplicates, this would allow two readers to move simultaneously through a book, meeting in partnerships to talk and think about the chapters they've read. The duplicate copies would allow readers to have deeper and more text-specific book talks, while growing and researching theories as they read with each other. Duplicates also help books gain social clout in a classroom—allowing the enthusiasm of several readers to urge even more readers to pick the book up. If teachers are looking for ways to supplement these libraries, buying some duplicate copies would be a perfect way to start.

Many of the libraries contain a very small number of multiple (four or five) copies of books intended for use in guided reading and strategy lessons. Once children are reading chapter books, we find teachers are wise to help children into a new series by pulling together a group of four readers, introducing the text, and guiding their early reading. Teachers may also want to offer extra support to children as they read the second book in a series, and so we suggest having a duplicate of this next book as well, so that each child can read it with a partner, meeting to retell and discuss it.

The Levels Within the Libraries

We've leveled many, but purposely not all, of the books in every classroom library. The fact that we have leveled these books doesn't mean that teachers should necessarily convey all of these levels to children. We expect teachers will often make these levels visible on less than half of their books (through the use of colored tabs), giving readers the responsibility of choosing appropriate books for themselves by judging unmarked books against the template of leveled books. "This book looks a lot like the green dot books that have been just-right for me, so I'll give it a try and see if I have a smooth read," a reader might say. It is important that kids learn to navigate different levels of difficulty within a classroom library on their own or with only minimal support from a teacher.

We do not imagine a classroom lending library that is divided into levels as discrete as the levels established by Reading Recovery© or by Gay Su Pinnell and Irene Fountas' book, *Guided Reading: Good First Teaching for All Children* (Heinemann, 1996). These levels were designed for either one-to-one tutorials or intensive, small group guided reading sessions, and in both of these situations a vigilant teacher is present to constantly shepherd children along toward more challenging books. If a classroom lending library is divided into micro-levels and each child's entire independent reading life is slotted into a micro-level, some children might languish at a particular level, and many youngsters might not receive the opportunities to read across a healthy range of somewhat-easier and somewhat-harder books. Most worrisome of all, because we imagine children working often with reading partners who "like to read the same kinds of books as you do," classroom libraries that contain ten micro-levels (instead of say, five more general levels) could inadvertently convey the message that many *children* as well as many *books* were off-limits as partners to particular readers.

There are benefits to micro-levels, however, and therefore within a difficulty level (or a color-dot), some teachers might ascribe a plus sign to certain books, signifying that this book is one of the harder ones at this level. Teachers can then tell a child who is new to a level to steer clear of the books with plus signs, or to be sure that he or she receives a book introduction before tackling a book with this marker.

When assigning books to levels, we have tried to research the difficulty levels that others have given to each text and we have included these levels in our guides. Fairly frequently, however, our close study of a particular text has led us to differ somewhat from the assessments others have made. Of course leveling books is and always will be a subjective and flawed process; and therefore teachers everywhere *should* deviate from assigned levels, ours and others, when confident of their rationale, or when particularly knowledgeable about a reader. You can turn to the tables at the back of this section, on pages xxvii–lx, to learn more about our leveling system.

Building the Libraries

When we started this project two years ago, we initiated some intensive study groups, each designed to investigate a different terrain in children's literature. Soon, a group led by Lynn Holcomb, one of the first Reading Recovery teachers in Connecticut, was working to select books for a K–1 library. Members of this group also learned from Barbara Peterson, author of *Literary Pathways: Selecting Books to Support New Readers* (Heinemann, 2001), who conducted groundbreaking research at Ohio State University, examining how readers actually experience levels of text complexity. The group also learned from Gay Su Pinnell, well-known scholar of literacy education and coauthor with Irene Fountas of many books including *Guided Reading*. Of course, the group learned especially from intensive work with children in classrooms. The group searched for books that:

- Represent a diverse range of shapes, sizes, authors, and language patterns as possible. The committee went to lengths to be sure that when taken as a whole, primary-level libraries looked more like libraries full of real books than like kits full of "teaching materials."

- Use unstilted language. A book that reads, "Come, Spot. Come, Spot, come," generally would not be selected.

- Contain many high frequency words. If one book contained just one word on a page ("Scissors/paste/paper/etc.") and another book contained the reoccurring refrain of "I see the scissors./ I see the paste." we selected the second option.

- Carry meaning and were written to communicate content with a reader. If the book would probably generate a conversation or spark an insight, it was more apt to be included than one that generally left a reader feeling flat and finished with the book.

- Represent the diversity of people in our world and convey valuable messages about the human spirit.

A second group, under the leadership of Kathleen Tolan, an experienced teacher and staff developer, spent thousands of hours studying early chapter books and the children who read them. This group pored over series, asking questions: Is each book in the series equally difficult? Which series act as good precursors for other series? Do the books in the series make up one continuous story, or can each book stand alone? What are the special demands placed on readers of this series?

Yet another group, led by Gaby Layden, staff developer at the Project, studied nonfiction books to determine which might be included in a balanced, independent reading library. The group studied levels of difficulty in nonfiction books, and found authors and texts that deserved special attention. Carefully, they chose books for teachers to demonstrate and for children to practice working through the special challenges of nonfiction reading.

Meanwhile, renowned teacher-educator Isoke Nia, teacher extraordinaire Kathy Doyle, and their team of educators dove into the search for the very best chapter books available for upper-grade readers. Isoke especially helped us select touchstone texts for writing workshops—books to help us teach children to craft their writing with style, care, and power.

Teacher, staff developer, and researcher Annemarie Powers worked full-time to ensure that our effort was informed by the related work of other groups across the city and nation. We pored over bibliographies and met with librarians and literature professors. We searched for particular kinds of books: books featuring Latino children, anthologies of short stories, Level A and B books which looked and sounded like literature. We researched the classrooms in our region that are especially famous for their classroom libraries, and took note of the most treasured books we found there. All of this information fed our work.

Reading Instruction and the Classroom Library: An Introduction to Workshop Structures

These classroom libraries have been developed with the expectation that they will be the centerpiece of reading instruction. When I ask teachers what they are really after in the teaching of reading, many answer, as I do, "I want children to be lifelong readers. I cannot imagine anything more important than helping children grow up able to read and loving to read. I want students to initiate reading in their own lives, for their own purposes."

There is, of course, no one best way to teach reading so that children become lifelong readers. One of the most straightforward ways to do this is to embrace the age-old, widely shared belief that children benefit from daily opportunities to read books they choose for their own purposes and pleasures (Krashen 1993, Atwell 1987, Cambourne 1993, Smith 1985, Meek 1988).

More and more, however, we've come to realize that students benefit not only from opportunities to read, read, read, but also from instruction that responds to what students do when they are given opportunities to read. I have described the reading workshop in my latest publication, *The Art of Teaching Reading* (Calkins 2001). The reading workshop is an instructional format in which children are given long chunks of time in which to read appropriate texts, and also given explicit and direct instruction. Teachers who come from a writing workshop background may find it helpful to structure the reading workshop in ways that parallel the writing workshop so that children learn simultaneously to work productively inside each of the two congruent structures. Whatever a teacher decides, it is important that the structures of a reading workshop are clear and predictable so that children know how to carry on with some independence, and so that teachers are able to assess and coach individuals as well as partnerships and small groups.

Many teachers begin a reading workshop by pulling students together for a minilesson lasting about eight minutes (unless the read aloud is, for that day, incorporated into the minilesson, which then adds at least twenty minutes). Children then bring their reading bins, holding the books they are currently reading, to their assigned "reading nooks." As children read independently, a teacher moves among them, conferring individually with a child or bringing a small group of readers together for a ten- to fifteen-minute guided reading or strategy lesson. After children have read independently for about half an hour, teachers ask them to meet with their partners to talk about their books and their reading. After the partners meet, teachers often call all the readers in a class together for a brief "share session" (Calkins 2001). The following table shows some general guidelines for the length of both independent reading and the partnership talks based on the approximate level of the texts students are reading in the class.

How Long Might a Class Have Independent Reading and Partnership Talk?		
Class Reading Level	*Independent Reading Duration*	*Partnership Talk Duration*
Library A	10 minutes	20 minutes
Library B	15 minutes	20 minutes
Library C	20 minutes	20 minutes
Library D	30 minutes	10 minutes
Library E	40 minutes	10 minutes
Library F	40 minutes	10 minutes
Library G	40 minutes	10 minutes

Periodically, the structure of the minilesson, independent reading, partnership, and then share time is replaced by a structure built around book clubs or "junior" book clubs, our own, reading-intensive version of reading centers.

Minilessons

During a minilesson, the class gathers on the carpet to learn a strategy all readers can use not only during the independent reading workshop but also throughout their reading lives. The content of a minilesson comes, in part, from a teacher deciding that for a period of time, usually a month, he needs to focus his teaching on a particular aspect of reading. For example, many teachers begin the year by devoting a month to reading with stamina and understanding (Calkins 2001). During this unit, teachers might give several minilessons designed to help children choose books they can understand, and they might give others designed to help readers sustain their reading over time. Another minilesson might be designed to help readers make more time for reading in their lives or to help them keep a stack of books-in-waiting to minimize the interval between finishing one book and starting another.

The minilesson, then, often directs the work readers do during independent reading. If the minilessons show students how to make sure their ideas are grounded in the details of the text, teachers may establish an interval between independent reading time and partnership conversations when children can prepare for a talk about their text by marking relevant sections that support their ideas.

Sometimes minilessons are self-standing, separate from the interactive read aloud. Other minilessons include and provide a frame for the day's read aloud. For example, the teacher may read aloud a book and direct that day's talk in a way that demonstrates the importance of thinking about a character's motivations. Then children may be asked to think in similar ways about their independent reading books. Perhaps, when they meet with a partner at the end of reading, the teacher will say, "Please talk about the motivations that drive your central characters and show evidence in the text to support your theories."

Conferences

While children read, a teacher confers. Usually this means that the teacher starts by sitting close to a child as he or she continues reading, watching for external behaviors that can help assess the child. After a moment or two, the teacher usually says, "Can I interrupt?" and conducts a few-minute-long conversation while continuing the assessment. A teacher will often ask, "Can you read to me a bit?" and this, too, informs any hunches about a child and his or her strengths and needs as a reader. Finally, teachers intervene to lift the level of what the child is doing. The following table offers some examples of this.

General Examples of the Conferring That Can Help Readers Grow	
If, in reading, the child is . . .	*Teachers might teach by . . .*
able to demonstrate a basic understanding of the text	nudging the child to grow deeper insights, perhaps by asking: ■ Do any pages (parts) go together in a surprising way? ■ Why do you think the author wrote this book? What is he (she) trying to say? ■ If you were to divide the book into different sections, what would they be? ■ How are you changing as a reader? How are you reading this book differently than you've read others? ■ What's the work you are doing as you read this?
talking mostly about the smallest, most recent details read	generalizing what kind of book it is, giving the child a larger sense of the genre. If it is a story, we can ask questions that will work for any story: ■ How is the main character changing? ■ How much time has gone by? ■ What is the setting for the story? If the text is a non-narrative, we could ask: ■ What are the main chunks (or sections) in the text? ■ How would you divide this up? ■ How do the parts of this text go together? ■ What do you think the author is trying to teach you?
clearly enthralled by the story	asking questions to help the reader tap into the best of this experience to use again later. ■ What do you think it is about this story that draws you in? ■ You seem really engaged, so I'm wondering what can you learn about this reading experience that might inform you as you read other books. ■ When I love a book, as you love this one, I sometimes find myself reading faster and faster, as if I'm trying to gulp it down. But a reading teacher once told me this quote. "Some people think a good book is one you can't put down, but me, I think a good book is one you must put down—to muse over, to question, to think about." Could you set some bookmarks throughout this book and use them to pause in those places to really think and even to write about this book? Make one of those places right now, would you?

Partnerships

When many of us imagine reading, we envision a solitary person curled up with a book. The truth is that reading is always social, always embedded in talk with others. If I think about the texts I am reading now in my life and ask myself, "Is there something *social* about my reading of those texts?" I quickly realize that I read texts because people have recommended them. I read anticipating conversations I will soon have with others, and I read noticing things in this one text that I have discussed with others. My reading, as is true for many readers, is multilayered and sharper because of the talk that surrounds it.

There are a lot of reasons to organize reading time so that children have opportunities to talk with a reading partner. Partner conversations can highlight the social elements of reading, making children enjoy reading more. Talking about books also helps children have more internal conversations (thoughts) as they read. Putting thoughts about texts out into the world by speaking them allows other readers to engage in conversation, in interpretations and ideas, and can push children to ground their ideas in the text, to revise their ideas, to lengthen and deepen their ideas.

For young children, talking with a partner usually doubles the actual unit of time a child spends working with books. In many primary classrooms, the whole class reads and then the teacher asks every child to meet with a partner who can read a similar level of book. Each child brings his bin of books, thus doubling the number of appropriate books available to any one child. The child who has already read a book talks about it with the other child, giving one partner a valuable and authentic reason to retell a book and another child an introduction to the book. Then the two readers discuss how they will read together. After the children read aloud together, the one book held between them as they sit hip to hip, there is always time for the partners to discuss the text. Sometimes, teachers offer students guidance in this conversation.

More proficient readers need a different sort of partnership because once a child can read short chapter books, there are few advantages to the child reading aloud often. Then too, by this time children can sustain reading longer. Typically in third grade, for example, individuals read independently for thirty minutes and then meet with partners for ten minutes to talk over the book. Again, the teacher often guides that conversation, sometimes by modeling—by entertaining with the whole-class read-aloud text—the sort of conversations she expects readers will have in their partnerships.

Book Clubs

Teaching children to read well has a great deal to do with teaching children to talk well about books, because the conversations children have in the air between one another become the conversations they have in their own minds as they read. Children who have talked in small groups about the role of the suitcase in Christopher Paul Curtis's book, *Bud, Not Buddy* will be far more apt to pause as they read another book, asking, "Might *this* object play a significant role in this book, like the suitcase did in *Bud, Not Buddy*?"

When we move children from partnership conversations toward small-group book clubs, we need to provide some scaffolding for them to lean on at first. This is because partnerships are generally easier for children to manage than small group conversations. It is also generally easier for students to read for thirty-minute reading sessions with ten-minute book talks than it is to read for a few days in a row and then sustain extended book talks, as they are expected to do in book clubs.

Children need some support as they begin clubs. One way to do this is to begin with small book club conversations about the read aloud book—the one book we know everyone will be prepared to talk about. Another way to get started with book clubs is for the teacher to suggest that children work in small groups to read multiple copies of, say, a mystery book. The teacher will plan to read a mystery book aloud to the class during the weeks they work in their clubs. Meanwhile, each group of approximately four readers will be reading one mystery that is at an appropriate level for them. The whole class works on and talks about the read-aloud mystery, and this work then guides the small group work. On one day, for example, after reading aloud the whole-class mystery, the teacher could immerse the class in talk about what it's like to read "suspiciously," suspecting everything and everyone. For a few days, the class can try that sort of reading as they listen to the read aloud. Meanwhile, when children disperse to their small groups to read their own mysteries, they can read these books "suspiciously."

Eventually the book clubs can become more independent. One small group of children might be reading several books by an author and talking about what they can learn from the vantage point of having read so many. Another group might read books that deal with a particular theme or subject. Either way, in the classrooms I know best, each book club lasts at least a few weeks. Teachers observe, and coach and teach into these talks, equipping kids with ways to write, talk, and think about texts. However, teachers neither dominate the clubs nor steer readers toward a particular preordained interpretation of a text. Instead, teachers steer readers toward ways of learning and thinking that can help them again and again, in reading after reading, throughout their lives.

Library Ⓓ Contents Description

Library D consists of

I.	Independent Reading & Partner Reading			
	Chapter Books (Levels 5–10)	Level 5	25 Titles	29 Texts
		Level 6	34 Titles	41 Texts
		Level 7	68 Titles	74 Texts
		Level 8	94 Titles	108 Texts
		Level 9	59 Titles	70 Texts
		Level 10	14 Titles	18 Texts
	Nonfiction		56 Titles	56 Texts
	Picture Books		26 Titles	26 Texts
	Poetry		10 Titles	10 Texts
	Short Stories		5 Titles	5 Texts
II.	Guided Reading		27 Titles	108 Texts
III.	Book Club/Literature Circle		17 Titles	102 Texts
IV.	Author Study		10 Titles	20 Texts
V.	Read Alouds		7 Titles	7 Texts
VI.	Books to Support the Writing Process		4 Titles	4 Texts
	Total Number of Texts in Library D		**456 Titles**	**502 Texts**

(Because of substitutions made in the ordering process, this number may not be precise.)

Group Description	Level	#	Author	Title	ISBN	Publisher	Quantity	Heinemann Write-Up
CORE								
Independent Reading			Tunnell, Michael	*Missing May*			1	
	5	1	Bonsall, Crosby	Who's Afraid of the Dark?	64440710	Harper Collins	1	
		2	Cox, Rhonda	Andi's Wool	1572741104	Richard C. Owen Publishers	1	
		3	Hoff, Syd	Happy Birthday Danny and the Dinosaur	64442373	Harper Trophy	1	Y
		4	Kuskin, Karla	City Dog	395900166	Clarion Books	1	Y
		5	Pilkey, Dav	Dragon's Series/Dragon's Fat Cat	531070689	Orchard Books	1	
		6	Pilkey, Dav	Dragon's Series/A Friend for Dragon	531070549	Orchard Books	1	Y
		7	Rylant, Cynthia	Dog Heaven	590417010	Scholastic Inc.	1	
		8	Scafffe, Bronwen	And Billy Went Out to Play	157255116X	Mondo Publishing	1	
		9	Ziefert, Harriet	When the TV Broke	140365400	Penguin Puffin	1	
	6	1	Adler, David	Young Cam Jansen Series/the Ice Skate Mystery	141300124	Penguin Putnam	1	Y
		2	Adler, David	Young Cam Jansen Series/the Pizza Shop Mystery	670888613 (hc)	Penguin Putnam	1	Y
		3	Asch, Frank	Bears Bargain/Moonbear Series	671678388	Simon & Schuster	1	
		4	Barbour, Karen	Little Nino's Pizzeria	152463216	Harcourt Brace	1	
		5	Benchley, Nathaniel	Small Wolf (I Can Read Books Series)	6004915	Harper Collins	1	
		6	Cole, Joanna	Bony Legs	590405160	Scholastic Inc.	1	
		7	Cronin, Doreen	Click, Clack, Moo, Cows That Type	689832133	Simon & Schuster	1	Y
		8	Galdone, Paul	Three Bears, The	395288118	Clarion Books	1	Y
		9	Hoff, Syd	Oliver	6028708X	Harper Collins	1	Y
		10	Kessler, Leonard	Last One is a Rotten Egg	64442624	Harper Collins	1	
		11	Minarik, Else Holmelund	Little Bear Series/Little Bear's Friend	64440516	Harper Collins	1	Y

Group Description	Level	#	Author	Title	ISBN	Publisher	Quantity	Heinemann Write-Up
		12	Novak, Matt	Newt	64442365	Harper Collins	1	
		13	O'Connor, Jane	Lulu and the Witch Baby	6024626X	Harper Collins	1	Y
		14	Paulsen, Gary	Dogteam	440411300	Bantam Doubleday Dell	1	Y
		15	Robins, Joan	Addie Meets Max	64441164	Harper Collins	1	Y
		16	Rylant, Cynthia	Henry and Mudge Series/and the Bedtime Thumps	689801629	Simon & Schuster	1	
		17	Rylant, Cynthia	Henry and Mudge Series/and the Forever Sea	689810172	Simon & Schuster	1	Y
		18	Rylant, Cynthia	Henry and Mudge Series/First Book	689810059	Simon & Schuster	1	Y
		19	Rylant, Cynthia	Henry and Mudge Series/Get the Cold Shivers	689810156	Simon & Schuster	1	
		20	Rylant, Cynthia	Mr. Putter & Tabby/Bake the Cake	152002146	Harcourt Brace	1	Y
		21	Rylant, Cynthia	Mr. Putter & Tabby/Fly the Plane	152010602	Harcourt Brace	1	
		22	Rylant, Cynthia	Mr. Putter & Tabby/Walk the Dog	152562591	Harcourt Brace	1	
	7	1	Bonsall, Crosby	Case of the Double Cross, The	6444029X	Harper Collins	1	
		2	Bonsall, Crosby	Case of the Scaredy Cats, The	64440478	Harper Collins	1	
		3	Bunting, Eve	Ducky	395751853	Clarion Books	1	
		4	Byars, Betsy	Golly Sisters Series/Golly Sisters Go West, The	64441326	Harper Collins	1	
		5	Byars, Betsy	Golly Sisters Series/Hooray for the Golly Sisters!	64441563	Harper Collins	1	
		6	Christopher, Matt	Dog That Pitched a No Hitter, The	316141038	Little Brown & Co	1	
		7	Cowley, Joy	Lavender the Library Cat	868677108	Rigby	1	
		8	Cushman, Doug	Aunt Eaters Mystery Christmas	64442217	Harper Collins	1	
		9	Giff, Patricia Reilly	Powder Puff Puzzle	44047180X	Bantam Doubleday Dell	1	
		10	Greenfield, Eloise	On My Horse	694005835	Harper Collins	1	
		11	Grimes, Nikki	Meet Danitra Brown	590224379	Scholastic Inc.	1	

Group Description	Level	#	Author	Title	ISBN	Publisher	Quantity	Heinemann Write-Up
		12	Havill, Juanita	Jamaica and Brianna	395779391	Houghton Mifflin	1	Y
		13	Havill, Juanita	Jamaica and the Substitute Teacher	395905036	Houghton Mifflin	1	
		14	Havill, Juanita	Jamaica's Find	590425048	Scholastic Inc.	1	Y
		15	Hoban, Lillian	Arthur's Honey Bear	64440338	Harper Trophy	1	Y
		16	Hoban, Lillian	Arthur's Loose Tooth	64440931	Harper Collins	1	Y
		17	Little, Jean	Emma's Magic Winter	6443706X	Harper Collins	1	
		18	Maitland, Barbara	Bookstore Ghost, The	141300841	Penguin Puffin	1	
		19	Marshall, Edward	Fox Series/Fox and His Friends	590265687	Scholastic Inc.	1	Y
		20	Marshall, Edward	Fox Series/Fox at School	140365443	Penguin Puffin	1	Y
		21	McCully, Emily	Grandma's at the Lake	64441776	Harper Trophy	1	
		22	McMullan, Kate	Fluffy Series/Fluffy Meets the Dinosaurs	590523104	Scholastic Inc.	1	
		23	McMullan, Kate	Fluffy Series/Fluffy's Funny Field Trip	439206731	Scholastic Inc.	1	Y
		24	Rylant, Cynthia	Poppleton and Friends	590847880	Scholastic Inc.	1	Y
		25	Rylant, Cynthia	Poppleton Has Fun	590848410	Scholastic Inc.	1	Y
		26	Sharmat, Marjorie Weinman	Nate the Great/Mushy Valentine	440410134	Bantam Doubleday Dell	1	
	8	1	Abbott, Tony	Danger Guys Series/The Golden Lizard	64420116	Harper Collins	1	
		2	Adler, David	Cam Jansen Series/and the Chocolate Fudge Mystery	590129023	Scholastic Inc.	1	Y
		3	Avi	Abigail Takes the Wheel	64442810	Harper Collins	1	
		4	Bos, Burny	Molesons/Meet the Molesons	1558584099	North South Books	1	
		5	Bos, Burny	Molesons/More from the Molesons	1558587780	North South Books	1	
		6	Brown, Marc	Arthur Adventure Series/Arthur's Loose Tooth	64440931	Harper Collins	1	
		7	Bulla, Clyde Robert	Paint Brush Kid, The	679892826	Random House	1	Y

Group Description	Level	#	Author	Title	ISBN	Publisher	Quantity	Heinemann Write-Up
		8	Cazet, Denys	Minnie & Moo Go to Paris	78943928X	DK Publishing	1	
		9	Cazet, Denys	Minnie & Moo Save the Earth	789439298	DK Publishing	1	
		10	Christopher, Matt	Hit-Away Kid	316140074	Little Brown & Co	1	
		11	Christopher, Matt	Stranger in Right Field	316106771	Little Brown & Co	1	
		12	Coerr, Eleanor	Josefina Story Quilt, The	64441296	Harper Collins	1	Y
		13	Cosby, Bill	Little Bill Series/Best Way to Play	590956175	Scholastic Inc.	1	
		14	Cuyler, Margery	Invisible in the Third Grade	590928813	Scholastic Inc.	1	Y
		15	Delton, Judy	Pee Wee Scouts/Grumpy Pumpkins (#5)	440400651	Bantam Doubleday Dell	1	Y
		16	Giff, Patricia Reilly	Clue at the Zoo, The	440403189	Dell Publishing	1	
		17	Giff, Patricia Reilly	Fish Face	440425573	Dell Publishing	1	
		18	Giff, Patricia Reilly	Kids of Polk Street School/Candy Corn Contest	44041072X	Dell Publishing	1	Y
		19	Giff, Patricia Reilly	Kids of Polk Street Series/Snaggle Doodles	44048068X	Dell Publishing	1	Y
		20	Grimes, Nikki	Dime a Dozen, A	803722273	Dial Books	1	
		21	Hesse, Karen	Lester's Dog	517583577	Random House	1	Y
		22	Howe, James	Pinky & Rex Series/And the Bully	689808348	Simon & Schuster	1	Y
		23	Howe, James	Pinky & Rex Series/And the Mean Old Witch	689828799	Simon & Schuster	1	
		24	Howe, James	Pinky & Rex Series/New Baby	68982548X	Aladdin	1	Y
		25	King-Smith, Dick	Cuckoobush Farm	688076807	William Morrow & Co	1	Y
		26	Kline, Suzy	Horrible Harry Series/the Drop of Doom	590290681	Scholastic Inc.	1	Y
		27	Kline, Suzy	Song Lee and the Leech Man	140372555	Viking Penguin	1	
		28	Parish, Peggy	Amelia Bedelia Series/Helps Out	38072796X	William Morrow & Co	1	Y
		29	Sachar, Louis	Marvin Redpost: Why Pick on Me?	679819479	Random House	1	Y

Group Description	Level	#	Author	Title	ISBN	Publisher	Quantity	Heinemann Write-Up
		30	Spinelli, Jerry	Bathwater Gang, The	316807796	Little Brown & Co	1	
		31	Spinelli, Jerry	Blue Ribbon Blues	679887539	Stepping Stone	1	Y
		32	Spinelli, Jerry	Tooter Pepperday	679847022	Stepping Stone	1	Y
		33	Stanley, Diane	Moe the Dog in Tropical Paradise	698117611	Penguin Putnam	1	Y
	9	1	Bulla, Clyde Robert	Shoeshine Girl	64402282	Harper Trophy	1	Y
		2	Cameron, Ann	Julian's Glorious Summer	394891171	Random House	1	
		3	Conrad, Pam	Pedro's Journal: A Voyage with Christopher Columbus	590462067	Scholastic Inc.	1	Y
		4	Dahl, Roald	George's Marvelous Medicine	140346414	Penguin Publishing	1	Y
		5	Danziger, Paula	Amber Brown Series/ is not a Crayon	59045899X	Scholastic Inc.	1	Y
		6	Danziger, Paula	Amber Brown Series/ Sees Red	590947281	Scholastic Inc.	1	Y
		7	Danziger, Paula	Amber Brown Series/You Can't Eat Your Chicken Pox, Amber Brown	590502077	Scholastic Inc.	1	Y
		8	Herman, Charlotte	Max Malone Series/the Great Cereal Ripoff	805018433	Henry Holt & Co	1	
		9	Herman, Charlotte	Max Malone Series/the Magnificent	805035486	Henry Holt & Co	1	
		10	Hesse, Karen	Sable	805057722	Henry Holt & Co	1	
		11	Kline, Suzy	Mary Marony and the Chocolate Surprise	440413265	Bantam Doubleday Dell	1	Y
		12	Kline, Suzy	Mary Marrony Hides Out	440411351	Bantam Doubleday Dell	1	Y
		13	Kline, Suzy	Song Lee and the Hamster Hunt	141307072	Penguin Puffin	1	Y
		14	Kline, Suzy	Song Lee in Room 2B	141304081	Penguin Puffin	1	Y
		15	Warner, Gertrude	Boxcar Children Series/Canoe Trip Mystery	590475355	Scholastic Inc.	1	
	10	1	Cleary, Beverly	Ramona Quimby, Age 8	380709562	William Morrow & Co	1	Y
		2	Dahl, Roald	James & the Giant Peach	140374248	Penguin Publishing	1	
		3	Hesse, Karen	Just Juice	590033824	Scholastic Inc.	1	

Group Description	Level	#	Author	Title	ISBN	Publisher	Quantity	Heinemann Write-Up
		4	Koller, Jackie French	Dragonling, The	671867903	Pocket Books	1	
		5	Lansky, Bruce	Girls to the Rescue #1	671899791	Meadowbrook	1	
Anthologies of Short Stories		1	Canfield, Jack, Mark V. Hansen, Patty Hansen & Irene Dunlap	Chicken Soup for the Kid's Soul: 101 Stories of Courage, Hope and Laughter	1558746099	Health Communications	1	
		2	Carle, Eric	Flora and Tiger: 19 Very Short Stories From My Life	399232036	Philomel Books	1	
		3	Shannon, George	More Stories to Solve: Fifteen Folktales from Around the World	688129471	William Morrow & Co	1	
Author Studies		1	Henkes, Kevin	Chester's Way	688154727	Mulberry Books	1	Y
		2	Henkes, Kevin	Chrysanthemum	688147321	Mulberry Books	1	Y
		3	Henkes, Kevin	Owen	688114490	William Morrow & Co	1	Y
		4	Henkes, Kevin	Sheila, Rae, the Brave	688147380	Mulberry Books	1	Y
		5	Henkes, Kevin	Weekend with Wendell	688140246	Mulberry Books	1	Y
Teaching Writing		1	Baylor, Byrd	I'm in Charge of Celebrations	689806205	Simon & Schuster	1	Y
		2	Kesselman, Wendy	Emma	760706921	Barnes & Noble Books	1	Y
		3	Little, Jean	Hey World Here I Am	6440384X	Harper Collins	1	Y
		4	MacLachlan, Patricia	Through Grandpa's Eyes	64430413	Harper Trophy	1	Y
		5	Moss, Marissa	Amelia's Notebook	1562477846	Pleasant Company	1	Y
Picture Books		1	Allard, Harry	Miss Nelson is Missing	590118773	Scholastic Inc.	1	Y
		2	Collier, Bryan	Uptown	805057218	Henry Holt & Co	1	Y
		3	Corey, Shana	You Forgot Your Skirt, Amelia Bloomer	439078199	Scholastic Inc.	1	Y
		4	de Paola, Tomie	Nana Upstairs, Nana Downstairs	698118367	Penguin Puffin	1	Y
		5	DeFelice, Cynthia	Mule Eggs	531086933	Scholastic Inc.	1	
		6	Dorros, Arthur	Abuela	140562257	Penguin Puffin	1	Y
		7	Greenfield, Eloise	Night on Neighborhood Street	140556834	Penguin Publishing	1	Y

Group Description	Level	#	Author	Title	ISBN	Publisher	Quantity	Heinemann Write-Up
		8	Greenfield, Eloise	She Come Bringing Me That Little Baby Girl	64432963	Harper Trophy	1	Y
		9	Greenfield, Eloise	Under the Sunday Tree	64432572	Harper Collins	1	
		10	Grimes, Nikki	Come Sunday	802851347	Eerdmans William B. Publishing Co.	1	
		11	Howard, Elizabeth	Aunt Flossie's Hats	39572077X	Houghton Mifflin	1	Y
		12	Lyon, George Ella	One Lucky Girl	789426137	DK Publishing	1	Y
		13	Miles, Miska	Annie and the Old One	316571202	Little Brown & Co	1	Y
		14	Rathmann, Peggy	Officer Buckle & Gloria	399226168	Penguin Putnam	1	Y
		15	Ringgold, Faith	Tar Beach	590463810	Scholastic Inc.	1	Y
		16	Sans Souci, R.	Talking Eggs, The	590441892	Scholastic Inc.	1	Y
		17	Say, Allen	Grandfather's Journey	395570352	Houghton Mifflin	1	Y
		18	Steig, William	Amos & Boris	274403600	Farrar Strauss & Giroux	1	
		19	Stevens, Janet	Three Billy Goats Gruff	152863974	Harcourt Brace	1	
		20	Stewart, Sarah	Gardener, The	374325170	Farrar Strauss & Giroux	1	Y
		21	Zolotow, Charlotte	Hating Book, The	64431975	Harper Trophy	1	
		22	Zolotow, Charlotte	Mr. Rabbit & the Lovely Present	64430200	Harper Trophy	1	Y
Poetry		1	Kennedy, X.J.	Talking Like the Rain	316488895	Little Brown & Co	1	Y
		2	Rosen, Michael, ed.	Home	60217898	Harper Collins	1	
Read-Aloud Texts		1	Blume, Judy	Fudge-a-Mania	440404908	Bantam Doubleday Dell	1	Y
		2	Cooper, Floyd	Coming Home: From the Life of Langston Hughes	698116127	Putnam Publishing	1	
		3	Dahl, Roald	Fantastic Mr. Fox	140328726	Penguin Publishing	1	
		4	Flor Ada, Alma	My Name is Maria Isabel	68980217X	Simon & Schuster	1	Y
		5	Hesse, Karen	Lavender	805042571	Henry Holt & Co	1	Y
		6	Martin, Bill	Knots on a Counting Rope	440843057	William Morrow & Co	1	Y
		7	Mathis, Sharon	Hundred Penny Box, The	140321691	Penguin Publishing	1	Y

Group Description	Level	#	Author	Title	ISBN	Publisher	Quantity	Heinemann Write-Up
	5	8	Mowat, Farley	Owls In the Family	440413613	Bantam Doubleday Dell	1	
		9	Rauzon, Mark	Skin, Scales, Feathers & Fur	688102336	Lothrop Lee & Shepard	1	Y
		10	Robinson, Barbara	Best Christmas Pageant Ever, The	64402754	Harper Collins	1	Y
		11	Walsh, Jill Paton	Matthew and the Sea Singer	3774348693	Farrar Strauss & Giroux	1	Y

MODULE 1: More Independent Reading: Filling in the Lower Portion of the Library

Group Description	Level	#	Author	Title	ISBN	Publisher	Quantity	Heinemann Write-Up
		1	Cole, Joanna	Bully Trouble	394849493	Random House	1	
		2	Giles, Jenny	Sarah & the Barking Dog	76351957	Rigby	1	
		3	Giles, Jenny	Toy Farm, The	763519553	Rigby	1	
		4	Herman, Gail	What a Hungry Puppy	448405369	Grosset & Dunlap	1	
		5	Pilkey, Dav	Dragon's Series/Dragon Gets By	531070816	Orchard Books	1	
		6	Pilkey, Dav	Dragon's Series/A Friend for Dragon	531070549	Orchard Books	1	
		7	Rau, Dana	Secret Code, The	516207008	Children's Press/Rookie Readers	1	
	6	1	Adler, David	Young Cam Jansen Series/the Lost Tooth	141302739	Viking Penguin	1	
		2	Adler, David	Young Cam Jansen Series/the Pizza Shop Mystery	670888613 (hc)	Penguin Putnam	1	Y
		3	Asch, Frank	Bear Shadow/Moonbear Series	590440543	Scholastic Inc.	1	
		4	Cowley, Joy	Ha Ha Party, The	780249798	Wright Group	1	
		5	Cowley, Joy	Plants of My Aunt, The	790106973	Rigby	1	
		6	Douglas, Anne	Camp Knock Knock	440411262	Bantam Doubleday Dell	1	
		7	Hoban, Lillian	Silly Tilly's Thanksgiving Dinner	64441547	Harper Collins	1	
		8	Hoban, Lillian	Silly Tilly's Valentine	64442233	Harper Collins	1	
		9	Lobel, Arnold	Frog and Toad Series/Frog and Toad All Year	64440591	Harper Collins	1	Y
		10	Lobel, Arnold	Frog and Toad Series/Frog and Toad Together	64440214	Harper Trophy	1	Y

Group Description	Level	#	Author	Title	ISBN	Publisher	Quantity	Heinemann Write-Up
		11	Rylant, Cynthia	Henry and Mudge Series/In Puddle Trouble	689810032	Simon & Schuster	1	Y
		12	Rylant, Cynthia	Henry and Mudge Series/Take the Big Test	689808860	Simon & Schuster	1	
		13	Rylant, Cynthia	Mr. Putter & Tabby/Bake the Cake	152002146	Harcourt Brace	1	Y
	7	1	Allen, Laura Jean	Rollo and Tweedy and the Ghost at Dougal Castle	64441822	Harper Collins	1	
		2	Baker, Barbara	Digby and Kate and the Beautiful Day	525458557	Penguin Putnam	1	
		3	Bridwell, Norman	Clifford the Small Red Puppy	590442945	Scholastic Inc.	1	
		4	Carle, Eric	Very Quiet Cricket, The	399226842	Philomel Books	1	
		5	Chardiet, Bernice	School Friends/Best Teacher in the World, The	590681583	Scholastic Inc.	1	
		6	Chardiet, Bernice	School Friends/Martin and the Tooth Fairy	590433059	Scholastic Inc.	1	
		7	Chardiet, Bernice	School Friends/Merry Christmas, What's Your Name	590443348	Scholastic Inc.	1	
		8	Flor Ada, Alma	Surprise for Mother Rabbit, A	1581052146	Santillana USA Publishing Company		
		9	Havill, Juanita	Jamaica's Find	590425048	Scholastic Inc.	1	Y
		10	Krensky, Stephen	Lionel in the Spring	140384634	Viking Penguin	1	
		11	Krensky, Stephen	Lionel in the Winter	140383220	Penguin Puffin	1	
		12	Lewis, Rob	Grandpa Comes to Stay	1572552123	Mondo Publishing	1	
		13	Marshall, Edward	Fox Series/Fox at School	140365443	Penguin Puffin	1	Y
		14	Marshall, Edward	Fox Series/Fox on Wheels	140365419	Penguin Puffin	1	Y
		15	McMullan, Kate	Fluffy Series/Fluffy Goes to School	590372130	Scholastic Inc.	1	Y
		16	McMullan, Kate	Fluffy Series/Fluffy and the Fire Fighters	439129176	Scholastic Inc.	1	
		17	Mills, Claudia	Gus and Grandpa	374428476	Farrar Strauss & Giroux	1	

Group Description	Level	#	Author	Title	ISBN	Publisher	Quantity	Heinemann Write-Up
		18	Mills, Claudia	Gus and Grandpa and the Two-Wheeled Bike	374328218	Farrar Strauss & Giroux	1	
		19	O'Connor, J.	Molly the Brave & Me	394841751	Random House	1	
		20	Pomerantz, Charlotte	Outside Dog, The	64441873	Harper Collins	1	
		21	Sharmat, Marjorie Weinman	Nate the Great/Fishy Prize	440400392	Bantam Doubleday Dell	1	
		22	Sharmat, Marjorie Weinman	Nate the Great/Missing Key	044046191X	Bantam Doubleday Dell	1	
		23	Spirn, Michele Sobel	Know Nothings, The	64442268	Harper Trophy	1	
		24	Spirn, Michele Sobel	Know-Nothing Birthday, A	006444242X	Harper Collins	1	
		25	Spirn, Michele Sobel	Know-Nothings Talk Turkey, The	60281839	Harper Collins	1	

MODULE 2: More Independent Reading : Filling in the Uppr Portion of the Library

Group Description	Level	#	Author	Title	ISBN	Publisher	Quantity	Heinemann Write-Up
	8	1	Adler, David	Cam Jansen Series/Mystery of the Monster Movie	140360212	Viking Penguin	1	Y
		2	Adler, David	Cam Jansen Series/Mystery of the UFO	590461222	Scholastic Inc.	1	
		3	Blume, Judy	One in the Middle is a Green Kangaroo, The	440467314	Bantam Doubleday Dell	1	Y
		4	Brown, Jeff	Flat Stanley Series/Flat Stanley	64420299	Harper Trophy	1	
		5	Brown, Marc	Arthur Chapter Books Series/Locked In the Library	316115584	Little Brown & Co	1	
		6	Cosby, Bill	Little Bill Series/Best Way to Play	59052190X	Scholastic Inc.	1	
		7	Cosby, Bill	Little Bill Series/Shipwreck Saturday	590956205	Scholastic Inc.	1	
		8	Delton, Judy	Pee Wee Scouts/Send in the Clowns	44040732X	Dell Publishing	1	
		9	Howe, James	Pinky & Rex Series/Get Married	689825269	Simon & Schuster	1	Y
		10	Komaiko, Leah	Annie Bananie and the Pain sisters	44041038X	Bantam Doubleday Dell	1	
		11	Levy, Elizabeth	Invisible Inc Series/Schoolyard Mystery	590474839	Scholastic Inc.	1	

Group Description	Level	#	Author	Title	ISBN	Publisher	Quantity	Heinemann Write-Up
		12	Marshall, James	George and Martha Series/Rise and Shine	395280060	Houghton Mifflin	1	
		13	Moore, Miriam	Kwanzaa Contest, the	786811226	Hyperion Books	1	
		14	Osborne, Mary Pope	Magic Tree House Series/Dinosaurs Before Dark	679824111	Random House	1	Y
		15	Osborne, Mary Pope	Magic Tree House Series/Lions at Lunchtime	679883401	Random House	1	
		16	Parish, Peggy	Amelia Bedelia Series/Play Ball, Amelia Bedelia	64442055	Harper Trophy	1	Y
		17	Parish, Peggy	Amelia Bedelia Series/Thank You, Amelia Bedelia	64441555	Harper Trophy	1	Y
		18	Park, Barbara	Junie B. Jones and the Stupid Smelly Bus	679826424	Random House	1	
		19	Pilkey, Dav	Captain Underpants & the Perilous Plot of Professor Poopypants	439049970	Scholastic Inc.	1	
		20	Rylant, Cynthia	Cobble Street Cousins/A Little Shopping	68981710X	Simon & Schuster	1	
		21	Rylant, Cynthia	Cobble Street Cousins/Some Good News	689817134	Simon & Schuster	1	
		22	Sachar, Louis	Marvin Redpost: Class President	67988999X	Scholastic Inc.	1	Y
	9	1	Cameron, Ann	Julian's Glorious Summer	394891171	Random House	1	
		2	Cameron, Ann	Stories That Julian Tells, The	394828925	Alfred A. Knopf	1	Y
		3	Cleary, Beverly	Muggie Maggie	380710870	William Morrow & Co	1	Y
		4	Duffey, Betsy	How To Be Cool in Third Grade	141304669	Penguin Putnam	1	
		5	Giff, Patricia Reilly	Ballet Slippers Series/Not-So-Perfect Rosie	141300604	Penguin Puffin	1	Y
		6	Hurwitz, Johanna	Aldo Ice Cream	14034084X	Penguin Putnam	1	
		7	Roy, Ron	A to Z Mysteries/Absent Author (#1)	679881689	Random House	1	Y
		8	Roy, Ron	A to Z Mysteries/Bald Bandit (#2)	679884491	Random House	1	

Group Description	Level	#	Author	Title	ISBN	Publisher	Quantity	Heinemann Write-Up
		9	Rylant, Cynthia	Best Wishes	1878450204	Richard C. Owen Publishers	1	
		10	Warner, Sally	Lily Series/Accidental Lily	375801820	Alfred A Knopf	1	
		11	Warner, Sally	Lily Series/Leftover Lily	375803475	Alfred A Knopf	1	
		12	Yolen, Jane	Piggins	152616861	Harcourt Brace	1	Y
	10	1	Danziger, Paula	Amber Brown Series/Forever Amber Brown	590947257	Scholastic Inc.	1	
		2	Koller, Jackie French	Dragonling, The	671867903	Pocket Books	1	
		3	Lansky, Bruce	Girls to the Rescue #2	671573756	Meadowbrook	1	
		4	Park, Barbara	Almost Starring Skinnybones	394825918	Random House	1	
		5	Parlin, J.	Amelia Earheart	440401178	Dell Publishing	1	
		6	Ziefert, Harriet	Elemenopeo	395904935	Houghton Mifflin	1	

MODULE 3: Multiple Copies for Small Group Work

Group Description	Level	#	Author	Title	ISBN	Publisher	Quantity	Heinemann Write-Up
	5	1	Jonas, Ann	Quilt, The			1	Y
	6	1	Minarik, Else Holmelund	Little Bear Series/Little Bear	64440044	Harper Trophy	1	Y
	7	1	Rylant, Cynthia	Poppleton	59084783X	Scholastic Inc.	1	Y
		2	Sharmat, Marjorie Weinman	Nate the Great/Nate the Great and Me	812429958	Bantam Doubleday Dell	1	Y
	8	1	Conford, Ellen	Jenny Archer Series/Jenny Archer Author	316153532	Little Brown & Co	1	
		2	Delton, Judy	Pee Wee Scouts/Cookies & Crutches (#1)	440400104	Bantam Doubleday Dell	1	Y
		3	Giff, Patricia Reilly	Kids of Polk Street Series/Say Cheese	440476399	Dell Publishing	1	Y
		4	Howe, James	Pinky & Rex Series/Pinky and Rex	689823487	Simon & Schuster	1	
		5	Kline, Suzy	Horrible Harry Series/in Room 2B	140385525	Penguin Puffin	1	

Group Description	Level	#	Author	Title	ISBN	Publisher	Quantity	Heinemann Write-Up
		6	Levy, Elizabeth	Invisible Inc Series/The Mystery of the Missing Dog	590474847	Scholastic Inc.	1	
		7	Osborne, Mary Pope	Magic Tree House Series/Buffalo Before Breakfast	679890645	Random House	1	
		8	Parish, Peggy	Amelia Bedelia Series/Amelia Bedelia	64441555	Harper Trophy	1	Y
	9	1	Duffey, Betsy	Cody series/Hey, New Kid!	140384391	Penguin Puffin	1	
		2	Warner, Gertrude	Boxcar Children Series/Mystery at the Fair	590569023	Scholastic Inc.	1	
MODULE 4: Enrichment								
Author Studies		1	Viorst, Judith	Alexander & the Terrible, Horrible, No Good, Very Bad Day	689711735	Simon & Schuster	2	Y
		2	Viorst, Judith	Alexander, Who Used to Be…	689711999	Simon & Schuster	2	
		3	Viorst, Judith	Earrings!	689716699	Simon & Schuster	2	Y
		4	Viorst, Judith	Sunday Mornings	68970447X	Macmillan Publishing	2	
		5	Viorst, Judith	Tenth Good Thing About Barney, The	689712030	Simon & Schuster	2	Y
		6	Williams, Vera	Chair for My Mother, A	590331558	William Morrow & Co	2	Y
		7	Williams, Vera	Cherries and Cherry Pits	590412388	Scholastic Inc.	2	Y
		8	Williams, Vera	Music, Music for Everyone	688078117	William Morrow & Co	2	Y
		9	Williams, Vera	Something Special for Me	688065260	William Morrow & Co	2	
		10	Williams, Vera	Three Days on a River in a Red Canoe	688040721	William Morrow & Co	2	Y
Memoir		1	Aliki	Two of Us, The			1	
		2	Crews, Donald	Shortcut	688135765	William Morrow & Co	1	Y
		3	Rylant, Cynthia	Relatives Came, The	689717385	Simon & Schuster	1	
		4	Woodson, Jacqueline	We Had a Picnic This Sunday Past	786802421	Hyperion Books	1	Y
Nonfiction		1	Brenner, Barbara	Thinking About Ants	1572552093	Mondo Publishing	1	

Group Description	Level	#	Author	Title	ISBN	Publisher	Quantity	Heinemann Write-Up
		2	Burleigh, Robert	Home Run: The Story of Babe Ruth	152009701	Harcourt Brace	1	
		3	Hooper, Meredith	Pebble In My Pocket, The/A History of Our Earth	670862592	Viking Penguin	1	
		4	Jenkins, Steve	What Do You Do When Something Wants To Eat You?	395825148	Houghton Mifflin	1	
		5	Lasky, Kathryn	Most Beautiful Roof in the World, The	152008977	Harcourt Brace	1	
		6	Lauber, Patricia	Earthworms: Underground Farmers	606112855	Demco Media	1	
		7	Leedy, Loreen	Furry News, The/How to Make a Newspaper	823410269	Holiday House	1	
		8	Quantock, Rod	School Newspaper, The		Wright Group	1	
Nonfiction How-To		1	Bolton, Faye	Planning a Birthday Party			1	
		2	Lucuero, Jaime	How to Make Salsa	1572551194	Mondo Publishing	1	
		3	Schwarz, Renee	Papier-Mache	1550747274	Kids Can Press	1	
Poetry		1	Adolf, Arnold	Street Music: City Poems	60215232	Harper Collins	1	
		2	Kuskin, Karla	Near the Window Tree	60235403	Harper Collins	1	
		3	Nye, Naomi Shihab	Salting the Ocean	688161936	Harper Collins	1	
		4	Rogasky, B.	Winter Poems	59042873X	Scholastic Inc.	1	
		5	Siebert, Diane	Mojave	64432831	Harper Collins	1	
Qualities of Good Writing		1	Aragon, Jane Chelsea	Salt Hands	140503218	Penguin Putnam	1	
		2	Baylor, Byrd	Other Way to Listen, The	689810539	Simon & Schuster	1	Y
		3	Ray, Deborah	Stargazing Sky	517578166	Random House	1	
		4	Woodson, Jacqueline	Other Side, The	399231161	Putnam Publishing	1	

MODULE 5: Multiple Copies for Book Clubs

Group Description	Level	#	Author	Title	ISBN	Publisher	Quantity	Heinemann Write-Up
	7	1	Schade, Susan	Toad Takes Off	679869352	Random House	4	

Group Description	Level	#	Author	Title	ISBN	Publisher	Quantity	Heinemann Write-Up
		2	Van Leeuwen, Jean	Amanda Pig and Her Big Brother Oliver	140370080	Penguin Puffin	4	Y
	8	1	Bos, Burny	Molesons/Fun With the Molesons	735813531	North South Books	4	
		2	Cosby, Bill	Little Bill Series/Treasure Hunt	590956183	Scholastic Inc.	4	
		3	Dale, Jenny	Kitten Friends Series/Bob the Bouncy Kitten	689841094	Simon & Schuster	4	
		4	Giff, Patricia Reilly	Kids of Polk Street Series/Pickle Puss	440468442	Bantam Doubleday Dell	4	
		5	Kline, Suzy	Horrible Harry Series/the Dungeon	140386203	Penguin Publishing	4	Y
		6	Parish, Peggy	Amelia Bedelia Series/ the Surprise Shower	64440192	Harper Trophy	4	Y
		7	Pilkey, Dav	Captain Underpants & the Invasion of the Incredibly Naughty Cafeteria Ladies from Outer Space	439049962	Scholastic Inc.	4	
		8	Saunders, Susan	Black Cat Club/Creature Double Feature (#9)	64420736	Harper Trophy	4	
		9	Willner-Pardo, Gina	Spider Storch Series/Carpool Catastrophe	807575763	Albert Whitman	4	
	9	1	Cleary, Beverly	Mouse and the Motorcycle, The	380709244	William Morrow & Co	4	Y
MODULE 6: Nonfiction	5; 6; 7; 8; 9	1	Collard, Sneed	Animal Dads	618032991	Houghton Mifflin	1	Y
		1	Butterfield, Moira	Quick, Quiet, and Feathered	081727233X	Steck-Vaughn	1	
		2	Drew, David	Life of a Butterfly, The			1	
		3	Florian, Douglas	Chef, A	688111084	Greenwillow Books	1	
		4	Gibbons, Gail	From Seed to Plant	823410250	Holiday House	1	
		5	Gibbons, Gail	Moon Book, The	823413640	Holiday House	1	
		6	Scieszka, Jon	Math Curse, The	670861944	Penguin Publishing	1	
	6	1	Maestro, Betsy	Why Do Leaves Change Color?	64451267	Harper Trophy	1	Y

Group Description	Level	#	Author	Title	ISBN	Publisher	Quantity	Heinemann Write-Up
	6; 7; 8	1	McPherson, Jan	Tails Can Tell	780128782	Wright Group	1	
		2	Robinson, Fay	Great Snakes!	590262432	Scholastic Inc.	1	Y
	7; 8	1	Biddulph, Fred & Jeanne	Different Kinds of Bread	780227255	Wright Group	1	
		2	Esbensen, Barbara	Sponges Are Skeletons	64451844	Harper Collins	1	
		3	Lauber, Patricia	You're Aboard Spaceship Earth	64451593	Harper Trophy	1	Y
	7; 8; 9	1	Bull, Pam	Money	32201851X	Wright Group	1	Y
		2	Evans, Chelsea	Diary of a Sunflower	439186064	Scholastic Inc.	1	
		3	Heller, Ruth	Reason for a Flower, The	698115597	Penguin Putnam	1	Y
		4	Massam-Windsor, Jo	Animal Fibers	780214331	Wright Group	1	
	8	1	Adler, David	Picture Book of Eleanor Roosevelt, A	590559079	Scholastic Inc.	1	Y
		2	Adler, David	Picture Book of Helen Keller, A	823409503	Holiday House	1	
		3	Adler, David	Picture Book of Jesse Owens, A	590494392	Scholastic Inc.	1	
		4	Adler, David	Picture Book of Rosa Parks, A	82341177X	Holiday House	1	
		5	Aliki	My Five Senses	6445083X	Harper Trophy	1	Y
		6	Biddulph, Fred & Jeanne	Fibers Made by People	780214366	Wright Group	1	
		7	Pinkney, Andrea Davis	Duke Ellington	786801786	Hyperion Books	1	
	8; 9	1	Arnosky, Jim	All About Deer	439058740	Scholastic Inc.	1	
		2	Berger, Melvin	Germs Make Me Sick	64451542	Harper Collins	1	
		3	Dussling, Jennifer	Slinky Scaly Snakes	789434393	DK Publishing	1	Y
		4	Gibbons, Gail	Click: A Book About Cameras & Taking Pictures	439148723	Scholastic Inc.	1	Y
		5	Gibbons, Gail	How a House is Built	823412326	Holiday House	1	Y
		6	Jenkins, Martin	Wings, Stings, and Wriggly Things	763600369	Candlewick Press	1	
		7	Tyler, Michael	Frogs	1572551917	Mondo Publishing	1	Y

Group Description	Level	#	Author	Title	ISBN	Publisher	Quantity	Heinemann Write-Up
	8; 9; 10	1	Bolton, Faye	Animal Shelters	1572551925	Mondo Publishing	1	
		2	Golenbock, Peter	Teammates	152842861	Harcourt Brace	1	Y
		3	Moore, Helen	Beavers	1572551119	Mondo Publishing	1	Y
		4	Short, Joan	Platypus	157255195X	Mondo Publishing	1	Y
	8; 9; 11	1	Jakobsen, Kathy	My New York	316456535	Little Brown & Co	1	
	9	1	Dorros, Arthur	Follow the Water from Brook to Ocean	64451151	Harper Collins	1	
		2	Monjo, F. N.	Drinking Gourd, The	64440427	Harper Trophy	1	
		3	Onyefulu, Ilfeoma	A is for Africa	140562222	Penguin Publishing	1	Y
	9; 10	1	Hall, Katy	Skeletons! Skeletons!	590460765	Scholastic Inc.	1	Y
	9; 10; 11	1	Berger, Melvin & Gilda	Do Tornados Really Twist?	439148804	Scholastic Inc.	1	
		2	Berger, Melvin & Gilda	Why Don't Haircuts Hurt?: Questions and Answers about the Human Body	590130862	Scholastic Inc.	1	Y
		3	National Geographic	Our World: A Child's First Picture Atlas	792275764	National Geographic	1	Y
		4	Workman, Robin	Surfing the Information Highway	78024608X	Wright Group	1	
	10	1	Cherry, Lynne	Great Kapok Tree, The	15200520	Harcourt Brace	1	Y
		2	Ryder, Joanne	Tyrannosaurus Time	688136826	William Morrow & Co	1	
	10; 11	1	Garelick, May	What Makes a Bird a Bird?	1572550082	Mondo Publishing	1	Y
	10; 11; 12	1	Ancona, George	Pinata Maker, The	152000607	Harcourt Brace	1	
		2	Dendy, Leslie	Tracks, Scats and Signs	836821475	Gareth Stevens Publishing	1	
	11	1	Aliki	Dinosaur Bones	64450775	Harper Collins	1	
	11; 12; 13	1	Ferris, Jeri	Walking the Road to Freedom	876145055	Lerner Publishing Group	1	

Benchmark Books for Each Text Level

TC Level	Benchmarks: Books that Represent Each Level
1	*A Birthday Cake* (Cowley) *I Can Write* (Williams) *The Cat on the Mat* (Wildsmith)
2	*Rain* (Kaplan) *Fox on the Box* (Gregorich)
3	*It Looked Like Spilt Milk* (Shaw) *I Like Books* (Browne) *Mrs. Wishy-Washy* (Cowley)
4	*Rosie's Walk* (Hutchins) *The Carrot Seed* (Krauss) *Cookie's Week* (Ward)
5	*George Shrinks* (Joyce) *Goodnight Moon* (Brown) *Hattie and the Fox* (Fox)
6	*Danny and the Dinosaur* (Hoff) *Henry and Mudge* (Rylant)
7	*Nate the Great* (Sharmat) *Meet M&M* (Ross)
8	*Horrible Harry* (Kline) *Pinky and Rex* (Howe) *Arthur Series* (Marc Brown)
9	*Amber Brown* (Danziger) *Ramona Quimby, Age 8* (Cleary)
10	*James and the Giant Peach* (Dahl) *Fudge-A-Mania* (Blume)
11	*Shiloh* (Naylor) *The Great Gilly Hopkins* (Paterson)
12	*Bridge to Terabithia* (Paterson) *Baby* (MacLachlan)
13	*Missing May* (Rylant) *Where the Red Fern Grows* (Rawls)
14	*A Day No Pigs Would Die* (Peck) *Scorpions* (Myers)
15	*The Golden Compass* (Pullman) *The Dark Is Rising* (Cooper) *A Wizard of Earthsea* (Le Guin)

Descriptions of Text Levels One Through Seven

TEXT LEVEL ONE

This level roughly corresponds to the following levels in other systems:

Reading Recovery© (RR) Levels 1–2
Developmental Reading Assessment (DRA) Levels A–2

Text Characteristics for TC Level One

- The font is large, clear, and is usually printed in black on a white background.

- There is exaggerated spacing between words and letters. (In some books, publishers have enlarged the print but have not adjusted the spacing which can create difficulties for readers.)

- There is usually a single word, phrase, or simple sentence on a page, and the text is patterned and predictable. For example, in the book *I Can Read*, once a child knows the title (which is ideally read to a Level One reader) it is not hard for the child to read "I can read the newspaper," "I can read the cereal box." These readers are regarded as "preconventional" because they rely on the illustrations (that support the meaning) and the sounds of language (or syntax) and not on graphophonics or word/letter cues to read a sentence such as, "I can read the newspaper."

- Usually each page contains two or three sight words. A Level One book *may* contain one illustrated word on a page (such as "Mom," "Dad," "sister," "cat") but it's just as easy for a child to read "I see my mom. I see my Dad. I see my sister. I see my cat." because the sight words give the child a way into the text.

- The words are highly supported by illustrations. No one would expect a Level One reader to solve the word "newspaper." We would, however, expect a child at this level to look at the picture and at the text and to read the word "newspaper."

- Words are consistently placed in the same area of each page, preferably top left or bottom left.

Characteristics of the Reader

Readers in this group will demonstrate most of these behaviors.

- Remember the pattern in a predictable text

- Use picture cues

- Use left to right directionality to read one or two lines of print
- Work on matching spoken words with printed words and self-correcting when these don't "come out even"
- Rely on the spaces between words to signify the end of one word and the beginning of another. These readers read the spaces as well as the words, as the words are at first black blobs on white paper
- Locate one or two known words on a page

Benchmarks

The following titles are representative of the kinds of books found in this grouping.

A Birthday Cake, Joy Cowley
Cat on the Mat, Brian Wildsmith
The Farm, Literacy 2000/Stage 1
Growing Colors, Bruce McMillan
I Can Write, Rozanne Williams
Time for Dinner, PM Starters

Assessment

The following titles can be used to determine if a reader is ready to move on to the next grouping of books. This type of assessment is most effective if the text is unfamiliar to the reader. If these titles will be used as assessment texts, they should *not* be part of the classroom library.

My Home, Story Box
The Tree Stump, Little Celebrations
DRA Assessments A–2

We move children from Level One to Level Two books when they are consistently able to match one spoken word with one word written on the page. This means that they can point under words in a Level One book as they read and know when they haven't matched a spoken word to a written word by noticing that, at the end of the line, they still have words left on the page or they've run out of words. When children read multisyllabic words and compound words and point to multiple, instead of one, word on the page, we consider this a successful one-to-one match.

TEXT LEVEL TWO

This level roughly corresponds to the following levels in other systems:

Reading Recovery© (RR) Levels 3–4
Developmental Reading Assessment (DRA) Levels 3–4

Text Characteristics of TC Level Two

- There are usually two lines of print on at least some of the pages in these books, and sometimes there are three. This means readers will become accustomed to making the return sweep to the beginning of a new line.

- The texts are still patterned and predictable, but now the patterns tend to switch at intervals. Almost always, the pattern changes at the end of the book. The repeating unit may be as long as two sentences in length.

- The font continues to be large and clear. The letters might not, however, be black against white although this is generally the case.

- Children still rely on the picture but the pictures tend to give readers more to deal with; children need to search more in the picture to find help in reading the words.

- High frequency words are still helpful and important. The sentences in Level One books tend to begin with 2 to 3 high frequency words, for example, "I like to run. I like to jump." At this level, the pages are more apt to begin with a single high frequency word and then include words that require picture support and attention to first letters, for example, "A mouse has a long tail. A bear has a short tail."

- Sentences are more varied, resulting in texts that include a full range of punctuation.

Characteristics of the Reader

Readers in this group will demonstrate most of these behaviors.

- Get the mouth ready for the initial sound of a word

- Use left to right directionality as well as a return sweep to another line of print

- Locate one or two known words on a page

- Monitor for meaning: check to make sure it makes sense

Benchmarks

The following titles are representative of the kinds of books found in this grouping.

All Fall Down, Brian Wildsmith
I Went Walking, Sue Williams
Rain, Robert Kalan
Shoo, Sunshine

Assessment

The following titles can be used to determine if a reader is ready to move on to the next grouping. This type of assessment is most effective if the text is unfamiliar to a reader. If these titles will be used as assessment texts, they should *not* be part of the classroom library.

The Bus Ride, Little Celebrations, DRA 3
Fox on the Box, School Zone, DRA 4

We generally move children from Level Two to Level Three texts when they know how to use the pictures and the syntax to generate possibilities for the next word, when they attend to the first letters of unknown words. These readers will also read and rely on high frequency words such as *I, the, a, to, me, mom, the child's name, like, love, go,* and *and*.

TEXT LEVEL THREE

This level roughly corresponds to the following levels in other systems:

Reading Recovery© (RR) Levels 5–8
Developmental Reading Assessment (DRA) Levels 6–8

Text Characteristics of TC Level Three

It is important to note that this grouping includes a wide range of levels. This was done deliberately because at this level, readers should be able to select "just right" books for themselves and be able to monitor their own reading.

- Sentences are longer and readers will need to put their words together in order to take in more of the sentence at a time. When they are stuck, it's often helpful to nudge them to reread and try again.

- The pictures are not as supportive as they've been. It's still helpful for children to do picture walks prior to reading an unfamiliar text, but now the goal is less about surmising what words the page contains and more about seeing an overview of the narrative.

- Readers must rely on graphophonics across the whole word. If readers hit a wall at this level, it's often because they're accustomed to predicting words based on a dominant pattern and using the initial letters (only) to confirm their predictions. It takes readers a while to begin checking the print closely enough to adjust their expectations.

- Children will need to use sight words to help with unknown words, using parts of these familiar words as analogies, helping them unlock the unfamiliar words.

- The font size and spacing are less important now.

- Words in the text begin to include contractions. We can help children read these by urging them to look all the way across a word.

Characteristics of the Reader

Readers in this group will demonstrate most of these behaviors.

- Reread and self-correct

- Read with some fluency

- Cross check one cue against another

- Monitor for meaning: check to make sure what has been read makes sense and sounds right

- Recognize common chunks of words

Benchmarks

The following titles are representative of the kinds of books found in this grouping.

Bears in the Night Stan and Jan, Berenstain
The Chick and the Duckling, Ginsburg
It Looked Like Spilt Milk, Charles G. Shaw
Mrs. Wishy-Washy, Joy Cowley

Assessment

The following titles can be used to determine if a reader is ready to move on to the next grouping. This type of assessment is most effective if the text is unfamiliar to a reader. If these titles will be used as assessment texts, they should *not* be part of the classroom library.

Bread, Story Box, DRA 6
Get Lost Becka, School Zone, DRA 8

We move a child to Level Four books if that child can pick up an unfamiliar book like *Bread* or *It Looked Like Spilt Milk* and read it with a little difficulty, but with a lot of independence and with strategies. This reader should know to reread when she is stuck, to use the initial sounds in a word, to chunk word families within a word, and so on.

TEXT LEVEL FOUR

This level roughly corresponds to the following levels in other systems:

Reading Recovery© (RR) Levels 9–12
Developmental Reading Assessment (DRA) Levels 10–12

Text Characteristics of TC Level Four

- In general, the child who is reading Level Four books is able to do more of the same reading work he could do with texts at the previous level. This child reads texts that contain more words, lines, pages, and more challenging vocabulary.

- These texts contain even less picture support than earlier levels.

- Fluency and phrasing are very important for the Level Four reader. If children don't begin to read quickly enough, they won't be able to carry the syntax of the sentence along well enough to comprehend what they are reading.

- These books use brief bits of literary language. That is, in these books the mother may turn to her child and say, "We shall be rich."

- These books are more apt to have a plot (with characters, setting, problem, solution) and they tend to be less patterned than they were at the previous level.

Characteristics of the Reader

Readers in this group will demonstrate most of these behaviors.

- Reread and self-correct

- Read with fluency

- Integrate cues from meaning, structure, and visual sources

- Monitor for meaning: check to make sure what has been read makes sense, sounds right, and looks right

- Make some analogies from known words to figure out unknown words

- Read increasingly difficult chunks within words

Benchmarks

The following titles are representative of the kinds of books found in this grouping.

The Carrot Seed, Ruth Krauss
Cookie's Week, Cindy Ward
Rosie's Walk, Pat Hutchins
Titch, Pat Hutchins

Assessment

The following titles can be used to determine if a reader is ready to move on to the next grouping. This type of assessment is most effective if the text is unfamiliar to a reader. If these titles will be used as assessment texts, they should *not* be part of the classroom library.

Are You There Bear?, Ron Maris, DRA 10
The House in the Tree, Rigby PM Story Books
Nicky Upstairs and Downstairs, Harriet Ziefert
William's Skateboard, Sunshine, DRA 12

We move a child to Level Five books if that reader can independently use a variety of strategies to work through difficult words or parts of a text. The reader must be reading fluently enough to reread quickly, when necessary, so as to keep the flow of the story going. If a reader is reading very slowly, taking too much time to work through the hard parts, then this reader may not be ready to move on to the longer, more challenging texts in Level Five.

TEXT LEVEL FIVE

This level roughly corresponds to the following levels in other systems:

Reading Recovery© (RR) Levels 13–15
Developmental Reading Assessment (DRA) Level 14

Text Characteristics

- Sentences in Level Five books tend to be longer, more varied, and more complex than they were in previous levels.

- Many of the stories are retold folktales or fantasy-like stories that use literary or story language, such as: "Once upon a time, there once lived, a long, long time ago. . . ."

- Many books may be in a cumulative form in which text is added to each page, requiring the reader to read more and more text as the story unfolds, adding a new line with every page turn.

- The illustrations tend to be a representation of just a slice of what is happening in the text. For example, the text may tell of a long journey that a character has taken over time, but the picture may represent just the character reaching his destination.

- There will be more unfamiliar and sometimes complex vocabulary.

Characteristics of the Reader

Readers in this group will demonstrate most of these behaviors.

- Reread and self-correct regularly

- Read with fluency

- Integrate a balance of cues

- Monitor for meaning: check to make sure what has been read makes sense, sounds right, and looks right

- Demonstrate fluent phrasing of longer passages

- Use a repertoire of graphophonic strategies to problem solve through text

Benchmarks

The following titles are representative of the kinds of books found in this grouping.

George Shrinks, William Joyce
Goodnight Moon, Margaret Wise Brown
Hattie and the Fox, Mem Fox
Little Red Hen, Parkes

Assessment

The following titles can be used to determine if a reader is ready to move on to the next grouping. This type of assessment is most effective if the text is unfamiliar to a reader. If these titles will be used as assessment texts, they should *not* be part of the classroom library.

> *The Old Man's Mitten,* Bookshop, Mondo
> *Who Took the Farmer's Hat?,* Joan Nodset, DRA 14

We move children from Level Five to Level Six texts when they are consistently able to use a multitude of strategies to work through challenges quickly and efficiently. These challenges may be brought on by unfamiliar settings, unfamiliar language structures, unfamiliar words, and increased text length. The amount of text on a page and the length of a book should not be a hindrance to the reader who is moving on to Level Six. The reader who is ready to move on is also adept at consistently choosing appropriate books that will make her a stronger reader.

TEXT LEVEL SIX

This level roughly corresponds to the following levels in other systems:

> Reading Recovery© (RR) Levels 16–18
> Developmental Reading Assessment (DRA) Level 16

Text Characteristics of TC Level Six

- The focus of the book is evident at its start

- Descriptive language is used more frequently than before

- Dialogue often tells a large part of the story

- Texts may include traditional retellings of fairy tales and folktales

- Stories are frequently humorous

- Considerable amount of text is found on each page. A book in this grouping may be a picture book, or a simple chapter book. These books offer extended stretches of text.

- Texts are often simple chapter books, and often have episodic chapters in which each chapter stands as a story on its own

- Texts often center around just two or three main characters who tend to be markedly different from each other (a boy and a girl, a child and a parent)

- There is limited support from the pictures

- Texts includes challenging vocabulary

Characteristics of the Reader

Readers in this group will demonstrate most of these behaviors.

- Reread and self-correct regularly

- Read with fluency

- Integrate a balance of cues

- Demonstrate fluent phrasing of longer passages

- Use a repertoire of graphophonic strategies to problem solve through text

Benchmarks

The following titles are representative of the kinds of books found in this grouping.

Danny and the Dinosaur, Syd Hoff
The Doorbell Rang, Pat Hutchins
Henry and Mudge, Cynthia Rylant
The Very Hungry Caterpillar, Eric Carle

Assessment

The following titles can be used to determine if a reader is ready to move on to the next grouping. This type of assessment is most effective if the text is unfamiliar to a reader. If these titles will be used as assessment texts, they should *not* be part of the classroom library.

Bear Shadow, Frank Asch, DRA 16
Jimmy Lee Did It, Pat Cummings, DRA 18

TEXT LEVEL SEVEN

This level roughly corresponds to the following levels in other systems:

Reading Recovery© (RR) Levels 19–20
Developmental Reading Assessment (DRA) Level 20

Text Characteristics of TC Level Seven

- Dialogue is used frequently to move the story along

- Texts often have 2 to 3 characters. (They tend to have distinctive personalities and usually don't change across a book or series.)

- Texts may include extended description. (The language may set a mood, and may be quite poetic or colorful.)

- Some books have episodic chapters. (In other books, each chapter contributes to the understanding of the entire book and the reader must carry the story line along.)

- There is limited picture support

- Plots are usually linear without large time-gaps

- Texts tend to have larger print and double spacing between lines of print

Characteristics of the Reader

Readers in this group will demonstrate most of these behaviors.

- Reread and self-correct regularly

- Read with fluency, intonation, and phrasing

- Demonstrate the existence of a self-extending (self-improving) system for reading

- Use an increasingly more challenging repertoire of graphophonic strategies to problem solve through text

- Solve unknown words with relative ease

Benchmarks

The following titles are representative of the kinds of books found in this grouping.

A Baby Sister for Frances, Russell Hoban
Meet M&M, Pat Ross
Nate the Great, Marjorie Sharmat
Poppleton, Cynthia Rylant

Asessment

The following titles can be used to determine if a reader is ready to move on to the next grouping. This type of assessment is most effective if the text is unfamiliar to a reader. If these titles will be used as assessment texts, they should *not* be part of the classroom library.

Peter's Pockets, Eve Rice, DRA 20
Uncle Elephant, Arnold Lobel

More Information to Help You Choose the Library That is Best for Your Readers

Library A

Library A is appropriate if your children enter kindergarten in October as very emergent readers with limited experiences hearing books read aloud. Use the following chart to help determine if Library A is about right for your class.

Approximate Distribution of Reading Levels of a Class Matched to Library A		
Benchmark Book	Reading Level	Percentage of the Class Reading at about This Level
The Cat on the Mat, by Wildsmith	TC Level 1	45%
Fox on the Box, by Gregorich	TC Level 2	30%
Mrs. Wishy-Washy, by Cowley	TC Level 3	25%

Library B

Library B is appropriate for a class of children if, in October, they are reading books like *I Went Walking*. Use the following chart to help determine if Library B is about right for your class. (Note to New York City teachers: Many of your students would score a 3 on the ECLAS correlated with titles such as, *Things I Like to Do* and *My Shadow*.)

Approximate Distribution of Reading Levels of a Class Matched to Library B		
Benchmark Book	Reading Level	Percentage of the Class Reading at about This Level
The Cat on the Mat, by Wildsmith	TC Level 1	10%
Fox on the Box, by Gregorich	TC Level 2	10%
Mrs. Wishy-Washy, by Cowley	TC Level 3	30%
The Carrot Seed, by Krauss	TC Level 4	25%
Goodnight Moon, by Brown	TC Level 5	15%
Henry and Mudge, by Rylant	TC Level 6	5%
Nate the Great, by Sharmat	TC Level 7	5%

Library C

Library C is appropriate for a class of children if, in October, many of your students are approaching reading books like *Mrs. Wishy-Washy* and *Bears in the Night*. (Note to New York City teachers: Many of your students would be approaching a 4 on the ECLAS that would be correlated with *Baby Bear's Present* and *No Where and Nothing*.)

Approximate Distribution of Reading Levels of a Class Matched to Library C		
Benchmark Book	Reading Level	Percentage of the Class Reading at about This Level
Fox on the Box, by Gregorich	TC Level 2	8%
Mrs. Wishy-Washy, by Cowley	TC Level 3	8%
The Carrot Seed, by Krauss	TC Level 4	20%
Goodnight Moon, by Brown	TC Level 5	20%
Henry and Mudge, by Carle	TC Level 6	20%
Nate the Great, by Sharmat	TC Level 7	15%
Pinky and Rex, by Howe	TC Level 8	5%
Ramona Quimby, by Cleary	TC Level 9	2%
James and the Giant Peach, by Dahl	TC Level 10	2%

Library D

Use the following chart to help determine if Library D is right for your class.

Approximate Distribution of Reading Levels of a Class Matched to Library D		
Benchmark Book	Reading Level	Percentage of the Class Reading at about This Level
Good Night Moon, by Brown	Level 5	8%
Henry and Mudge, by Rylant	Level 6	20%
Nate the Great, by Sharmat	Level 7	25%
Pinky and Rex, by Howe	Level 8	30%
Ramona Quimby, by Cleary	Level 9	10%
James and the Giant Peach, by Dahl	Level 10	2%

Library E

Library E is appropriate for a class of children if, in October, a readers list tends to look approximately like the following chart.

Approximate Distribution of Reading Levels of a Class Matched to Library E		
Benchmark Book	*Reading Level*	*Percentage of the Class Reading at about This Level*
Nate the Great, by Sharmat	Level 7	10%
Pinky and Rex, by Howe	Level 8	25%
Ramona Quimby, by Cleary	Level 9	30%
James and the Giant Peach, by Dahl	Level 10	22%
Shiloh, by Naylor	Level 11	5%
Baby, by MacLachlan	Level 12	5%
Missing May, by Rylant	Level 13	2%
Scorpions, by Myers	Level 14	1%

Library F

Library F is appropriate for a class of children if, in October, a readers list tends to look approximately like the following chart.

Approximate Distribution of Reading Levels of a Class Matched to Library F		
Benchmark Book	*Reading Level*	*Percentage of the Class Reading at about This Level*
Pinky and Rex, by Howe	Level 8	2%
Ramona Quimby, by Cleary	Level 9	20%
James and the Giant Peach, by Dahl	Level 10	25%
Shiloh, by Naylor	Level 11	30%
Baby, by MacLachlan	Level 12	20%
Missing May, by Rylant	Level 13	2%
Scorpions, by Myers	Level 14	1%

Library G

Library G is appropriate for a class of children if, in October, a readers list tends to look approximately like the following chart.

Approximate Distribution of Reading Levels of a Class Matched to Library G		
Benchmark Book	*Reading Level*	*Percentage of the Class Reading at about This Level*
James and the Giant Peach, by Dahl	Level 10	10%
Shiloh, by Naylor	Level 11	10%
Baby, by MacLachlan	Level 12	30%
Missing May, by Rylant	Level 13	30%
Scorpions, by Myer	Level 14	20%

About the Guides

Soon we'd begun not only accumulating titles and honing arrangements for dream libraries, but also writing teaching advice to go with the chosen books. Our advice to the contributors was, "Write a letter from you to others who'll use this book with children. Tell folks what you notice in the book, and advise them on teaching opportunities you see. Think about advice you would give a teacher just coming to know the book." The insights, experience, and folk wisdom poured in and onto the pages of the guides.

A written guide accompanies many of the books in the libraries. These guides are not meant to be prescriptions for how a teacher or child should use a book. Instead they are intended to be resources, and we hope thoughtful teachers will tap into particular sections of a guide when it seems fit to do so. For example, a teaching guide might suggest six possible minilessons a teacher could do with a book. Of course, a teacher would never try to do all six of these! Instead we expect one of these minilessons will seem helpful to the teacher, and another minilesson to another teacher. The teaching guides illustrate the following few principles that are important to us.

Teaching One Text Intensely in Order to Learn About Many Texts

When you take a walk in the woods, it can happen that all the trees look the same, that they are just a monotony of foliage and trunks. It is only when you stop to learn about a particular tree, about its special leaf structure and the odd thickness of its bark, about the creatures that inhabit it and the seeds it lets fall, that you begin to see that particular kind of tree among the thickets. It is when you enter a forest knowing something about kinds of trees that you begin to truly see the multiplicity of trees in a forest and the particular attributes and mysteries of each one. Learning about the particulars of one tree leads you to thinking about all of the trees, each in its individuality, each with its unique deep structure, each with its own offerings.

The same is true of texts. The study of one can reveal not just the hidden intricacies of that story, but also the ways in which truths and puzzles can be structured in other writings as well. When one book holds a message in the way a chapter ends, it gives the reader the idea that any book may hold a message in the structure of its chapter's conclusions. When one book is revealed to make a sense that is unintended by the author, we look for unintended sense in other books we read. Within these guides, then, we hope that readers like you will find truths about the particular books they are written about, but more, we hope that you find pathways into all the books you read. By showing some lengthy thinking and meditations on one book, we hope to offer you paths toward thinking about each and every book that crosses your desk and crosses your mind.

Suggesting Classroom Library Arrangements

Many the attributes of a book, detailed in a guide, can become a category in a classroom library. If a group of students in a class seems particularly energized by the Harry Potter books, for example, the guide can be used to help determine which books could be in a bin in the library marked, "If You Like *Harry Potter*—Try These." The similarity between the *Harry Potter* books and the other books in this group may be not only in difficulty gradient, but also in content, story structure, popularity, or genre. That is, a class of children that like *Harry Potter* might benefit from a bin of books on fantasy, or from a collection of best-selling children's books, or from a bin of "Long-Books-You-Can't-Put-Down," or from stories set in imagined places. As you browse through the guides that accompany the books you have chosen, the connections will pop out at you.

Sometimes, the guides will help you determine a new or more interesting placement for a book. Perhaps you have regarded a book as historical fiction, but now you realize it could alternatively be shelved in a collection of books that offer children examples of "Great Leads to Imitate in Your Own Writing." Or, perhaps the guides will suggest entirely new categories that will appeal to your class in ways you and your students haven't yet imagined. Perhaps the guides will help you imagine a "Books That Make You Want to Change the World" category. Or maybe you'll decide to create a shelf in your library titled, "Books with Odd Techniques That Make You Wonder What the Author Is Trying To Do."

Aiding in Conferring

Teachers' knowledge of what to ask and what to teach a reader who says, "this book is boring" comes not only from their knowledge of particular students but also from their knowledge of the text they are talking about. Does "boring" mean that the book is too easy for the reader? Perhaps it means instead that the beginning few chapters of the book are hard to read—confusing because of a series of flashbacks. A guide might explain that the book under discussion has mostly internal, emotional action, and, if the reader is accustomed to avalanche-and-rattlesnake action in books, she may need some time to warm up to this unfamiliar kind of "quiet" action. The guide can point out the kinds of reactions, or troubles, other readers have had with particular books. With the guides at our fingertips, we can more easily determine which questions to ask students, or which pages to turn to, in order to get to the heart of the conference.

Providing a Resource for Curriculum Planning

One Friday, say, we leave the classroom knowing that our students' writing shows that they are thirsting for deeper, more complicated characters to study and imitate. As we plan lessons, we can page through the guides that correspond with some of the books in our library, finding, or remembering, books that students can study that depict fascinating characters.

On the other hand, perhaps we need a book to read aloud to the class, or perhaps we need to recommend a book to a particular struggling reader.

Maybe a reader has finished a book he loves and has turned to you to help him plan his reading for the next weeks. When designing an author study or an inquiry into punctuation and its effects on meaning, it also helps to have the guides with you to point out books that may be helpful in those areas. In each of these cases, and many more, the guides can be a planning aid for you.

Reminding Us, or Teaching Us, About Particular Book Basics

No teacher can read, let alone recall in detail, every book that every child will pick up in the classroom. Of course, we read many of them and learn about many more from our colleagues, but there are far too many books in the world for us to be knowledgeable about them all. Sometimes, the guides will be a reminder of what you have read many years ago. Sometimes, they will provide a framework for you to question or direct your students more effectively than you could if you knew nothing at all about the book. "Probably, you will have to take some time to understand the setting before you can really get a handle on this book, why don't you turn to the picture atlas?" you might say after consulting the guide, or "Sharlene is reading another book that is similar to this one in so many ways! Why don't you go pair up with her to talk." You might learn to ask, "What do you think of Freddy?" in order to learn if the student is catching on to the tone of the narrator, or you might learn you could hint, "Did you get to chapter three yet? Because I bet you won't be bored any more when you get there. . . ." The guides provide a bit of what time constraints deny us: thoughtful insights about the content or unusual features of a given book.

Showcasing Literary Intricacies in Order to Suggest a Reader's Thinking

Sometimes, when we read a book, our idea of the author's message is in our minds before we even finish the story. Because we are experienced readers, much of our inferring and interpreting, our understanding of symbols and contexts, can come to us effortlessly. In the guides, we have tried to slow down some of that thinking so that we can all see it more easily. We have tried to lay out some of the steps young readers may have to go through in order to come to a cohesive idea of what the story is about, or a clear understanding of why a character behaved the way she did. As experienced readers, we may not even realize that our readers are confused by the unorthodox use of italics to show us who is speaking, for example. We may not remember the days when we were confused by changing narrators, the days when it took us a few chapters to figure out a character wasn't to be believed. In these guides, we have tried to go back to those days when we were more naïve readers, and have tried to fill in those thoughts and processes we are now able to skip over so easily.

By bringing forth the noteworthy features of the text, features experienced readers may not even notice, we are reminded of the thinking that our students need to go through in order to make sense of their reading. It gives us an idea of where to offer pointers, of where readers may have gone off in an unhelpful direction, or of where their thinking may need to go instead of where it has gone. By highlighting literary intricacies, we may remember that every bit about the construction of texts is a navigation point for students, and every bit is something we may be able to help students in learning.

Providing a Community of Readers and Teachers

The guides are also intended to help teachers learn from the community of other teachers and readers who have used particular texts already. They make available some of the stories and experiences other teachers have had, in order that we might stand on their shoulders and take our teaching even higher than they could reach. These guides are intended to give you some thinking to go with the books in your classroom library, thinking you can mix with your own ideas.

In the end, we don't all have a community of other teachers with whom we can talk about children's literature. The guides are meant not to stand in for that community, but instead to provide a taste, an appetizer, of the world of supportive professional communities. We hope that by reading these guides and feeling the companionship, guidance and insight they offer, teachers will be nudged to recreate that experience for the other books that have no guides, and that they will ask their colleagues, librarians, and the parents of their students to talk with them about children's literature and young readers. Then, when teachers are creating these guides for themselves, on paper or in their minds' eyes, we will know this project has done the work for which it was created.

Bibliography

Atwell, Nancie. 1987. *In the Middle: Writing, Reading, and Learning with Adolescents*. Portsmouth, NH: Boynton/Cook.

Calkins, Lucy. 2001. *The Art of Teaching Reading*. New York: Addison-Wesley Educational Publishers, Inc.

Cambourne, Brian. 1993. *The Whole Story: Natural Learning and the Acquisition of Literacy in the Classroom*. Auckland, NZ: Ashton Scholastic.

Krashen, Stephen. 1993. *The Power of Reading: Insights from the Research*. Englewood, CO: Libraries Unlimited.

Meek, Margaret. 1988. *How Texts Teach What Readers Learn*. Thimble Press.

Smith, Frank. 1985. *Reading Without Nonsense*. 2nd ed. New York: TC Press.

A Chair For My Mother
Vera B. Williams

Book Summary

In this vividly illustrated story, a young girl describes her family's quest for an armchair. After they lose everything in a fire and get a new apartment, she, her mother and her grandmother save their coins in a big glass jar, working toward the moment when they will have enough for the chair. In the end, the family's perseverance earns them the "wonderful, beautiful, fat, soft armchair" they have wanted so much.

Basic Book Information

All but two pages in this 29-page book share the same layout: full-page illustrations are on the left of each pair of facing pages, and two or three paragraphs of text are on the right. Beneath the text is a small, simple illustration as well. *A Chair For My Mother* was named a Caldecott Honor Book. Its other accolades include The Boston Globe/Horn Book Award for Illustration and an American Library Association Notable Book selection. Vera B. Williams lives in Brooklyn.

Noteworthy Features

In many ways, the story of *A Chair For My Mother* is quite accessible. The girl, her mother, her grandmother and their cat are the only characters mentioned more than once, and thus the only characters readers need to remember from page to page. The girl herself narrates. Her voice is colloquial and clear. There is, however, a subtle shift in time, present to past to present: the fifth page of text flashes back to the fire one year earlier. A large capital letter accentuates the start of each new time, with a very large "M" at the start of the book, another large "M" at the start of the flashback and an equally large "T" at the start of the final, present-tense segment.

Much of the story is conveyed through the illustrations. For example, the narrator never explicitly states that work exhausts her mother but the image of her mother, shoes off, eyes closed, body slumped awkwardly around the kitchen table suggests why a comfortable armchair in which to relax might be so important. The small illustrations beneath the text also provide information. The narrator says that "it took a while" to find her cat after the fire; the tail poking from a garbage can under the text implies where the cat hid. The borders around facing pages convey yet more.

Teaching Ideas

A Chair For My Mother is a wonderful read aloud, but children should be able to hold this book and scrutinize its rich illustrations at their own pace. This book provides excellent opportunities for readers to practice using

Illustrator
Vera B. Williams

Publisher
Morrow, 1982

ISBN
0590331558

TC Level
8

pictures to expand their comprehension. On a first or second time through the book, readers might note details in Williams' large paintings opposite the text, inferring as much as they can. What do the thirteen coins at the bottom of the enormous jar on the second page tell about how far this family is from buying a new chair? What do the family's expressions say about how they are feeling when they have finally purchased a stuffed chair and loaded it onto their truck? During later readings, readers might also note smaller details, such as the borders. For example, they can see how the borders around the three pages in which the narrator and her mother return to find their home on fire go from a sunny blue sky with cottony clouds to angular orange flames shooting upward to drooping, blackened tulips. They might notice a more hopeful mood when those singed tulips give way on the next page to a border of rejuvenated, upright flowers.

When readers get together in partnerships to talk over what they notice about the book, teachers may want to nudge them to use every bit of information possible, from the pictures and from the text, to develop theories about the characters. Students may note that one member of the family, the mother, appears to support three. This may explain why the family cannot simply buy everything they need to furnish their new apartment, and why their neighbors treat them so generously. They can also infer the characters' attitudes and emotions. For instance, what does it say about the grandmother's sense of self that, when thanking the neighbors for the gifts, she says, "It's lucky we're young"? In what ways *is* she young?

Book Connections

Vera B. Williams has illustrated many of the books she has authored, including *Cherries And Cherry Pits*; *Something Special For Me*; and *Music, Music For Everyone*, which also involves collecting coins in a jar. Tomie dePaola's *The Art Lesson* and Patricia Polacco's *Chicken Sunday* are two other picture books at this level that have been illustrated by the author. *Aunt Flossie's Hats (and Crab Cakes Later)*, written by Elizabeth Fitzgerald Howard, is yet another realistic picture book at this level. Many of its facing pages are laid out similarly to those in *A Chair For My Mother*, with whole-page paintings on one side, text opposite them, and small illustrations beneath the text.

Genre
Picture Book

Teaching Uses
Partnerships; Read Aloud; Independent Reading

A Field Guide to the Classroom Library, Lucy Calkins and the Teachers College Reading and Writing Project, Heinemann, ©2002 Teachers College, Columbia University; http://www.heinemann.com/fieldguides

A Is for Africa

Ifeoma Onyefulu

Book Summary

In *A Is for Africa*, each letter of the alphabet introduces us to a phrase in the Nigerian Igbo culture. The words are chosen to represent all of Africa. They usually refer to artifacts found in everyday life, such as pots, beads, canoes, rivers, feathers and drums.

Basic Book Information

This 25-page, nonfiction picture book, structured alphabetically, focuses on African culture in general and Igbo culture in particular. One or two letters are on each page, followed by a word that begins with that letter and several sentences describing the word's cultural importance. In addition, a colorful photograph that depicts scenes in Nigeria accompanies each word.

The author's note at the book's beginning explains that, although the scenes are Nigerian, they represent all of Africa. Reading this note is not crucial to a basic understanding of *A Is for Africa*. As it follows an alphabet book format, this picture book has no index, table of contents or any other such reference structures often found in nonfiction books.

Noteworthy Features

A Is for Africa's modern photographs of rural Nigeria are inviting and intriguing. The short text chunks separated by the familiar alphabet make the text less intimidating to readers, despite the usually unfamiliar content.

Teaching Ideas

This book can counterbalance some of the skewed images of Africa so prevalent in popular culture. It is important to note, however, that *A Is for Africa* depicts only village life, and only certain aspects of it. Readers should also be aware of Africa's bustling cities, its industries and its diversified economy.

Every situation in *A Is for Africa* is described as a happy one. While the text does not condescend toward village life, there is no mention that many people have no refrigerators or running water, or of the health problems that can be associated with that. The many reasons for these conditions are not mentioned, just as the conditions themselves are passed over lightly.

The author also generalizes about the cultures and peoples of Africa in the opening note and in several places in the text. Teachers may or may not point these instances out to readers, depending on the needs and purposes of the reader. This book's generalizations might lead to interesting work on questioning texts while reading. A teacher might introduce such questioning with a query such as, "Why do you think the author would portray *all*

Illustrator
Ifeoma Onyefulu

Publisher
Puffin Books, 1993

ISBN
0140562222

TC Level
9

Africans as welcoming or warm?" Students may go on to develop their own questions, such as "What is the author's point of view?" and "What has the author left out of the book?"

Book Connections

A Is for Africa is very similar both in structure and content to *J is for Jambo*, an alphabet book about the Swahili language and some of the cultures of East Africa. Students might explore other nonfiction books that follow an alphabet structure, such as Jerry Pallotta's *The Desert Alphabet Book* or Joseph Bruchac's *Many Nations: An Alphabet of Native America*.

Genre
Picture Book; Nonfiction

Teaching Uses
Independent Reading; Partnerships; Content Area Study; Critique

A Field Guide to the Classroom Library, Lucy Calkins and the Teachers College Reading and Writing Project, Heinemann, ©2002 Teachers College, Columbia University; http://www.heinemann.com/fieldguides

A Picture Book of Eleanor Roosevelt

David A. Adler

Book Summary

This biography leads readers first through Eleanor Roosevelt's seemingly harsh, though privileged, childhood and her happy boarding school years. The reader then learns of the politics in her family, her uncle Theodore Roosevelt, and of her courtship with her distant cousin Franklin Roosevelt. The book describes her life and work as first lady and touches on the hard times the country endured during the Depression and World War II. The book describes and extols her morality and ends with a note of appreciation for her from everyone in the world.

Basic Book Information

This 30-page picture book is one in a series of 28 biographies by David A. Adler, each about a particular historical figure. Each page in this book has about one paragraph of text and a large watercolor illustration. A timeline of major events in Roosevelt's life is listed on the back page. David Adler is the author of the *Cam Jansen* and *Young Cam Jansen* series.

Noteworthy Features

The book is arranged chronologically, starting with Eleanor Roosevelt's birth and ending with her death. The text itself is mid-sized and presents no special graphic challenges. There are no headings or any other textual structures to aid in foreseeing the book's organization or to aid in using the book for reference purposes, though the illustrations support the words on every page.

Teaching Ideas

Readers will benefit from hearing a bit about Eleanor Roosevelt before they read this book. This is not because the book itself is complex, but because it does not mention her political role until the midpoint of the book, when it says that her husband sought public office. It will thus take a while for readers who are not familiar with her to understand why Eleanor Roosevelt became famous in the first place.

The biography touches on the issues of the Great Depression, World War II and prejudice. In conferring with students during independent reading time, teachers may want to focus on what readers have learned from these brief references to historical events and about how readers can, simply from context, learn a bit about the issues of the time. Unless they become mindful of the fact that they are reading about unfamiliar events, readers who lack prior knowledge may overlook all the historical information woven into this text.

Series
David A. Adler biographies

Illustrator
Robert Casilla

Publisher
Scholastic, 1991

ISBN
0590559079

TC Level
8

Readers will probably be most drawn into the details of Roosevelt's shyness and homeliness as a girl. These features make her an unlikely candidate for fame. Readers should know, however, that many biographies portray people who achieved things their youth might not have predicted, much as another common biographical structure shows subjects' early experiences building directly into the work of their adulthood.

At the end of the book, the author presents a list of "Important Dates." In that list are Eleanor's birth followed by the date of her marriage, her husband's term as governor of New York, his election to the presidency and other dates related to him. After the date of his death, there are two dates that indicate jobs Eleanor had, and then the date of her death. Readers may want to mull over this list. Why did the author choose so many important dates in Franklin Delano Roosevelt's life when the subject of the biography is Eleanor Roosevelt? Was she famous only because she was married to a president? Why did the author choose these particular events instead of others? Which other dates could appear there instead of, or alongside, the ones that are there? This is a form of critique that can help children be aware that even lists of facts have opinions and points of view implicit in them.

Book Connections

This book could be used in conjunction with Barbara Cooney's book *Eleanor*, also about Eleanor Roosevelt, and the book *Amelia and Eleanor Go for a Ride* by Pam Munoz Ryan, about the night flight of two great women. Children may also become interested in David A. Adler's other picture biographies.

Genre
Biography; Picture Book; Nonfiction

Teaching Uses
Independent Reading; Content Area Study; Critique

Abuela

Arthur Dorros

Book Summary

A little girl goes with her grandmother to the park. While there, she imagines taking a flying trip around the city with her grandmother. The girl talks about all the places they would see and all the relatives they would visit, imagining all the conversations they would have. The girl remembers she is still in the park with her *abuela*, whom she loves greatly. The two go for a boat ride together.

Basic Book Information

Abuela has 34 unnumbered pages with large illustrations accompanying each page's text. While the narration is in English, there is simple, referenced, italicized dialogue in Spanish throughout this imaginative story. More complicated phrases are first quoted and/or italicized in Spanish and then paraphrased in English as the girl, who narrates the story, reflects on what her grandmother says. Usually, the context provides clues about how to translate the Spanish (e.g., "'Mira,' Abuela would say, pointing. And I'd look ..."). For students who do not speak Spanish or cannot translate it in context, there is a glossary, which also provides tips on pronunciation.

Noteworthy Features

Most people love the colorful, detailed, and playful illustrations in the story. Children are often enthralled with the picture in which the girl and her grandmother are soaring over the bustling, happy city. The book's multiple Spanish phrases mixed with the English story bring to print the bilingual experience many students have.

Every Spanish phrase the grandmother speaks is translated by her granddaughter in the phrases just following it, either directly, or via the girl's replies. Readers who need the glossary should get into the habit of checking in the back of a book for a glossary whenever they are reading a book that contains foreign words that they don't understand and feel uncomfortable skipping.

Teaching Ideas

The Spanish words in the text present engaging possibilities for practicing how to use context clues to figure out unknown vocabulary. Those students who do not already read Spanish should see the ways in which the little girl repeats her grandmother's words in English, and then uses the English words to understand the Spanish. Students who don't speak Spanish can use the glossary to see if they are getting the gist of the Spanish words. Students can apply this skill of informed, contextualized guessing to any unfamiliar

Illustrator
Elisa Kleven

Publisher
Trumpet, 1991

ISBN
0140562257

TC Level
8

words they encounter while reading - even to words already in English.

The trickiest part of this story could be understanding the time in which things happen, and managing the tenses of the story. The structure of time in the book is not at all simple, and following it takes quite a bit of skill. The book starts out in the present tense, with the girl and her grandmother going to the park. Once she imagines flying, the tense changes. The girl speaks in the future conditional tense about what *would* happen first and then what *would* happen next. After her lengthy daydream, the girl remembers she is in the park, and switches back to the present tense. From there, she and Abuela go on a real, present-tense adventure in a boat. The illustrations for both reality and daydream are in the same style. Thus, catching the switch from reality to fantasy and back to reality can be tricky, as only the tense shifts provide cues. If such a misunderstanding occurs, however, it might be a perfect time to intervene and explain about "would" and what the word suggests.

In the writing workshop, this book can be set alongside other books, such as *Jamaica's Find*, or *Tar Beach* to show that the story, and the plot, does not always revolve around external events. Sometimes the important events during a day in the park (or any other day) are the *internal* events and sometimes they are the *interpersonal* events. This can be a significant lesson for young writers who tend to retell what they did and to overlook all mention of what they thought or imagined or wished they had done.

Book Connections

Gary Soto has written several books that mix Spanish with English, including *Chato's Kitchen*. *Tar Beach* is a bit similar to this book in content and illustrations. Interesting conversations could result from comparing and contrasting the messages, content and structure of these two books. *Grandma's Cookie Jar* by Louise Dundas and *Knots on a Counting Rope* by Bill Martin Jr. and John Archambault have similar themes of grandchildren and grandparents telling stories. Readers who want to read more by Arthur Dorros will probably enjoy *Alligator Shoes*.

Genre
Picture Book

Teaching Uses
Teaching Writing; Language Conventions; Read Aloud; Partnerships

A Field Guide to the Classroom Library, Lucy Calkins and the Teachers College Reading and Writing Project, Heinemann, ©2002 Teachers College, Columbia University; http://www.heinemann.com/fieldguides

Addie Meets Max

Joan Robins

Book Summary

When Max moves into the neighborhood, Addie is sure she is not going to like him or his mean dog. After Addie's mother invites Max for lunch, Addie shares pizza and chocolate chip cookies with him, helps him bury his lost tooth in the backyard and meets his friendly dog, Ginger. Addie and Max become friends.

Basic Book Information

Addie Meets Max is a 32-page-long *Early I Can Read Book* with 3-5 sentences and bright illustrations on each page. Each illustration matches some part of the text on the page. There is simple referenced dialogue throughout the story. Print is large and well spaced.

Noteworthy Features

Using simple yet meaningful language, this book conveys Addie's first feelings of trepidation and her ensuing change of heart. The theme of new friendship is well written and one to which readers can relate. The illustrations add to the warm, enjoyable quality of the book.

Teaching Ideas

Addie Meets Max is a good book for readers who are just beginning to read independently with some fluency and stamina. The sentences are simple and straightforward, though somewhat longer and more descriptive than those in very early *I Can Read* books. The story is long enough so that early readers will not race through it, yet short enough to be read during the independent work time of a single reading workshop.

If a teacher wanted to support children by giving this book an introduction, the teacher might say something like: "This is a story about a little girl named Addie who makes a new friend, Max. At first she feels as if she will never like him, because she doesn't really know him. But then she talks and plays with him a little and discovers that he is a lot like her. That happened to me almost every time I started a new grade in school. I felt shy and nervous too. Do you ever feel that way, like Addie does?"

This book is also a good book to use in a strategy lesson designed to coach readers to infer as they read. Bringing together 2-4 children for whom this would be a just-right read, the teacher might say, "We've been talking a

Series
Addie and Max books

Illustrator
Sue Truesdell

Publisher
Harper & Row Publishers, 1985

ISBN
0064441164

TC Level
6

lot about the *thinking work* you guys do as you read and especially about how authors don't always come right out and say everything. They want you to think as you read. Authors expect you to fill in the parts of the story that they leave out. Today I want to show you something else authors do. They sometimes say one thing and expect you, as smart, thinking readers, to *think something else* entirely! So for example in *The Gingerbread Boy*, the fox says, 'Get on my nose and I'll carry you across the river.' Smart readers know the fox plans to eat the gingerbread boy, so they don't really believe the fox's words. In this book, when you read the first few pages, you'll see the author has written things we're not supposed to believe completely. Why don't you each read a bit, and I'll stop you after a few minutes."

In the beginning of the story, Addie's reasons for not wanting to meet or become friends with Max are made up. She tells her mother she will not be friends with him because his dog is mean (when the dog is actually friendly) or because Max has knocked her off her bike (when they actually collided with each other). In conferences, teachers may want to point out these inconsistencies and ask readers to infer the real reason Addie does not want to meet Max: she is shy and apprehensive. Teachers may direct readers to look more closely at the illustrations, particularly at the characters' faces. Teachers may ask leading questions such as: "How is Addie really feeling?" "Do you think she really doesn't want a new friend?" "Why is she telling her mother that Max caused their bicycle accident when it really doesn't seem to be what happened?" "What's really going on in the story?" The answers to these questions can inform a discussion about how the author sometimes tells the story without directly stating it in words.

This book can also be used to teach a dialogue through a strategy mini-lesson or guided reading lesson. Teachers can select a page of text that includes dialogue and share it with readers on an overhead projector or on photocopies. Teachers can read the text, changing their voices for the parts that are written in dialogue, and ask the readers why they do so. Readers can look for and discuss the quotation marks, references and placement of dialogue on the page. Readers can practice reading the dialogue in the characters' voices.

Book Connections

Addie Meets Max is one of three books about the same characters. The others are *Addie Runs Away* and *Addie's Bad Day*. Other titles that are similar in vocabulary, length and content are the *Henry and Mudge* series by Cynthia Rylant and the *Little Bear* books by Else Holmelund Minarik. Crosby Newell Bonsall's *And I Mean It, Stanley* is perfect for teaching readers that we are not always expected to believe what a character says. Just an excerpt section of that book could be read aloud in a strategy mini-lesson to help a small group of children doing similar work in *Addie's Bad Day*.

Genre
Short Chapter Book

A Field Guide to the Classroom Library, Lucy Calkins and the Teachers College Reading and Writing Project, Heinemann, ©2002 Teachers College, Columbia University; http://www.heinemann.com/fieldguides

Teaching Uses
Independent Reading; Small Group Strategy Instruction; Language Conventions

Amanda Pig and Her Big Brother Oliver

Jean Van Leeuwen

Book Summary

This is a story about the relationship between Amanda and her older brother, Oliver, and the trials of being the oldest or the youngest child in a family. Amanda tries and fails to be like Oliver, but in doing so discovers her own strengths and learns independence. The *Oliver Pig* books each contain four or five short stories about Oliver Pig, Mother, Father, Grandfather and Oliver's baby sister, Amanda. The stories are all based on the author's recollection of real incidents that happened when her children were young. Van Leeuwen skillfully recreates the drama of childhood in a way that shows how her characters feel and that allows readers to empathize with them.

Basic Book Information

Each chapter in this 56-page book can stand alone as an individual story, and each chapter title refers to its theme or main event. There are large color illustrations on every page and each illustration matches the text.

Noteworthy Features

Because this book is part of a series, readers may already be acquainted with the characters. Regardless, each chapter in *Amanda Pig and Her Big Brother Oliver* stands alone. This may make the book easier for beginning readers who might struggle with carrying the story across many pages, though the chapters all tell a continuing saga, focusing on sibling relationships and family roles. Though chapter titles are accompanied by large illustrations on the same page, chapters are not numbered, which may cause readers to overlook chapter breaks.

In each chapter, the activity in which Amanda is trying to participate always fails comically. It is the humor (in both words and illustrations) that keeps readers reading. Dialogue, not narration, tells most of the story. The sentences are short and straightforward, making it a good book for students who need more practice with dialogue-driven text and making inferences.

Teaching Ideas

Although this book does not explicitly tell the reader what the characters are feeling, the author does a magnificent job showing feelings. Readers will readily relate to the stories, making it easier for them to make inferences. Even students who do not have brothers and sisters know these basic emotions that arise between siblings. This makes the book a good choice for

Illustrator
Ann Schweninger

Publisher
Puffin Books, 1982, 1982

ISBN
0140370080

TC Level
7

A Field Guide to the Classroom Library, Lucy Calkins and the Teachers College Reading and Writing Project, Heinemann, ©2002 Teachers College, Columbia University; http://www.heinemann.com/fieldguides

strategy lessons on using both inference and background information to understand reading.

If this is the first time reading from this series of books, it may be helpful for a teacher to give a reader or a small group of readers brief character sketches. In order to orient the reader or readers so that they can pick up on the upcoming sibling rivalry, teachers might invite a small conversation on the readers' own experiences with siblings.

A teacher will want to notice ways in which this book (and others like it) are more challenging than, say, Else Holmelund Minarik's *Little Bear* and Arnold Lobel's *Mouse Tales*. The episodes in the *Oliver Pig* books are more elaborate and detailed. Readers need to consolidate more subordinate details that go together to comprise the main plot line in *Little Bear* or *Mouse Tales*. It will be good for readers to retell the *Oliver Pig* books while they read, as retelling can help them capture the main gist of the various episodes.

Teachers can use this book for independent reading or fit it under a number of other organizational structures. For example, some teachers decide to highlight the strategies that readers use when they really want to think deeply about their characters. To do such work, teachers tend to select a book with a rich, quirky, dynamic character and read the book aloud, before readers disperse to independent reading. Embedded into the read aloud work with the one chosen book would be lots of "lessons" on what readers do to think about a character:

Readers notice what the character says and does, and they develop theories about the "kind of person" this character is.

Readers notice how other characters relate to this character, and use that information to embellish their theories.

Readers notice times when the character does not fit into the readers' expectations. Does this information suggest the initial theory was not complex enough? Is the character changing? Is the character behaving uncharacteristically?

Readers try to understand the motivations that underlie a character's actions, even when readers say things like, "I'd *never* yell and pound the floor like that character does."

Each of these "lessons" about the sort of thinking a reader does can also angle book talks. Once children have noticed, for example, the physical appearance of a character and wondered how this does and does not fit with the character's personality, then they can read independently with the same questions in mind; choosing books that contain strong characters will allow readers to practice similar work on their own.

Book Connections

Students may become interested in the other nine books in the *Oliver Pig* series. Judy Blume's *The Pain and The Great One* deals with similar themes of rivalry between older and younger siblings.

Genre
Short Chapter Book

A Field Guide to the Classroom Library, Lucy Calkins and the Teachers College Reading and Writing Project, Heinemann, ©2002 Teachers College, Columbia University; http://www.heinemann.com/fieldguides

Teaching Uses
Independent Reading; Character Study; Small Group Strategy Instruction

Amber Brown Sees Red

Paula Danziger

Book Summary

Amber has noticed that she is going through a growth spurt, which bothers her. Amber is ambivalent about her mother's fiancé, Max; Amber still loves her dad and feels torn and unsure about how this will affect her. When Dad announces he wants joint custody, Amber suffers from being in the middle. When Dad arrives home from Paris, Amber suddenly decides everything will be okay.

Basic Book Information

Amber Brown Sees Red is a 116-page chapter book. There are no chapter titles. Illustrations occur every several pages and support the text. Paula Danziger is the award-winning author of many books, including *The Cat Ate My Gymsuit, The Pistachio Prescription,* and *Can You Sue Your Parents for Malpractice?* The character of Amber was inspired by Danziger's niece, Carrie.

There are currently six books in the *Amber Brown* series. The books get longer and more complex as Amber ages, and the later books sometimes allude to events in earlier books. The author reintroduces characters and past events in each new book so that it is not necessary for readers to read them in sequence.

Noteworthy Features

Amber Brown Sees Red uses a straightforward plot with a linear time structure. There is a subplot, about school, but this comes in and out in an easily recognized setting change. Amber narrates the story in the first person. As a narrator, Amber likes to use colloquialisms. This can be thought of as kid language or puns, like "skunkorama" and "scrunchies." This book uses several idioms, most notably "Sees Red." Often students do not know that seeing red means being angry.

Difficult issues such as divorce are treated and explained honestly in the text. This book helps students reflect on the inevitable emotional impact that divorce has on children.

There is a lot of dialogue in this book that is not always easy to follow. Quite often, the author does not reference who is speaking, relying instead on paragraph changes to indicate new speakers. Occasional big words such as "apprehend" may need some support. Sentences are of varied length and complexity. Sentence fragments are present in Amber's internal monologues.

Series
Amber Brown books

Illustrator
Tony Ross

Publisher
Scholastic, 1998

ISBN
0590947281

TC Level
9

Teaching Ideas

Amber Brown Sees Red works well as a read aloud or book club book because of the conversation it engenders about divorce. This book also makes a good choice for partnership reading and reading centers dedicated to character development. Readers should pay special attention to inferring the causes of Amber's anger.

Amber thinks a lot during her narration, which makes this book a good one for introducing the concept of internal monologue. Issues such as how much the reader trusts the narrator should be addressed. Students can take their learning about narrators to their other books and other writing projects.

Book Connections

Amber Brown Sees Red is the sixth book in the Amber Brown series. Amber ages as the books progress, which may make them best read in sequence. If readers are interested in series books at this level, they might try *The Bailey School Kids*. *Junie B. Jones* and the *Marvin Redpost* series are a bit easier, and offer similar opportunities for studying character. The *Flower Girls* series would make a good follow-up series.

Genre
Short Chapter Book

Teaching Uses
Independent Reading; Read Aloud; Book Clubs

A Field Guide to the Classroom Library, Lucy Calkins and the Teachers College Reading and Writing Project, Heinemann, ©2002 Teachers College, Columbia University; http://www.heinemann.com/fieldguides

Amelia Bedelia Helps Out

Peggy Parish

Book Summary

Amelia is a housemaid who has responsibilities such as cleaning the house and preparing and cooking dinner for her employers, Mr. and Mrs. Rogers. Amelia is hard working and well meaning, but easily confused. In this story, the reader is introduced to Amelia Bedelia's niece, Effie Lou, and a friend of the Rogers, Miss Emma. Amelia Bedelia and Effie Lou set out to help Miss Emma get her house ready for her garden club's afternoon tea party, but Amelia Bedelia is comically baffled by the jobs on her list. In the end, Amelia's baking skills save the day.

Basic Book Information

Amelia Bedelia Helps Out is one continuous story without chapters. There are supportive, humorous pictures on every page that help readers understand Amelia Bedelia's unusual work habits.

Both children and adults laugh aloud as they read these funny books. Usually, Amelia is given instructions that she tries to follow *exactly*, but she confuses homophones and ends up creating giant fiascoes everywhere she goes. The *Amelia Bedelia* books do not need to be read in any particular order. However, the initial book in the series, *Amelia Bedelia*, introduces the recurring characters of Amelia, Mr. Rogers and Mrs. Rogers, so it may help to read this book first.

Noteworthy Features

Amelia Bedelia books are much more difficult than they at first appear. The text has many features that make texts accessible for students beginning work with longer books, such as referenced dialogue, linear plot structures, a large and well-spaced typeface, and illustrations that match the text on each page. However, some students may struggle to understand the humor of these books. Often, Peggy Parish uses terms with which students may not be familiar. In *Amelia Bedelia Helps Out*, for example, Mrs. Rogers asks Amelia to "sow" grass seeds and "stake" green beans. Students who have little experience gardening may not understand how 'sowing' seeds relates to planting, or that 'staking' vines involves training them up along a vertical structure. Thus, students can find themselves in the embarrassing position of no less confused than a character they know tends to be dizzy and befuddled.

Amelia Bedelia is nonetheless a humorous and lovable character. After reading a couple of books in this series, readers grow to expect silly things from Amelia's well-intentioned work habits. Young readers may not know what Mr. and Mrs. Rogers have in mind when they give their maid orders, but they will likely develop a sense that another disaster is coming up and

Series
Amelia Bedelia books

Illustrator
Lynn Sweat

Publisher
Harper Trophy, 1979

ISBN
0380534053

TC Level
8

that it will be something involving a humorous play on words.

The setting in this book is different from the others in the series. Although Amelia says good-bye to Mr. Rogers on the first page when he drops her off at Miss Emma's house, she still works for Mr. and Mrs. Rogers as their housekeeper. Readers may be confused by this, not realizing that Amelia works occasionally for other people as well as for the Rogers.

Teaching Ideas

In a conference with one or more children who are reading *Amelia Bedelia*, a teacher may want to talk about the concept of homonyms, words that look alike and sound alike but have different meanings. Homonyms are fundamental to the humor in this book. The same problem could be approached through a discussion of literal versus figurative meanings. Whether or not the term "homonym" is used in teaching, even young children should be able to grasp the concept, which has probably caused similar misunderstandings in their interactions with other people and with books. (Indeed, many children's jokes are based on words or phrases that have multiple meanings). English language learners may be even more tuned in to this communicative challenge and could benefit from a discussion of homonyms.

Some children who can produce a word-perfect performance of these books still may not get the jokes because the books require a rarified vocabulary. If readers don't know what it means to "dress the turkey," to "write bread-and-butter letters," or to "stake the string beans," they will run into some difficulties with these books. That can be half the fun of it, but only if readers understand puns and figurative language enough to comprehend at least a fair percentage of this book. A picture walk through the text may help the reader envision just what kinds of tasks Amelia is asked to perform.

Reading easier books filled with puns can be a good preface to the *Amelia Bedelia* series. Readers can develop finesse by reading Fred Gwynne's *A Chocolate Moose for Dinner* and *The King Who Rained*.

Children who are just beginning to read chapter books will often find themselves reading either mystery books (such as the *Boxcar Children*, *Nate the Great*, and *Cam Jansen*) or else humorous books (such as the *Wayside School* or *Joshua Adams* books). It might be reasonable, therefore, for teachers to do some whole-class work with humorous books. The whole class might listen to a read aloud of an *Amelia Bedelia* book and talk about the special kind of work that readers of this book (and perhaps other humorous books) need to do. Teachers may ask their classes to choose their independent books from a collection of humorous books.

During a read aloud discussion or mini-lesson, children might notice that when they read (or listen to) *Amelia Bedelia*, they are leaning forward to co-author the funny parts. The text says that Amelia is to "stake the string beans;" as good readers, they get pleasure out of being one step ahead of the text, imagining what Amelia will do. After a mini-lesson explaining how readers of humor try to beat the author to the punch line, it will be time for independent reading. Teachers may preface independent reading by saying, "Today, when you are reading your independent books, keep an eye out for sections of the text that you expect will turn out to be funny, and see if you

A Field Guide to the Classroom Library, Lucy Calkins and the Teachers College Reading and Writing Project, Heinemann, ©2002 Teachers College, Columbia University; http://www.heinemann.com/fieldguides

can predict what the punch lines will be."

Of course, there are a host of other things readers will notice as they read *Amelia Bedelia*, including the fact that from time to time something funny in the text will fly right over their heads. They should be encouraged to reread to see if on closer inspection they can "get the joke."

Book Connections

Amelia Bedelia Helps Out is similar in difficulty to *Cam Jansen* by David Adler, *Pinky and Rex* by James Howe, and *The Golly Sisters* series by Betsy Byars. It is more difficult than *Frog and Toad* by Arnold Lobel and the *Fox* series by Edward Marshall. Once children can successfully read *Amelia Bedelia* and other books of similar difficulty, they may find themselves well prepared to read the *Horrible Harry* series by Suzy Kline, *The Zack Files* series by Dan Greenburg, and *Freckle Juice* by Judy Blume.

Genre
Short Chapter Book; Picture Book

Teaching Uses
Independent Reading; Language Conventions; Character Study; Small Group Strategy Instruction

A Field Guide to the Classroom Library, Lucy Calkins and the Teachers College Reading and Writing Project, Heinemann, ©2002 Teachers College, Columbia University; http://www.heinemann.com/fieldguides

Amelia's Notebook

Marissa Moss

Book Summary

Amelia's Notebook looks likes the real, handwritten notebook of a creative 9-year-old girl-full of exclamations, jokes, art, cross-outs, stories, and marginalia. Amelia describes moving long-distance to a new house with her mother and annoying older sister, Cleo. Funny, dramatic and opinionated, Amelia finds a way to stay close to an old best friend and begin to make new friends in school.

Basic Book Information

The *Amelia* series covers a variety of topics, from Amelia's move to a reunion with her father to a fire at school. The books are consistent: all use a humorous tone and busy, colorful presentation to address realistic problems many children experience.

Noteworthy Features

Amelia's character and her relationships come through clearly in the notebook. Amelia is a well-developed character whose problems and emotions will seem familiar to many readers. Other characters are not particularly detailed, but Amelia renders them with an artistic flair that makes them memorable.

The art in Amelia's notebook breaks up and supplements the text. In addition, the art shows aspects of Amelia's character that the straightforward writing cannot. Through the cartoon-like drawings, the highlighted words, and the artifacts like postcards and a necklace, readers gain a feel for Amelia's homesickness, her dramatic personality, and her sense of humor. Her simultaneous irreverence and her genuine warmth toward others are as appealing as her drawings.

Amelia's Notebook demonstrates the multiple uses of a journal. While Amelia's journal is on the simplest level a chronicle of events, it also contains her artwork, fiction and important items such as a letter from her best friend, Nadia. Because the notebook captures Amelia's feelings about moving, her sister, and her friends, it models how journals can serve as outlets for emotions.

Teaching Ideas

To support writing workshop, children might study how Amelia makes her notebook her own, and think about how each one of them could personalize his or her own writer's notebook. Readers might discuss how Amelia's notebook fits into the whole of her life, and think about their own writer's notebooks. Amelia's multiple uses for her journals can suggest ways

Illustrator
Marissa Moss

Publisher
Pleasant Company, 1999

ISBN
1562477846

TC Level
9

A Field Guide to the Classroom Library, Lucy Calkins and the Teachers College Reading and Writing Project, Heinemann, ©2002 Teachers College, Columbia University; http://www.heinemann.com/fieldguides

children can expand their own work with notebooks. How can each student customize their writing to reflect who they are?

A character study on Amelia could involve, in part, tracking the changes in Amelia's attitudes toward her old friend Nadia, her art, her sister Cleo, and her parents. Part of the study could include a comparison between Amelia and Amber Brown (another humorous, vibrant child of divorced parents) of the series by Paula Danziger..

Book Connections

Other books in the Amelia series include: *Amelia Writes Again*; *Amelia Works It Out; Luv, Amelia Luv, Nadia* ; *Amelia's Family Ties* and *Madame Amelia Tells All*. The *Amber Brown, Ramona, Henry and Mudge* series are books that have similarly well-developed protagonists who evolve over time.

Genre
Memoir; Picture Book

Teaching Uses
Teaching Writing; Partnerships; Character Study

Animal Dads

Sneed B. Collard III

Book Summary

This book is a collection of descriptions of fatherhood in the animal world. It details some of the jobs animal fathers undertake for their children, from the nest building of the megapod to the birthing of male seahorses. The book mentions animal fathers that leave their young, such as the gopher tortoise, and animal fathers that stay, such as the wolf. In total, the book describes nineteen different jobs that animal fathers perform in the rearing of their offspring.

Basic Book Information

This nonfiction picture book is about 40 pages long. Each page or two-page spread contains a full-color, realistic paper collage illustration of an animal father. There is one short topic sentence for the page in large font, and then a short paragraph elsewhere on the page that gives details about the animal in smaller font. There is no index and no table of contents.

Noteworthy Features

At first glance, the book looks as though it could be read on two levels: one where readers read only the large-type, topic sentence for each page, and one where readers read everything on the page, both the large and the smaller print. Reading the larger print alone, however, would confuse readers. The topic sentences are general enough that they do not provide insight into the behavior of the animal father depicted in the illustration. For example, a sentence might read, "They shelter us from harm" and the picture might show baby fish swimming next to their father. Reading the small print, however, reveals that the father cichlid fish opens his mouth to let his babies swim inside until they are out of harm's way.

Since the book has no index and no table of contents, it is not easy for young readers to look up one particular animal. To find out about the fathering habits of one particular animal-or even to find out if that animal is in the book-readers have to take in every page. Of course, they could skim through all the pictures and try to recognize the animal they are studying in order to read more about it if it is pictured.

The paper collages of this text are very realistic, and quite beautiful and unusual.

Teaching Ideas

This book has extremely clear examples of topic sentences that tell the main idea of the paragraph that follows. In the writing workshop, *Animal Dads* can make a strong model for children who are beginning to explore

Illustrator
Steve Jenkins

Publisher
Houghton Mifflin, 1997

ISBN
0618032991

TC Level
5; 6; 7; 8; 9

A Field Guide to the Classroom Library, Lucy Calkins and the Teachers College Reading and Writing Project, Heinemann, ©2002 Teachers College, Columbia University; http://www.heinemann.com/fieldguides

paragraph structure.

It can be interesting to look at this book with children with the question, "What does it seem that the author thinks animal fathers *don't* do?" The book assumes that most readers will expect animal fathers to do very little, and that animal fathers would probably not be involved much with child rearing. These underlying assumptions are not explicitly stated, though the text subtly implies them. For example, the book offers the questions, "Babysitting dads?" and "Housecleaning dads?" and answers each with a very firm yes. This implies that readers might not be accustomed to seeing fathers who actively rear children and perform domestic tasks. The term "babysitting" suggests temporary paternal attention, as if regular, ongoing childcare were (at least among human males) wildly atypical.

Book Connections

Sneed B. Collard has written more than children's books. Among his nonfiction works are *Our Wet World*, *Leaving Home*, *Creepy Creatures* and *Tough Terminators: Nature's Most Amazing Animals.*. Students who are just beginning to read informational books at this level can read more about animals in books such as Carolyn MacLulich's *Insects*. For students with more experience with nonfiction, the Mondo animal series makes a good follow-up.

Genre
Nonfiction; Picture Book

Teaching Uses
Independent Reading; Partnerships; Content Area Study; Reading and Writing Nonfiction

Annie and the Old One

Miska Miles

Book Summary

Annie, a young Navajo girl, enjoys a good life with her parents and grandmother in their snug hogan with their crops and animals. She spends a lot of time with her grandmother and loves her very much. One day, Annie's grandmother says she will die when the rug Annie's mother is weaving is finished. Annie cannot understand why her mother keeps weaving, and tries several ways to sabotage the process of the work. Annie's grandmother sees what is happening and helps her understand that time cannot be stopped. Finally, Annie understands and begins to weave the rug herself.

Basic Book Information

Annie and the Old One is a Newbery Honor Book. The illustrations are spare line drawings with several earth tones added in parts of some pictures.

Noteworthy Features

The pictures, while elegant and gentle in their tone, tend not to capture the attention of children who are merely glancing through the book. Many children will need to read a few pages or have a few pages read to them before the book will catch their interest. Even so, the book moves slowly and gradually builds intensity, so readers who prefer fast-paced stories may never finish the book independently.

Though the setting is unfamiliar to many readers, Annie's life here is presented clearly enough that her hogan and pumpkins and weaving tend to intrigue readers instead of scaring them away. The text does not explicitly define content-specific words and concepts, although readers can discern them from the context of the story and the accompanying illustrations.

This book's strength, however, is that it is beautifully written and has the power to move the listener or reader. For this reason, *Annie and the Old One* might be best read aloud to the class with the reverence it deserves. The hope is for children to feel the power of this piece of literature.

Teaching Ideas

The subject of the book is Annie's reaction to the approaching death of her grandmother. This subject can be particularly sensitive, so teachers should use it carefully with students. Some children can connect to this story from their own losses, or imagine how upset they would be if a grandparent's death were imminent. This connection to Annie tends to make readers feel close to her whether or not they can picture or imagine her Navajo environment. Personal connections can help children empathize with Annie's character and read the book more deeply.

Illustrator
Peter Parnall

Publisher
Little, Brown, and Company, 1971

ISBN
0316571202

TC Level
10

A Field Guide to the Classroom Library, Lucy Calkins and the Teachers College Reading and Writing Project, Heinemann, ©2002 Teachers College, Columbia University; http://www.heinemann.com/fieldguides

Personal response may also be the best platform from which to discuss the ending of the book, where Annie peacefully accepts the knowledge that flowers wither and die, that the sun rises and then sets, and that her grandmother will soon die. Some children may at first find Annie's acceptance strange or cold. Discussion and rereading can add to students' thinking on this topic.

Some children will also find it strange that Annie does not explain to her grandmother why she has been bad, or why she does not yell at her mother to stop the weaving, or why she does not explain to her teacher that she needs to call Annie's parents into school. This, too, can fuel discussion.

Book Connections

Although Miska Miles penned more than twenty books, only *Annie and the Old One* remains in print. Peter Parnall's illustrations, however, are still easy to find. Parnall's longtime collaboration with Byrd Baylor has produced *The Other Way to Listen*, which also features intergenerational conversations in the southwestern United States.

Knots on a Counting Rope, by Bill Martin Jr. and John Archambault, is yet another picture book of a Navajo child preparing for the death of a grandparent. Aliki's *The Two of Them* also deals with a grandchild preparing for the death of a grandparent.

Genre
Picture Book

Teaching Uses
Read Aloud; Independent Reading; Partnerships

Arthur's Honey Bear

Lillian Hoban

Book Summary

Arthur's Honey Bear is about a chimp named Arthur and his sister, Violet. Arthur decides that he is going to go through his old toys and games and have a tag sale. As he puts tags on all his items and sets them up for the sale, he resists putting his old "Honey Bear" up front. Several children come to the sale and find nothing they like. Finally, their friend Wilma arrives and asks about Arthur's Honey Bear. Arthur talks her out of buying the Honey Bear and then very reluctantly sells the bear to Violet, who proceeds to dress him up and play with him. Arthur struggles with his sadness about losing Honey Bear until he realizes that he is, in fact, Honey Bear's uncle. From then on, he and Violet happily share Honey Bear.

Basic Book Information

Arthur's Honey Bear is 64 pages long and does not contain chapters. Although most books of this level contain four or five self-contained chapters, this book contains one story that spans from cover to cover. This *I Can Read* book is part of a series involving Arthur the chimp. It is at a similar difficulty level as short chapter books of this length.

Noteworthy Features

Arthur's Honey Bear is warmly written and really captures Arthur's conflicted feelings about letting go of a toy from earlier in his childhood. The dialogue between Arthur and his sister, Violet, can feel quite real; children may recognize their relationships with their own siblings in this and other stories about Arthur and Violet.

Some of the text is broken into two, three or four words on a line, with four or five lines going together to make a completed sentence. For some readers, this layout may help them progress bit by bit through long lists of items in a sentence, but for many readers, it can be difficult to hold onto the words in one line as their eyes travel to another line, another, and another.

There are several sentences in the story in which the author uses italics for emphasis. Readers at this level may be unfamiliar with this writing device. Page 17 contains a 'hand-painted' sign for the tag sale that, because it is not in typed text, may be a little difficult for early readers to decode.

Teaching Ideas

As a read aloud, a teacher may do a short mini-lesson or strategy lesson on how readers use their voices (aloud or in their heads) appropriately when text is italicized. A teacher may show part of the text on an overhead projector or photocopies of the pages where text is italicized, so that many

Series
Arthur books

Publisher
Harper Collins, 1974

ISBN
0064440338

TC Level
7

A Field Guide to the Classroom Library, Lucy Calkins and the Teachers College Reading and Writing Project, Heinemann, ©2002 Teachers College, Columbia University; http://www.heinemann.com/fieldguides

readers can follow along. The teacher can read the text and ask children to describe how their voice changed when they came to the italicized parts.

This book can also be used for strategy lessons to help readers who are just beginning to read books that have more dialogue in them. The dialogue in *Arthur's Honey Bear* is fairly straightforward. It is always referenced, contained on one page and contextualized by narration. The dialogue never employs ellipses or dashes. Readers will not be overwhelmed by the amount of dialogue, but there is enough to make it important and meaningful for teachers to do several strategy lessons.

This dialogue study might include an emphasis on making a movie in one's mind so one already knows Violet is talking even before the text says, "said Violet." It could also include a pointer or two on intonation, although it is not helpful to push readers to read as if they were actors on a stage.

Because some readers read chapter books as if the challenge is simply to get through so many words and lines, it's helpful to encourage readers to stop often to talk about the text. One way to do this is look over a book (or section of a book) prior to reading it, and putting Post-It s in that will signal, "Stop-and-Talk." Because this book is quite long and is not separated into stories or chapters, assigning oneself some "stop and reflect places" can be especially useful. These stopping points can be used to reflect, retell, and reread and maybe to discuss the text with a partner or group.

Teachers may use *Arthur's Honey Bear* as a starting point on studying what it means to read books within a series. The *Arthur* books retain the same main characters, the same level of vocabulary, and similarities in the context across the entire series. Readers can read, write and discuss ways in which the books are similar and different, how the author's voice is consistent from book to book and whether the characters grow and change.

Book Connections

Arthur's Honey Bear is one of several books about the same main characters. Other titles include *Arthur's Loose Tooth*, *Arthur's Pen Pal*, *Arthur's Christmas Cookies* and *Arthur's Prize Reader*. Similar in level, Jean Van Leeuwen's *Oliver Pig* is also built on the true-life dramas of growing up and of living with siblings. Children could profit from looking at and comparing these series. How are they similar? How are they different?

Genre
Short Chapter Book

Teaching Uses
Independent Reading; Small Group Strategy Instruction; Character Study

A Field Guide to the Classroom Library, Lucy Calkins and the Teachers College Reading and Writing Project, Heinemann, ©2002 Teachers College, Columbia University; http://www.heinemann.com/fieldguides

Aunt Flossie's Hats (and Crab Cakes Later)

Elizabeth Fitzgerald Howard

Book Summary

This book tells the story of two sisters, Sarah and Susan, who visit their great-great-aunt Flossie on Sundays. During their Sunday visits, they participate in a family ritual. First, they drink tea and eat cookies. When Aunt Flossie and the girls are finished, they open hatboxes. Then, Aunt Flossie tells a memory about what happened when she wore each hat. "The hats are her memories and each hat has a story."

Basic Book Information

This book is 31 pages long. It is a picture book illustrated with richly-colored oil paintings. The story is written in first-person narrative, told from the point of view of Susan, the elder sister. The author, Elizabeth Howard, says there was a strong oral storytelling tradition in her family; she really did have an Aunt Flossie who loved to tell stories.

Noteworthy Features

The text contains rich descriptions and the language in the book paints a clear picture of the actions in the story. Phrases like, "Thin floppy hats, the water rippled, and the hats floated by like a boat," in conjunction with the richly detailed paintings, enliven the text. The author uses dialogue frequently throughout the book, which brings the hat stories to life for the reader. Children may need assistance in understanding the story's time elements, as the text shifts forward and backward.

Throughout her hat stories, Aunt Flossie opens a window into her past and the family's history. Woven into the text is how the retelling of the stories makes Aunt Flossie reflect on and relive her past. By trying on the hats and recreating the stories they have come to know about each one, the girls also live the stories, too.

Teaching Ideas

This story is a fine example of the power of oral storytelling. Children can be introduced to the practice of passing stories down through generations. The text not only tells the story of Aunt Flossie's life, but also shows the interconnection of generations. While the hat stories of the past are told, new memories are being created.

As Aunt Flossie reveals the stories of her life, she is revisiting significant memories, feelings, and deep emotions. A student could be encouraged to

Illustrator
James Ransome

Publisher
Houghton Mifflin, 1995

ISBN
039572077X

TC Level
9

A Field Guide to the Classroom Library, Lucy Calkins and the Teachers College Reading and Writing Project, Heinemann, ©2002 Teachers College, Columbia University; http://www.heinemann.com/fieldguides

look carefully at her facial expressions and to take note of lines such as, "Aunt Flossie closed her eyes. I think she was seeing long ago." The teacher might ask, "What do you think Aunt Flossie is thinking about?" This can help students practice inferring. By closely examining the pictures, they can also find out more information about the characters.

This book may be used in a whole-class study of story. The book can prompt discussions about what makes a good story. Where do authors get ideas for their stories? Children can be encouraged to share their own family stories, traditions, and rituals, or to learn the stories of family members.

Book Connections

Elizabeth Fitzgerald Howard has written other family-themed picture books, including *Mac & Marie & the Train Toss Surprise* and *Virgie Goes to School with Us Boys*. Both books recount stories handed down to the author by her family.

Genre
Picture Book

Teaching Uses
Read Aloud; Partnerships; Independent Reading

A Field Guide to the Classroom Library, Lucy Calkins and the Teachers College Reading and Writing Project, Heinemann, ©2002 Teachers College, Columbia University; http://www.heinemann.com/fieldguides

Beavers

Helen H. Moore

Book Summary

The book's sections focus on defining and giving examples of animal relatives of beavers, explaining why beavers gnaw, outlining dam and lodge construction, discussing beaver family life, and describing the physical features of beavers that allow them to survive.

Basic Book Information

This nonfiction picture book is about 30 pages long with approximately one paragraph of text on each page, and occasional one-word labels on some pictures. All of the pages are illustrated with drawings instead of a mix of drawings and photographs, which makes the book unusual for Mondo animal series. As in the other books in the series, there is a short table of contents, in this case listing the seven sections of about four pages each. At the book's end there is a 25-word glossary and a short index.

Noteworthy Features

The illustrations in *Beavers* lend the animals a cute, fuzzy and happy appearance. This can lead readers to feel more attached to the creatures and therefore more interested in them. On the other hand, the mood of these illustrations can leave readers with the feeling that the book itself is not very scientific and may make the book more appealing as a read aloud text for first or second graders than as an independent reading book for third graders.

The table of contents and index effectively reference the text, leaving little room for frustration for children using the book to find answers to their questions about beavers, or using it to find out basic information about the creatures. It could be a great beginning nonfiction research book for that reason, and a good choice for a shared reading experience designed to show children how one reads informational texts differently than narratives.

Teaching Ideas

Beavers is well suited to a read aloud designed to show children how readers approach informational texts. A teacher could, for example, begin such a read aloud by saying to the class, "I love to study the pictures in information books because they teach me so much, even before I read any words. Please turn to your partner and talk about what you can learn about beavers just by looking at the cover picture" This invitation gets everyone involved. Teachers can write down on chart paper everything students notice about the appearance, size, and habits of beavers. Teachers could then read the title page, noting the picture of the mother and baby beaver. "I wonder if

Illustrator
Terri Talas

Publisher
Mondo, 1996

ISBN
1572551119

TC Level
8; 9; 10

most beavers only have one baby?" they might muse aloud, soliciting talk about litters of dogs and cats. "I hope the book will tell us." Teachers can step back from the work with this particular nonfiction text and comment, "This is what I do when I read nonfiction books. I learn things that get me asking questions and hoping to learn more."

Teachers may want to show children that one great way to read nonfiction is to stop often and think, "So, the big thing the book is saying is...." Readers tend to lock onto small, intriguing details, and while such engagement is commendable, it is crucial for readers to pay attention to the big points the author is trying to make.

Readers may want to learn where beavers live, but oddly enough, the book never directly addresses this question. It will be fun for children to encounter this dead-end, however, and to learn that they can nevertheless gather some information about beaver habitat and survival needs of the creatures from the pictures. Some teachers use this question, and the process of figuring out the answer, to help children realize that they can sometimes find the answers to their questions even when those answers are not directly stated.

The book also leaves room for readers to ask questions about the larger context of the life of beavers. Why do some people consider them a nuisance and a pest? Why would others consider them precious to nature and the environment? How would the ecosystem change if they were to become extinct? What is their broad role in nature?

Book Connections

Some teachers use this book to go alongside fictional books about beavers, such as Avi's *Poppy and* Rye. Other informational books on animals written at similar levels include Kevin J. Holmes' *Bats, Bears and Bees*. Gary Davis' *Coral Reef* and *Limestone Caves* provide information on ecosystems.

Genre
Nonfiction; Picture Book

Teaching Uses
Reading and Writing Nonfiction; Content Area Study; Independent Reading

Blue Ribbon Blues

Jerry Spinelli

Book Summary

In this sequel to *Tooter Pepperday*, Tooter has adjusted to her move from the suburbs to the farm, and is ready to enter her goat in the county fair. The story, however, is less about the goat contest than about her relationship with Jack, her neighbor. The story of *Blue Ribbon Blues* revolves around Jack's and Tooter's contrasting kindness and tartness.

Although his own animal will be competing against hers, Jack teaches Tooter how to show her goat. After her little brother paints her goat, which forces it out of the competition, Tooter tries to get her brother to paint Jack's goat, too. In the end, she rises to her better nature and saves Jack's goat from a coyote. Jack brings Tooter the blue ribbon he wins at the show. Tooter thinks he's done this to make her feel bad, but he actually gives her the ribbon in gratitude for saving his animal.

Basic Book Information

Blue Ribbon Blues has 69 pages, divided over ten chapters. Black-and-white illustrations appear every four or five pages. The author, Jerry Spinelli, is well known for his *Maniac Magee,* which won the 1991 Newbery Medal.

Noteworthy Features

Blue Ribbon Blues is a sequel to *Tooter Pepperday*. It can stand alone, but since the action begins where the other book ends, and since *Tooter Pepperday* helps readers understand Tooter's quirky personality, it makes sense for readers to read these books in order.

Blue Ribbon Blues is slightly more challenging than *Tooter Pepperday*. Its complex dialogue requires readers to do some inferring. There are a few places where readers need to infer important things, such as Tooter's brother's name. Early in the book, Aunt Sally talks jokingly about Tooter's anxiety over the goat show. She says, "Young Miss Pepperday isn't afraid of anything," and readers may need help understanding that Aunt Sally knows Tooter is not as tough as she would like everyone to believe. More importantly, towards the very end of the book, Tooter takes her brother to paint Jack's goat. Readers are left to infer that Tooter is doing this out of spite, so that his goat, like hers, will be disqualified. There is also inference required for readers to understand why Tooter is surprised when Jack gives her the blue ribbon, and to understand why he does this. Readers will have

Series

Blue Ribbon Blues, Tooter Pepperday

Illustrator

Donna Kae Nelson

Publisher

Random House, 1998

ISBN

0679887539

TC Level

8

A Field Guide to the Classroom Library, Lucy Calkins and the Teachers College Reading and Writing Project, Heinemann, ©2002 Teachers College, Columbia University; http://www.heinemann.com/fieldguides

to follow these twists to learn the lesson about kindness the book aims to teach.

As in the first book, Aunt Sally uses countrified expressions such as, "Well, bless my bunions. I never would have thunk it." Reading some of Aunt Sally's country talk aloud to puzzled readers might them help hear Aunt Sally's voice and understand it better.

Chapter titles focus the reader's attention on the chapter topic. For example, the chapter entitled "Mama Tooter" deals with Tooter's frustration that the chick she hatched will not act like her child and respond to her commands. There are no flashbacks or dramatic jumps in time or space. Time moves along in a step-by-step fashion, and the story occurs over a few weeks. Most time gaps are signaled in the text.

Teaching Ideas

The title and cover of this book can help students preview it, if they need such a preview. Teachers might explain to children who are unfamiliar with the term "blue ribbon" that it is an award for first place. They might also ask children what else they associate with the color blue. In one class, children connected blue to sadness and speculated that the book might be about losing the contest and not getting a blue ribbon. The students then looked at the cover illustration showing someone scrubbing blue paint off a goat and the group surmised that the paint could be part of the problem. This ritual of studying a book's cover can often help readers know what kind of book they are about to read and can help their comprehension of the story.

Some children will benefit from being asked to retell the plot of this book with a partner because it takes some effort to keep things straight and to understand the dialogue enough to keep track of the actions. They could also decide to study Tooter's character, identifying traits with Post-its or in a notebook. Being aware of Tooter's sassy and guarded nature helps readers see how surprising it is when she acts out of character to save Jack's goat. The book sets readers up to contrast Tooter with Jack, spotlighting traits that make them different.

Students can also trace the development of Tooter's character over this book and its antecedent, *Tooter Pepperday*. Work around inference, which is important to figuring out why Tooter and Jack behave as they do, can help this character study.

Book Connections

Tooter Pepperday, also by Jerry Spinelli, and the *Junie B. Jones* series, by Barbara Park, as well as the *Zack Files* series, by Dan Greenburg, are similar in difficulty. *The Magic Treehouse* series by Mary Pope Osborne and the *Marvin Redpost* series by Louis Sachar might be possible series to read next.

Genre
Short Chapter Book

A Field Guide to the Classroom Library, Lucy Calkins and the Teachers College Reading and Writing Project, Heinemann, ©2002 Teachers College, Columbia University; http://www.heinemann.com/fieldguides

Teaching Uses
Independent Reading; Partnerships; Character Study

A Field Guide to the Classroom Library, Lucy Calkins and the Teachers College Reading and Writing Project, Heinemann, ©2002 Teachers College, Columbia University; http://www.heinemann.com/fieldguides

Cam Jansen and the Chocolate Fudge Mystery

David A. Adler

Book Summary

Cam Jansen is a fifth-grade detective with a photographic memory. She and her friend Eric Shelton are selling chocolate door-to-door to raise money for their school. As they are selling some chocolate to a nice elderly couple, they notice several suspicious things happening. A woman wearing sunglasses and a raincoat - when it is not sunny or rainy out - carries a big garbage bag to a neighbor's garbage can. The house next door to the elderly couple's looks empty, and yet there is a box of fresh groceries at the back door. Several newspapers piled up at the front door make the house appear unoccupied, but all of the newspapers are from the same date. Cam Jansen cannot resist piecing these clues together, along with clues she has memorized, in order to figure out what the mystery is about. With the help of Eric, the elderly couple, and her father, she tracks down a bank robber and his accomplice, saving the day.

Basic Book Information

Cam Jansen and the Chocolate Fudge Mystery is 58 pages long with eight chapters. The chapters are untitled. There are one or two black-and-white illustrations per chapter. The illustrations are not always on the same page as the corresponding text, and often match only a small detail of the content. There is quite a bit of dialogue throughout the book. The dialogue is always referenced, but is often embedded in the sentence, or at the beginning or end of a string of several sentences.

This book is part of a series that currently includes over 20 titles. Adler's Cam Jansen is loosely based on a student in his own first grade class whom everyone thought had a photographic memory. Much of the series includes many of the same characters. All of the books in the series are consistent in level, and in the way Cam and her friends go about solving each case.

Noteworthy Features

Although most of the text is straightforward, there are some small areas that may be confusing to readers at this level. The author often uses italics to indicate strange noises, people thinking or Cam using her photographic memory. For example, on pages 9-10, the text reads:

"Crinkle! Crinkle! 'Shh,' Cam said.

Eric whispered, 'I can't help it. It's the rice cakes. They make noise when they move around in the bag.'"

That Cam's efforts to solve the case lead her all over the neighborhood

Series
Cam Jansen Mystery

Illustrator
Susanna Natti

Publisher
Scholastic, 1993

ISBN
0590129023

TC Level
8

may also confuse readers. Although all the changes in the setting are defined in the text, the changes come quickly, one right after the other. Finally, Cam's father, the two criminals, the elderly couple and several police officers all make appearances at crucial points in the story. Their roles are important to recognize and understand, in order to follow the story.

Teaching Ideas

Cam Jansen and the Chocolate Fudge Mystery, like all of the books in the *Cam Jansen* series, is a good book for children who are beginning a study of, or who already enjoy, the genre of mystery. In mini-lessons about how to tackle mysteries during independent reading, teachers might push students to look closely to see what the first few pages reveal. Later, the class (or small group) could talk about what they learned and realize that readers tend to learn the identity of a crime-solver, whether he or she has a sidekick, and what the mystery will be.

Alternatively, a teacher may want to encourage children to do the same thing most mystery readers do, which is to act as if they, too, were crime solvers hunting for clues. To do this, a teacher might introduce the book saying, "*Cam Jansen and the Chocolate Fudge Mystery* is about a girl named Cam who is trying to solve a mystery with her friend Eric. While she is selling chocolate to raise money for her school, she notices a lot of things that just don't make sense. For example, she sees a woman wearing a raincoat when the sky does not show any signs of rain. She gets very curious and starts to try to figure out the answers to all of the questions she is starting to have. While you are reading today, try to notice all of the things that just don't make sense to you. Remember those things, because that is how a detective tries to 'solve a case.'"

Book Connections

There are many other titles in the *Cam Jansen* series. Some titles include *Cam Jansen and the Mystery of the Dinosaur Bones*, *Cam Jansen and the Mystery of the Babe Ruth Baseball*, *Cam Jansen and the Mystery of the Monster Movie*, and *Cam Jansen and the Mystery of Flight 54*. Mystery series that are somewhat more difficult are *The A to Z Mysteries*, the *Magic Tree House* series and *The Polka Dot Private Eye* series. The *Young Cam Jansen* series and the *Nate the Great* series are somewhat easier.

Genre
Short Chapter Book; Mystery

Teaching Uses
Independent Reading; Small Group Strategy Instruction; Interpretation

A Field Guide to the Classroom Library, Lucy Calkins and the Teachers College Reading and Writing Project, Heinemann, ©2002 Teachers College, Columbia University; http://www.heinemann.com/fieldguides

Cam Jansen and the Mystery of the Monster Movie

David A. Adler

Book Summary

Cam Jansen and the Mystery of the Monster Movie is about a fifth-grade detective with a photographic memory. Cam, her friend Eric Shelton, and her parents go to see an old monster movie called *Shoe Escape*. After a moviegoer makes a scene in the lobby, the movie suddenly stops in the middle, and it is revealed that the second reel of film is missing. As Cam, Eric, and Cam's mother hunt for clues, including the clues stored in Cam's photographic memory, Cam realizes that she has seen a celebrity from the missing movie *in* the theater, but that now that celebrity is missing as well. Eventually they track down the movie star and discover that she, believing the movie has ruined her film career, has stolen the second reel of film. Cam returns the missing reel to the theater and is rewarded with three months of free movies for herself and her family.

Basic Book Information

Cam Jansen and the Mystery of the Monster Movie has 58 pages, each containing 4-6 short paragraphs, and is divided into eight untitled chapters. There is quite a bit of referenced dialogue throughout the book.

This book is part of a series that currently includes over twenty titles. Adler's Cam Jansen is loosely based on a student in his own first-grade class whom everyone thought had a photographic memory. Much of the series includes many of the same characters. All of the books in the series are consistent in level, and in the way Cam and her friends go about solving each case.

Noteworthy Features

There are two features of this book (as well as of all the Cam Jansen books) that are essential to the plot: one is Cam's photographic memory, and the other is the mystery genre itself. These two features demand that the first two chapters be filled with details. For example, on page 13, the text states:

"Cam and Eric rushed to their seats. As they sat down, soft marching music began to play. The music became louder, and the screen lit up with a picture of a marching band. At first the screen showed the marcher's faces. Then it showed their feet and their shoes. Then two words seemed to shoot out on to the screen: 'Shoe Escape.' There were pictures of the movie stars: Joe Roberts, Angela Kane, and Robert Allen. After their faces and names were shown on the screen, their shoes were shown."

The details are included by the author, for Cam to memorize, so that she

Series
Cam Jansen Mystery

Illustrator
Susanna Natti

Publisher
The Viking Press, 1984

ISBN
0140360212

TC Level
8

can later use her photographic memory to recall them to help her solve the mystery. They are also an integral part of a mystery story. Readers need to be aware of all the details so that they may begin to solve the mystery on their own. It is up to the reader to figure out which details are significant and which are not. And, of course, all the details lend themselves to the fun of being stumped as the mystery unfolds. Although these details are essential to the mystery, they can also be difficult for readers - especially those who are unfamiliar with the mystery genre-to hold onto as they read.

The mystery revolves around a missing reel of film. Double features, movie projectors, projection rooms, reels of film, concession stands, theater managers and movie theaters are all important elements of this mystery, so it is important for readers to have some understanding of all these things to enjoy and understand the book fully.

There are a few quick setting changes over the course of the story. The mystery begins as Cam and her family are outside the movie theater, but quickly leads them to the concession stand, the theater seats, back to the concession stand, up to the projection room, back to the lobby, to Cam's mother's car, to the house of Angela Kane, and back to the movie theater. All of these setting changes are well defined in the text, but may cause some challenges to early readers.

There are several minor characters, including Cam's parents, two movie managers, the projectionist, and Angela Kane, who make appearances at crucial points in the story. The roles they play are small but important in moving along the plot.

The text in *Cam Jansen and the Mystery of the Monster Movie* is not written with difficult vocabulary or concepts, but it appears easier than it is. Because it is a mystery, there are several things that are crucial for readers to attend to, such as plot twists, people wearing disguises, people lying and smallbut significant details.

Teaching Ideas

Cam Jansen and the Mystery of the Monster Movie, like all of the books in the *Cam Jansen* series, is a good book for children who are beginning a study of, or who already enjoy, the genre of mystery/detective books. Students may read this book independently, though teachers can also use it as a read-aloud to model good reading behaviors in this genre, which is common as a type of early chapter book.

In this fashion, readers can look for, discuss, and write about things that seem universal in all mysteries: how the detectives are alike in their methods, what literary devices the authors use consistently, how red herrings provide false clues to throw readers off, and the like.

Teachers may also use this book as part of a study of books in the same series. Readers may choose several titles from the same series and compare them. Readers can read, write, and discuss ways in which the books are similar and different, and how the author's voice, setting, characters, and plot are consistent, or not, throughout.

Although the characters in the *Cam Jansen* series are not particularly well developed, there are some consistent qualities that appear in all of the titles. Readers who are just beginning to do character studies will find some opportunities in the stories to note recurring characteristics, consistent relationships of characters to each other, and characters' strengths and weaknesses (e.g., Cam cannot keep herself from following her suspicions, even if they lead her into a dangerous situation; Eric is less outgoing and more cautious than Cam).

Book Connections

There are many other titles in the *Cam Jansen* series. Some titles include *Cam Jansen and the Mystery of the Dinosaur Bones*, *Cam Jansen and the Mystery of the Babe Ruth Baseball*, and *Cam Jansen and the Mystery of Flight 54*. Mystery series that are somewhat more difficult are *The A to Z Mysteries*, the *Magic Tree House* series and *The Polka Dot Private Eye* series. The *Young Cam Jansen* series and the *Nate the Great* series are somewhat easier.

Genre
Short Chapter Book; Mystery

Teaching Uses
Independent Reading; Read Aloud; Author Study; Character Study

A Field Guide to the Classroom Library, Lucy Calkins and the Teachers College Reading and Writing Project, Heinemann, ©2002 Teachers College, Columbia University; http://www.heinemann.com/fieldguides

Chrysanthemum

Kevin Henkes

Book Summary

When she is born, her parents can see she is a perfect baby mouse, and want to give her a perfect name. So they do: Chrysanthemum. At first, she loves her name. But then she goes to school. All the mice children there have short names, and her long name makes her the butt of jokes. Chrysanthemum goes home feeling miserable about her name. Her parents cheer her up with her favorite food, but the next day the same thing happens all over again. Then, on the third day, the class meets the new music teacher. She is wonderful and all the kids love her. When she hears the class making fun of Chrysanthemum, the music teacher tells them that she, too, has a lengthy, floral name: Delphinium. The teacher adds that if her new baby is a girl, she may well name her Chrysanthemum. Suddenly everyone wishes they had a name like a flower and Chrysanthemum goes home, proud and happy.

Basic Book Information

This is a short picture book with Kevin Henkes' fun, detailed illustrations. Henkes fans will undoubtedly recognize the mouse community where this book takes place.

Noteworthy Features

Within the story of *Chrysanthemum* there are many small patterns that can help children if they notice and rely on them. Several times in a row, sentences begin in the same way. Three times, Henkes writes, "She loved the way it sounded when...." The author repeats three times that "She loved the way it looked when...." Each time this is followed by Chrysanthemum's name said three times. There are other patterns in the prose. When Chrysanthemum's father speaks, he tends to use strings of three inviting, unusual vocabulary words. The phrases "absolutely perfect" and "absolutely dreadful" come up many times, as does the sentence, "Chrysanthemum wilted." Several different times her classmate Victoria gets up during nap time to say something mean about her, and each time, her teacher has the same reply. There are other repetitions and patterns in the book, and if children are sensitive to them as they come along, it will support them in their reading by giving them the rhythm to fill in with the words and by letting them know generally what is coming next.

Teaching Ideas

This is a book that deserves to be read, reread, discussed, studied, and read some more. Many teachers first read it aloud early in the year as a book that

Illustrator
Kevin Henkes

Publisher
Trumpet, Scholastic, 1991

ISBN
0688147321

TC Level
7

A Field Guide to the Classroom Library, Lucy Calkins and the Teachers College Reading and Writing Project, Heinemann, ©2002 Teachers College, Columbia University; http://www.heinemann.com/fieldguides

spotlights the importance of building a trusting and respectful community. This book can lead to whole-class conversations about the times when each one of us has felt unsafe, and about the importance of kindness. Children may notice that it is the music teacher who comes to Chrysanthemum's rescue, though it could have been one of her peers. "What could they have said?" teachers can ask children. "In this room, this year, can we try to have the courage to speak out on behalf of children like Chrysanthemum?" A book such as this one can evoke conversations not only on one day, but also on other days when situations arise that push us to recall and discuss *Chrysanthemum* again.

Readers should think deeply about the character of Chrysanthemum. A teacher could use the one-to-one conference format to help students think about ways to study the characters. Some of these ways could be: marking with Post-its revealing details about the character, making a two-column chart with the first column describing a character's action and the second column describing possible reasons for the action, or having a conversation with a partner about the character.

Alternatively, the teacher could suggest that every child read, thinking about character, and could do some work on character study around the read-aloud book as well, challenging readers to do the same thinking alone and in their independent reading partnerships.

The changes in Chrysanthemum's character make for interesting discussions about peer pressure and self-esteem and about being different. Children tend to have a lot to say about these issues. If the class or a particular reader is looking closely at a character (in this instance, at Chrysanthemum), it is entirely likely that readers will soon talk about Chrysanthemum's feelings with reference only to their own experiences. They might say, "Chrysanthemum feels bad. I know, because when I was six, I felt bad because...." It is worthwhile to support the way readers draw on their own lives in order to empathize with the characters, but it is also important for readers to ground what they say in a close study of the text, and not just in personal connections. It is usually easy for children to root their ideas and conversations in *Chrysanthemum*, as opposed to only their own experiences, because this text has so much in it to draw them back.

In encouraging readers to find ways to understand Chrysanthemum, it can be helpful to invite them to examine details. Her dresses reflect how she feels each day as she goes to school, as does the speed at which she moves. Chrysanthemum's dreams are also worth studying because they reflect her emotional state.

Chrysanthemum is one of very few picture books that contains an epilogue. This might be a perfect time to talk about what epilogues are and what purpose they serve-both of which will probably be apparent to children from reading this one. Other chapter books with epilogues might be shown, especially if there are any that the teacher has already read aloud or that are familiar to children for some other reason. Sometimes, children love the idea of epilogues and end up including them in their own writing.

Book Connections

Kevin Henkes has written multiple books about this mouse neighborhood, including *Sheila Rae, the Brave*; *Julius, the Baby of the World*; *Lilly's Purple*

A Field Guide to the Classroom Library, Lucy Calkins and the Teachers College Reading and Writing Project, Heinemann, ©2002 Teachers College, Columbia University; http://www.heinemann.com/fieldguides

Plastic Purse and *Wemberly Worried*.

Genre
Picture Book

Teaching Uses
Character Study; Partnerships; Read Aloud; Independent Reading

City Dog
Karla Kuskin

Book Summary

Noted poet and writer of *The Philharmonic Gets Dressed* (Harper, 1982), Karla Kuskin, tells the story of a city dog's first trip to the country in verse. This city dog is wild with freedom and glee as she experiences the country for the first time.

Basic Book Information

The book begins, "We took the dog to the country...." On each page, the dog is both befuddled by, and overjoyed with, the new experience of the vast countryside. The verse is a free-form rhyming scheme, which makes it a little hard to predict. The very last page holds the poem in its entirety, stanza by stanza.

City Dog has won numerous awards, among them, the John Burroughs Outstanding Nature Book for Children and the *New York Times* Notable Book of the Year. Karla Kuskin is the winner of the NCTE Award for Excellence in Poetry for Children.

Noteworthy Features

This is a 31-page book where the text averages from three words to eight lines on the page. Text usually runs along the bottom of each page, but is also incorporated. On a couple of two-page spreads the illustrations alone tell the story, especially on pages 28-29, as the moon rises and we watch City Dog chase after fireflies and play in a wide-open field.

Kuskin uses language to create imagery that readers may find unusual, refreshing and, possibly, a bit ponderous. Phrases such as, "...the melon yellow moon looked down at the pretty city dog..." combine so much imagery that some readers may need for it to be broken down.

Teaching Ideas

When used as a read aloud, *City Dog* can be used to show young readers how to use inference to develop understanding of a character in a story. You may first need to have a general discussion about ways in which the city and the country differ, in order to allow all students some understanding of the environments. One teacher remarked to her gathered class, "It's interesting that the story begins here, as they pack up the dog and leave the city. As readers, we don't really know what it was like in the city. It doesn't say, does it? The only way we can find out is by looking at City Dog and figuring out from the dog's behavior how different the city and the country are. What do we know about this City Dog?"

The class responded with exclamations of the dog's wild behavior as the

Illustrator
Karla Kuskin

Publisher
Clarion, 1994

ISBN
0395900166

family drove to the country and when they arrived there. One student said, "I think that she [the dog] is acting out so much because she was kept inside so much in the city." The teacher, who had been waiting for this, replied with, "And that use of what you know about the world and the story is called an inference. You used what the book gave you and figured out the rest."

Teachers often like to use this book while teaching poetry. Kuskin uses alliteration (the repetition of the same beginning sounds, *crabs, crows*) and rhyming words *sea, me*. These techniques can be pointed out as being both intentional and important. The book may also be used as an example of vivid descriptive writing. Kuskin not only uses rhyme, but she also uses metaphor, personification (the countryside *rolls around*) and other figurative language to bring the dog in the country to life. In writing workshops, student writers may want to try using some of these techniques themselves.

This is a book that could also be used as an example of alternatives to the common "What I did on summer vacation" writing. City Dog goes to the country, very much like some children go on vacation in the summer. Rather than a humdrum listing of, "First we did this, then this, then this," the beginning, middle, and end of *City Dog* whirl around the emotions the new environment inspired.

When used in guided reading lessons teachers may call attention to the *-s* and/or *-ing* endings by asking, "What's the same about all of these words?" (e.g., *holes, bikes, toes* or *walking, barking, rolling*). If the children are able to do this, the teacher may generate other similar words to show how to link this information to solve other words.

Book Connections

City Mouse & Country Mouse by Isabelle Chantellard shows a similar contrast of setting with city and country.

Genre
Picture Book

Teaching Uses
Independent Reading; Read Aloud; Interpretation; Character Study; Teaching Writing; Small Group Strategy Instruction; Whole Group Instruction; Language Conventions

Dogteam

Gary Paulsen

Book Summary

It is a cold and moonlit night. The dogs are harnessed to the sled and off they go, into the chilly air. Paulsen tells this story of a dogsled night run with precise details and crisp language.

Basic Book Information

This is a 26-page full-color picture book. Very often there are several lines of text per page, many of which are part of sentences that run on and on from page to page.

Noteworthy Features

This story is told in the first person plural, we. The "we" includes the dogs and their human leader, as in "And so *we* run. Part of the night and dark and cold and moonlight and steam from *our* breaths..." [emphasis added]. The dog team and leader become one collective voice. Readers of all ages need to recognize this point of view, as it could be confusing.

Because the sentences are very long, readers may become confused. Readers need to be alerted to the fact that the style of this writing purposefully dramatizes the running of the dogs. At the end of the book, the dogs talk to each other. The point of view shifts from "we" to "you." This may confuse students.

Teaching Ideas

Dogteam can be used as an example of fine writing in the classroom. Meandering sentences such as, "Away from camp, away from people, away from houses and light and noise and into only the one thing, into only winter night they fly away and away and away," capture the sense of the dogs' steady movement forward. While we want children to recognize run-on sentences and understand when they are inappropriate in their own writing, they should know that they might use run-ons as an *intentional* stylistic device. *Dogteam* shows how this technique can be used effectively.

Gary Paulsen is a dogsled racer himself and his expert knowledge exemplifies the maxim, "write what you know." His wife, Ruth Wright Paulsen, has used her own familiarity with the subject to illustrate the text. *Dogteam* and the Paulsens can be used to encourage young writers to write about what they know well and are passionate about.

In a writing workshop, students can examine certain twists, such as the shift from "we" to "you" at the ending. This book could be revisited in a mini-lesson in which the teacher helps readers to consider the point of view in a book. Teachers can make transparencies of particular pages from this

Illustrator
Ruth Wright Paulsen

Publisher
Dell Picture Yearling
Books, 1995

ISBN
0440411300

TC Level
6

and other books in which authors make interesting choices about point of view. Children can discuss whatever they notice in these excerpts about how such decisions contribute to meaning. *Ereth's Birthday* (or any of the *Poppy* series) by Avi, and *Marianthe's Story: Painted Words and Spoken Memories* by Aliki, could join with this text in such a strategy mini-lesson.

Book Connections

Gary Paulson has written full-length books on dog sledding, and these, or John Reynolds Gardiner's *Stone Fox*, could be used as part of a text set on dog sledding. Other books that model how authors make careful decisions about their use of conventions (as Paulsen does with long sentences) include Cynthia Rylant's *Whales* for sentence fragments, Jacqueline Woodson's We *Had a Picnic This Sunday Past* for dialogue, Judy Blume's *Fudge-A-Mania* for italics, and Jerry Spinelli's *Fourth Grade Rats* for parentheses.

Genre
Picture Book

Teaching Uses
Teaching Writing; Read Aloud; Language Conventions

A Field Guide to the Classroom Library, Lucy Calkins and the Teachers College Reading and Writing Project, Heinemann, ©2002 Teachers College, Columbia University; http://www.heinemann.com/fieldguides

Frog and Toad Together

Arnold Lobel

Book Summary

In the first chapter, Toad writes a list of things to do, crossing off tasks he completes. When his list blows away, Toad becomes upset. Frog sits with him until it is late. They write, "Go to Sleep" in the sand, and after Toad crosses it out, they do. In the next chapter "The Garden," Toad plants seeds and assumes they are scared to grow immediately. Frog advises him to wait patiently, but Toad sits with them and tries to coax them to shoot upward. After a few days, Toad's garden begins to grow, and he is exhausted from the effort. In the third chapter, Frog and Toad worry that they are eating so many cookies they will soon become sick. Frog proposes several ways to hide the cookies, but Toad knows they will retrieve them anyway. Frog finally scatters the cookies for birds, and Toad goes home to bake a cake. In "Dragons and Giants," Frog and Toad dodge a snake, falling rocks, and a hawk that all threaten them. While they flee frantically, they tell themselves they are brave. Frog and Toad return to Toad's house and fall asleep, feeling brave indeed. In the final chapter, Toad dreams that he is on stage, expertly performing tricks for Frog. With each stunt, Frog shrinks until he eventually disappears. Toad realizes he will be lonely without Frog and desperately searches for him. Frog awakens Toad. They eat a big breakfast and spend a long day together.

Basic Book Information

Frog and Toad Together, a Newbery Honor Book, is 64 pages long with five chapters divided into approximately 12 pages each. The text has large print with large spacing between words and lines. The sentence structure is simple yet has some complex sentences scattered throughout. There are supportive pictures on almost every page. The pictures are detailed and reflect the character's mood and the setting.

There are four titles in the *Frog and Toad* series. Frog and Toad have many adventures and always remain the best of friends. They have distinct personalities that unfold through the episodic chapters. Frog is always responsible and reasonable. He looks for solutions when there is a problem, and does not get ruffled very easily. Toad is more nervous, demanding, impatient, and easily discouraged. His quirky vulnerability and needs propel these stories forward.

Noteworthy Features

The sentence structure in *Frog and Toad Together* is usually simple, though there are some complex sentences scattered throughout. Dialogue is clearly

Series
Frog and Toad books

Illustrator
Arnold Lobel

Publisher
Harper Trophy, 1972

ISBN
0064440214

TC Level
6

referenced, often in the middle of one character's speech. The pictures are detailed and reflect the character's mood and the setting. Vocabulary is generally less challenging than in other books at this level.

As with the other titles in this series, each chapter of this book can stand alone. The only two characters readers must remember are Frog and Toad themselves, whose personalities are consistent throughout this book and the other three. As a result, *Frog and Toad Together* works well for students who do not have much experience with chapter books because readers can start almost anywhere in the book and follow the story of a chapter.

Teaching Ideas

Because the characters behave consistently, this series makes for excellent character studies. Readers can jot on Post-its recurring characteristics of both Frog and Toad. They can discuss the main characters' general patterns of behavior - Toad's anxious fumbling and Frog's steady practicality - especially in the first three chapters. Since friendship is such an important theme in these books, students should think carefully about what the friendship between Frog and Toad is actually like. In teacher-student conferences or in partnership discussions between students reading together, students might discuss whether Frog balances out Toad, or whether this friendship is as uneven as the size of the two characters.

Once students have read the book several times and are familiar with the basic events of the plot, they might engage in some challenging discussions about the final two chapters. Careful readers may note that, when a hawk flies over their heads, both Toad *and* Frog seem to be scared. Students can infer why Frog suddenly becomes fearful, and speculate about why he changes. Are Frog and Toad actually brave? How do they seem once they return to Toad's house? "The Dream" also raises engaging issues. What does it say about Toad that he dreams, each time he succeeds with another trick, Frog shrinks some more? What does this dream say about their friendship? As a point of comparison, students may look at Henry's dream at the end of *Henry and Mudge: The First Book*. Both dreams are rich with possible metaphors.

Book Connections

Frog and Toad Together is similar in difficulty to *Tales of Amanda Pig* by Jean Van Leeuwen, and the series, *The Adventures of Benny and Watch*, created by Gertrude Chandler Warner. It is more difficult than *Sammy the Seal* by Syd Hoff, and *Joe and Betsy the Dinosaur* by Lillian Hoban. Once children have read *Frog and Toad Together* and other books of similar difficulty, they may find themselves well prepared to read books from the *Pinky and Rex* series by James Howe, and *The One in the Middle Is the Green Kangaroo* by Judy Blume.

Genre
Short Chapter Book

A Field Guide to the Classroom Library, Lucy Calkins and the Teachers College Reading and Writing Project, Heinemann, ©2002 Teachers College, Columbia University; http://www.heinemann.com/fieldguides

Teaching Uses
Independent Reading; Character Study; Interpretation

Frogs
Michael Tyler

Book Summary

This book discusses and illustrates some of the more than 4,000 types of frogs in the world, including their physical features. It explains how frogs make sounds, draw breath, grow, and reproduce. The book also offers tips for caring for frogs and for cleaning up frog environments to help them survive.

Basic Book Information

This nonfiction picture book has 32 pages and about 1400 words. Each page contains roughly one paragraph of text, less per page than the average book in the Mondo animal series. The text is organized into sections by topic, each with a heading, and each listed in the table of contents. There are several clear diagrams. The end of the book has one page that contains a 25-word index, and a list of the precise scientific names as well as the common names of the frogs depicted in the photographs.

Noteworthy Features

The text in *Frogs* is larger and more widely spaced than that in many of the other books in the Mondo animal series. The full-color, well-chosen pictures and short, separated bursts of text also make this book stand out in the series. The pictures are sure to draw in readers to find out more about what is in them. The text, however, is only casually linked to the pictures, so the illustrations do not always provide context clues. Though each page appears to stand on its own, three or four pages generally go together as paragraphs under a subheading.

The text is organized into sections by topic, each with a heading listed in the table of contents. These headings divide the text unevenly: sometimes they are followed by a paragraph of text, sometimes by several pages of it. These categories are also not necessarily uniform in importance or parallel in structure. For example, one section is called "Features of Frogs," and it could be argued that a separate section, "Frog Calls," could fall under the "Features of Frogs" category. Nonetheless, the text can read like one long description of frogs, and so the categories of information need not be perfectly organized or clear for the reader to learn a lot.

Sentences are often compound and complex.

Teaching Ideas

Using all of the visual supports in *Frogs* can help children become better readers of nonfiction. A picture walk before reading can make a good entry point. Most of the photographs in the first twenty pages do not directly

A Field Guide to the Classroom Library, Lucy Calkins and the Teachers College Reading and Writing Project, Heinemann, ©2002 Teachers College, Columbia University; http://www.heinemann.com/fieldguides

Series
Mondo Animals

Publisher
Mondo, 1987

ISBN
1572551917

TC Level
8; 9

relate frogs to the accompanying text, but readers should pause to look carefully and glean whatever information they can. The sequential photographs of a burrowing frog on pages 8-9, the three distinct habitats on page 11, the dotted motion drawing of a leaping frog on page 13, and the puffy-throated frogs on page 16 all suggest topics that might come.

Readers might also notice the headings of different sections, and skim the index at the back to preview topics. Later, as students read more slowly, they might again study the images. They might, for example, imagine the moisture held by the environments depicted on page 11, noticing just how parched the red desert soil is compared to the lush greens in the photograph beneath it. How might such habitats affect frogs? Readers will also want to notice when the illustrations do *not* match the text.

Understanding the common features of nonfiction is important. Students should know how captions work. They should take the small font size of the captions as a clue that the text they hold is different from the main text of the book. Parenthetical labels such as "above" and "below left" may not be intuitively clear to some readers, and how readers handle captions is something to assess during teacher-student conferences. What readers make of sequential images such as the burrowing frog on pages 8-9 and the four stages of tadpole development on page 22, and how they connect such images to the main text, can also tell a lot about what children understand. Children should also know how the table of contents and index can help them find particular parts of this or other nonfiction books without reading each page.

If children are reading this book in partnerships, they can talk to each other about what they have learned about frogs. They can do this even if they are reading different nonfiction books on separate topics, with both partners telling what they now know about the topics they have explored.

Book Connections

If a reader becomes interested in a topic, it is helpful to begin by reading somewhat easier books. Gail Gibbon's *Frogs* would fit this description. The reader might next want to read Sabrina Crewe's *The Frog*, a much longer text that introduces vocabulary and concepts such as predator, amphibian, and camouflage. Michael Tyler's *Frogs* book is more challenging than these. Students may also enjoy other books in the Mondo animal series.

Genre
Nonfiction; Picture Book

Teaching Uses
Content Area Study; Reading and Writing Nonfiction; Independent Reading; Partnerships

A Field Guide to the Classroom Library, Lucy Calkins and the Teachers College Reading and Writing Project, Heinemann, ©2002 Teachers College, Columbia University; http://www.heinemann.com/fieldguides

Fudge-A-Mania
Judy Blume

Book Summary

First, Peter Hatcher, soon to be a seventh grader, learns that his little brother, Fudge, has concocted a plan to marry Sheila Tubman, Peter's sworn enemy. Next, Peter learns that his family and the Tubmans will be sharing a house in Maine for three weeks in the summer. But once in Maine, Peter finds that the situation is not as he imagined: he discovers that a famous retired baseball player lives in the house next door, he helps Fudge out of a few scrapes, he meets Isobel who has eyes like "the best chocolate," his friend Jimmy comes up for a visit and Fudge gives up the idea of marrying Sheila Tubman.

Basic Book Information

Fudge-A-Mania is final installment in a three-book series: *Tales of a Fourth Grade Nothing*, *Superfudge* and *Fudge-A-Mania*. *Fudge-A-Mania* has 147 pages broken into 14 chapters. The chapters range in length from 3 to 15 pages. A table of contents lists chapter titles and page numbers.

Noteworthy Features

Fudge-A-Mania takes place over a three-week period. While there is no central plot line, the chapters do build on and refer back to one another to some extent. Though some children will mistakenly regard each chapter as quite separate, they are, in fact, parts of a whole.

Fudge is a central character in this book, but *Fudge-A-Mania* is really Peter's story. Peter narrates, and some readers miss out on this essential characteristic of the story. Because of the title, readers sometimes expect Fudge to be the narrator. Readers may want to discuss why the book is named for Fudge and not for Peter.

The dialogue in the book is realistic and amuses most readers. Among the realistic spoken parts of the book are that Fudge asks a lot of questions and causes some verbal mix-ups, that Peter teases Fudge and that Peter argues with both Fudge and Sheila. Also realistic is the fact that Sheila and Peter do not become friends at the end of the book. In fact, they promise always to hate each other. Readers may enjoy that the ending is not pat.

Explanations of idiomatic expressions and definitions of terms are woven into the text, as are reminders of safety rules. For example, when the group goes sailing, hypothermia is defined, and everyone is instructed to wear life jackets. Chapter titles are catchy and intriguing, such as "Dizzy from Izzy" and "Green Gurgling Gas." The title of one chapter, "The I.S.A.F. Club," may confuse readers until they learn that I.S.A.F stands for "I Swallowed a Fly."

Teachers should be aware that some of Peter's private thoughts appear in italics. However, italics are also used for emphasis in dialogue between other

Series
Fudge books

Publisher
Yearling/Bantam
Doubleday Dell, 1990

ISBN
0440404908

TC Level
10

characters. The multiple uses of italics may be confusing to some readers and may need to be explained. Readers may also have a hard time keeping track of the minor characters who appear in the book.

Teaching Ideas

If students have read these books as a series, they may want to talk with partners or in small groups about how Peter has changed since his introduction in *Tales of a Fourth Grade Nothing*. They could talk about the most memorable messes Fudge has created for Peter, and discuss what is happening to the boys' personalities as they mature.

Students can also discuss how the antics in *Fudge-A-Mania* are different from the antics in *Superfudge*.

During teacher-student conferences, it is important to ask, "Who is telling this story?" Students can be asked to cite evidence in the first two chapters that indicates that it is Peter who is telling the story. They should understand that Peter's thinking and point of view color everything we learn as readers. Then they might be asked to think about how the story might be different if it were Fudge or Sheila Tubman telling it. In fact, in Chapter 9, Fudge begins writing his own book called *Tell Me a Fudge*.

There are several occasions in the book when Peter acts like a typical big brother. Sometimes that means losing patience with Fudge, and other times it means helping him out of a mess. Readers can connect Peter's role in his family to their roles in their own families. In what ways does Peter feel both protective of and frustrated by Fudge, and do readers feel this way about their siblings, too? How can this personal connection with the character inform their reading and inform their lives?

Time passes in this story and readers can note how the author makes that happen. Phrases such as "the next morning" in the beginning of Chapter 8 can be pointed to as signals that indicate the passage of time.

Since *Fudge-A-Mania* contains so much dialogue, students who read it in a book club might assume roles of particular characters and read their parts aloud. Chapter 5 would lend itself nicely to being read aloud. First, students could scan the chapter and then list all the characters that appear. Then they can discuss what is happening in the chapter, what the characters are feeling, and how a reader could express those feelings. Next, students could be selected for the various parts. Before the readers begin, they can quickly review the use of quotation marks, reminding each other that they are only reading aloud what is in quotation marks. For example, when the text says, "'I can't stand that smell,' Sheila said," the reader playing the part of Sheila needs to be reminded only to read aloud, "I can't stand that smell." "Sheila said" falls to whomever is reading the part of Peter; that person is responsible both for Peter's spoken dialogue and for the narration. Besides bringing the story alive for those who participate and those who view the drama, this activity might reinforce an understanding of direct quotations, help students to differentiate clearly between characters, and encourage reading with expression.

Book Connections

Students will be able to understand the characters' development better if

A Field Guide to the Classroom Library, Lucy Calkins and the Teachers College Reading and Writing Project, Heinemann, ©2002 Teachers College, Columbia University; http://www.heinemann.com/fieldguides

they have already read the first two books in this series, *Tales of a Fourth Grade Nothing* and *Superfudge. Forever Amber Brown*, another later book in a series, is written at a comparable level to *Fudge-A-Mania*, as is *Ramona Quimby, Age 8*.

Genre
Chapter Book

Teaching Uses
Partnerships; Read Aloud; Independent Reading

A Field Guide to the Classroom Library, Lucy Calkins and the Teachers College Reading and Writing Project, Heinemann, ©2002 Teachers College, Columbia University; http://www.heinemann.com/fieldguides

George's Marvelous Medicine

Roald Dahl

Book Summary

George Kranky does not have a sweet, kindly grandmother. George's grandma is a "selfish, grumpy old woman" with "pale brown teeth and a small puckered-up mouth like a dog's bottom." In retaliation for her constant bossing, George replaces his grandmother's medicine with a potion that he hopes will blow off the top of her head. After his grandmother takes a spoonful, her innards catch on fire. She inflates and then grows so tall that she sticks out of the chimney.

George's father, after recovering from the shock, realizes just how "marvelous" this medicine could be to a farmer. In an attempt to have the biggest cows and hens (maybe he could cure world hunger with their eggs) in the county, he gets George to mix him up a batch. The only problem is that George cannot remember all of the ingredients in his concoction. George's failed attempts create a farm of misshapen animals and eventually shrink his grandmother into nothingness.

Basic Book Information

The 89-page book contains 15 chapters that are outlined in the table of contents. There are humorous illustrations by Quentin Blake on every other page. Roald Dahlis the author of the acclaimed *Matilda, James and the Giant Peach* and *Charlie and the Chocolate Factory*.

Noteworthy Features

The structure of *George's Marvelous Medicine* generally supports readers since it is in chronological order and all jumps in time are explained in the text. It contains a single plot line and only four characters. The entire book is set on the Krankys' farm.

The story itself is told by a third-person narrator who gets inside George's head and tells readers just how the boy is feeling. The narrator also provides humorous commentary on the unfolding events.

For inexperienced readers, retaining the developing plot for the duration of the book may still be difficult, and so these readers may benefit from opportunities to meet with a partner, to page through what they've read so far and retell it. The chapter titles give a glimpse of what the upcoming chapter will be about.

Teaching Ideas

This book contains all of the trademark features of a Roald Dahl book, including silly rhyming songs, concoctions that disfigure nasty people, a protagonist who rises from poverty to do something extraordinary, and

Illustrator
Quentin Blake

Publisher
Penguin Group, 1981

ISBN
0140346414

TC Level
9

Quentin Blake's marvelously funny illustrations. It would be a good idea to group all of Dahl's books together in a classroom library, much like you would a chapter book series. Since there is such a formula to his books a child can get hooked on reading all of them.

At first, teachers may think that the best way to introduce this text is with the big disclaimer, "Kids, don't try this at home." Feeding your grandma nail polish remover is never a solution to your problems, no matter how cantankerous she is. Dahl, however, does this work for us. He creates such ludicrous scenarios that children can easily infer that the story is in jest. As in *Charlie and the Chocolate Factory*, Dahl skillfully creates a world in which anything is possible. The cartoon-like illustrations further enhance the ridiculousness of the story.

Teachers may use *George's Marvelous Medicine* in a writing workshop to focus on how to write descriptively and humorously. Dahl uses many adjectives to create vivid and funny pictures in readers' heads. Students will be able to see that, when they write with many synonyms to describe the same thing, the adjectives intensify the description, the words "screechy," "shrill," "awful," "snapping" and "shouting" all work together to convey how horrible grandma's voice is.

A source of confusion for readers may be the dialogue throughout the book. Some children may develop an ear for Dahl's sarcasm, but others may not. Reading aloud can help, since a teacher can relay some of the sarcasm through vocal intonation. Children reading with partners may then pick up on the facetious outlook in Dahl's books, discussing what tone they would use if reading aloud.

There are also plays on words that the reader may not pick up on, such as when George is mixing the medicine and adds "half a pint of ENGINE OIL-to keep Grandma's engine running smoothly," and "Some ANTIFREEZE-to keep her radiator from freezing up in the winter." During independent reading conferences or whole-class read alouds, teachers may want to monitor whether students understand these double meanings.

Book Connections

George's Marvelous Medicine may excite children to read *Matilda, Charlie and the Chocolate Factory* and other Roald Dahl books.

Genre
Chapter Book

Teaching Uses
Independent Reading; Book Clubs

Great Snakes!

Fay Robinson

Book Summary

In simple, rhyming language, this book lists and describes snakes to readers. We see snakes with spots, snakes with diamonds, snakes eating rats, and snakes eating crocodiles. We see snake eggs and snake skin and snake fangs. The text in this case serves almost as captions to the detailed, realistic pictures of the snakes themselves.

Basic Book Information

This nonfiction picture book has 32 pages. Each page has one or more illustrations of snakes on a primarily white background and a line or two of text in large font. Since the book is written as a long, rhyming list of snake features, each line is not a complete sentence. At the end, three pages reproduce a miniature version of all of the book's pictures, with the name of each species below the illustration.

Noteworthy Features

The rhyming pattern in *Snakes* is not regular enough to help readers their first time through the text. On second or third or fourth readings, however, the rhyme may indeed facilitate the reading of the book.

Probably it is the pictures of the snakes in action that will attract readers to the book. Studying the illustrations in depth provides excellent support for the text. A picture of a snake swallowing a rodent gives readers at least as much information as the words, "Snakes eat . . . rats," and the picture can certainly help readers who rely heavily on illustrations to decipher these words.

Teaching Ideas

The small pictures and page numbers at the back of the book make an excellent introduction to the structure of an index. Although these pages are not, strictly speaking, an index, they can introduce readers to the concept that the text at the end of a book is sometimes a reference for the rest of the book, and can help them find parts of the main book itself. Readers could, for example, turn back to the page where they first saw the picture of the hognose snake and read the text, now knowing the snake's name from the "index."

This can also be a great book for children who are learning to draw or sketch what they see in science or ecology units. These illustrations are isolated pictures of the creatures themselves, with detail and realism. The fact that they are divorced from most of their background makes them easy to see as scientific drawings.

Illustrator
Jean Day Zallinger

Publisher
Scholastic, 1996

ISBN
0590262432

TC Level
6; 7; 8

A Field Guide to the Classroom Library, Lucy Calkins and the Teachers College Reading and Writing Project, Heinemann, ©2002 Teachers College, Columbia University; http://www.heinemann.com/fieldguides

The book opens and closes with the lines: "Every single snake is great!" There is a lot of room for discussion here. Do all people think that all snakes are great? Why do so many people hate snakes? Why do farmers sometimes kill snakes? What exactly is great about snakes? Kids can find a lot of things to say about these sentences, if they take them very seriously.

Book Connections

Fay Robinson's *Mighty Spiders!* and *Amazing Lizards!* would be good follow-ups to *Great Snakes!* Rigby's PM Animal Facts series offers a number of books for students who have begun to read at this level, including *Cats, Dogs* and *Guinea Pigs.* Students reading nonfiction at the upper end of this range might try Patricia Lauber's *You're Aboard Spaceship Earth* and Betsy Maestro's *Why Do Leaves Change Color?*

Genre
Nonfiction; Picture Book

Teaching Uses
Content Area Study; Partnerships; Reading and Writing Nonfiction

Happy Birthday, Danny and the Dinosaur!

Syd Hoff

Book Summary

Danny finds his friend the dinosaur at the museum and invites him to his sixth birthday party. He discovers that it is the dinosaur's birthday, too. The dinosaur is "a hundred million years and one day old!" They decide to celebrate together. They hang balloons, wear party hats, sing songs, play pin-the-tail-on-the-donkey, and blow out the candles on the birthday cake. At the end of the day, they make their birthday wish, which is to be together again the following year.

Basic Book Information

Happy Birthday, Danny and the Dinosaur! is part of the An I Can Read Book series. There are 32 pages and no chapter breaks. There are between one and four lines of text per page and most pages contain a single sentence. Each page is brightly illustrated with pictures that match at least one sentence on the page, but the picture alone won't tell readers what the text says.

Begun in 1958, Syd Hoff's *Danny and the Dinosaur* series, like Else Holmelund Minarik's *Little Bear* series, have been an important step into longer books. The dinosaur is huge, but in no way intimidating. He is instead friendly to Danny and the rest of the neighborhood kids.

Noteworthy Features

Children will love this simple funny tale of Danny and his dinosaur in the familiar world of birthday parties. For a text that is this simple, Syd Hoff does a good job of creating humor. He does this by placing the dinosaur in activities that are familiar for children, yet silly for a dinosaur. The story is simple, but because many children fantasize about having a dinosaur as a loyal pet, the story will hold the interest of most readers at this level. The *Danny and the Dinosaur* books offer the challenge of a single, continuous plot. The story in all the *Danny and The Dinosaur* books is made up of a series of linked and chronological episodes.

The majority of the text is written with high frequency words, such as *was, friend, said, would, rode, today, your, children, helped, asked,* and *everybody.* There is a sprinkling of more difficult words that may challenge the reader, such as *delighted, museum, million, balloons,* and *furniture.* Quotation marks and exclamation points are used simply throughout. Some of the sentences are compound. There is referenced dialogue (readers are

Illustrator
Syd Hoff

Publisher
Harper Collins, 1996

ISBN
0064442373

TC Level
5

explicitly told who the speaker is), with references always coming at the beginning or end of the sentence.

Teaching Ideas

Happy Birthday, Danny and the Dinosaur can be used as a read aloud, in a guided reading group, as an independent reading book for early readers, or as part of an author study of Syd Hoff. Readers can discuss the ways in which most Syd Hoff books are alike. For example, most Syd Hoff books have a child with an unlikely, talking animal friend. Readers can also discuss recurring characters such as Danny and the dinosaur.

The most obvious and strongest characteristic of books written by Syd Hoff is the humor. When introducing *Happy Birthday, Danny and the Dinosaur*, a teacher may say, "This is the story of a boy who has a dinosaur as a friend. They decide to have a birthday party together and do all sorts of birthday things, like wearing party hats, playing pin-the-tail-on-the-donkey, and making a wish on a birthday cake. Can you imagine having a dinosaur at your party? What funny things might happen? Could a dinosaur really come to your house?" Readers will enjoy discussing their fantasies of what it would be like to be visited by a dinosaur.

Primary grade readers who have mastered early reading skills, such as one-to-one matching, directionality, checking the picture against the text, or "getting their mouth ready" for an unfamiliar word can use this book to support those behaviors. At the same time, the book also enables children to attempt new skills, including reading text that does not have pictures that match each sentence, reading longer and often compound sentences, reading with quotation marks and punctuation, tackling harder words, and reading with increasing fluency, for longer and longer periods of time.

Teachers may work with readers on developing self-checking skills; strategies for figuring out unfamiliar words such as using context, rereading and looking for the unfamiliar word in other parts of the text; retelling; and how to talk about funny, interesting or confusing parts with other readers.

As it is written in the past tense, *Happy Birthday, Danny and the Dinosaur!* is a good book to use to help children pay special attention to words with -ed endings.

Book Connections

Happy Birthday, Danny and the Dinosaur! is one of three books about the same characters. The others are *Danny and the Dinosaur* and *Danny and the Dinosaur Go to Camp*. Other titles by Syd Hoff at a similar level include *Sammy the Seal, The Firehouse Cat, Captain Cat*, and *Oliver*. Before reading *Danny and the Dinosaur* books, children may want to read *Rex and Lilly*, a somewhat easier book that also has a dinosaur as a character.

Genre
Picture Book

A Field Guide to the Classroom Library, Lucy Calkins and the Teachers College Reading and Writing Project, Heinemann, ©2002 Teachers College, Columbia University; http://www.heinemann.com/fieldguides

Teaching Uses
Read Aloud; Character Study; Independent Reading; Small Group Strategy
Instruction; Author Study

Henry and Mudge and the Forever Sea

Cynthia Rylant

Book Summary

Henry and Mudge and the Forever Sea is one of a series of books about a boy and his loveable 180-pound dog who do everything together. It holds four self-contained, yet connected, stories. All the stories take place on a day at the beach. In the first story, "To the Beach," Henry, his father and Mudge prepare their individual bags for their day at the beach. The contents of each bag reflect the owners. Henry tells Mudge he will love his first time at the beach but warns, "Don't drink the water!" In the second story, "The Forever Sea," Henry and his father splash and play in the surf as Mudge, who is too scared to come in, watches from the shore. In the third story, "Brave Dog," Henry, Mudge, and Henry's father have a hot dog lunch and build sand castles. When Henry's father's fake lobster gets washed out to sea, Mudge ignores his fear and swims out to get the lobster. In the last story, "Good-bye, Crab," Henry, Mudge and Henry's father chase a crab for a while. When they realize they will not be able to catch it, Henry's father buys them all a second Sno-cone and they head home.

Basic Book Information

Henry and Mudge and the Forever Sea is one of a series of books about the same main characters written by Cynthia Rylant, a well-loved writer of countless popular children's books including *When I Was Young in the Mountains, The Relatives Came* and *Missing May*. It is part of the *Ready to Read* series. *Henry and Mudge and the Forever Sea* is 48 pages long and is separated into four stories, each of which has a title and is listed in a table of contents. Some of the illustrations take up whole pages, and some are at the top, middle or bottom of the page. The illustrations support some part of the text on each page. Pages range from having as little as two lines of text, with one word per line, to five or six lines of text. There is a little simple dialogue throughout the text, all of it referenced at the beginning or the end of the sentence.

This series focuses on the relationship between Henry and Mudge and their adventures together. The whole series does not have to be read in order, but *Henry and Mudge: The First Book* makes a good entry point because it describes how the pair originated. Books dealing with Annie, Henry's cousin, should be read in order because a story line develops over the course of the three Annie books. Many of the books in this series have short stories connected by a theme such as winter, moving, or a birthday.

Series
Henry and Mudge books

Illustrator
Sucie Stevenson

Publisher
Simon & Schuster, 1989

ISBN
0689810172

TC Level
6

Noteworthy Features

Henry and Mudge and the Forever Sea has less text and more obvious themes than many of the other Henry and Mudge titles. The writing and the humor are more direct than in many of the others as well. The setting stays the same throughout the book. This lends itself to an easier understanding of the content for readers at this level.

Teaching Ideas

Henry and Mudge and the Forever Sea can be used as a read aloud, for partner and group reading and for independent reading.

Henry and Mudge and the Forever Sea is a good book for readers who are just beginning to read longer, more challenging books. The divisions between the four stories offer natural stopping points. Teachers may use each story to instruct readers in setting independent reading goals by using a bookmark, Post-it, or reading partner. Taking one story at a time can help readers pace themselves at each sitting. At this point, readers can try out some important independent reading strategies, such as retelling what they've read; rereading difficult, enjoyable or funny parts; using a Post-it to mark places to which they want to come back and reread before discussion; rereading to "feel strong" in what they've read; or rereading what they've read so far before continuing on in a second or third sitting.

Because of its simplicity, teachers may use this book as a starting off point in this series, although it is probably a good idea to use this book as a follow-up to the first book, which introduces how Henry acquires Mudge. Readers can read, write, and discuss ways in which the books are different; how the author's voice is consistent from book to book; and whether the character, settings, and plots have remained the same or changed. For example, readers might say, "I notice that Henry's father really likes to have fun with Henry and Mudge. It reminds me of the time Henry's father jumped into a big puddle with Henry and Mudge in the book called *Henry and Mudge in Puddle Trouble*."

Book Connections

Henry and Mudge and the Forever Sea is part of a large series of books about the same characters. Some other titles include: *Henry and Mudge in Puddle Trouble, Henry and Mudge in the Green Time, Henry and Mudge Under the Yellow Moon, Henry and Mudge in the Sparkle Days,* and *Henry and Mudge Get the Cold Shivers.* Other books that are near the same level in vocabulary, content and theme include the *Little Bear* books by Else Holmelund Minarik, and, at a slightly more advanced level, the *Oliver Pig* books by Jean Van Leeuwen.

Genre
Short Chapter Book

A Field Guide to the Classroom Library, Lucy Calkins and the Teachers College Reading and Writing Project, Heinemann, ©2002 Teachers College, Columbia University; http://www.heinemann.com/fieldguides

Teaching Uses
Independent Reading; Character Study; Small Group Strategy Instruction

Henry and Mudge in Puddle Trouble

Cynthia Rylant

Book Summary

Henry and Mudge in Puddle Trouble is one in a series of books about a boy and his lovable 180-pound dog who do everything together. This is the second book of their adventures. There are three separate, yet connected stories in the book. In "The Snow Glory," Henry tries and tries to resist picking a beautiful flower in his garden. When he finally decides he can resist no longer, he confesses to Mudge, but Mudge eats it! At first, Henry is really angry, but quickly realizes that the flower never belonged to him anyway. In "Puddle Trouble," Henry and Mudge spend all afternoon splashing in a muddy puddle. Henry's father finds them in the middle of their adventure and it appears he is going to be really angry. At the last moment, when Henry is feeling remorseful, his father jumps in to play with them! In "The Kittens," Henry and Mudge are excited about, and then protective of, the kittens next door. Mudge "adopts" them. One day, while Henry is at school, Mudge saves the kittens from an uncertain fate, when a strange dog comes "sniffing around."

Basic Book Information

Henry and Mudge in Puddle Trouble is the second book in a series of books about the same characters, written by Cynthia Rylant. The book is 47 pages long, separated into three individual stories. The stories are listed in a table of contents. The stories do not rely upon each other, but they are connected by a subtle theme: it is a springtime book. Each story is between 12 and 15 pages long and is brightly illustrated. Some of the illustrations are full page, and some are at the top, bottom or middle of a page. Many of the sentences are short and straightforward, but there are several examples of longer, more complicated sentence structures and vocabulary. Simple question marks, exclamation points and quotation marks are used throughout the book.

This series focuses on the relationship between Henry and Mudge and their adventures together. The whole series does not necessarily have to be read in order. The books from the series that contain the character Annie, Henry's cousin, are best read sequentially because a storyline develops over the course of the three Annie books. Many of the books in this series have short stories connected by a theme such as winter, moving, or a birthday.

Noteworthy Features

The text of *Henry and Mudge in Puddle Trouble* is simply, yet beautifully written. There are many "big" concepts (of friendship, family, childhood fears, love, etc.) that are subtly woven into the text. For example, on page

Series
Henry and Mudge

Illustrator
Suçie Stevenson

Publisher
Aladdin, 1987

ISBN
0689810032

TC Level
6

18, the text states, "Henry knew it wasn't his snow glory. He knew it wasn't anybody's snow glory. Just a thing to let grow. And if someone ate it, it was just a thing to let go." There are many places in the series where these subtle themes are alluded to, but not directly written into the text. This adds to the depth and the interest level of these sweet stories. It also makes them great opportunities for discussions. There are many humorous sections in each story-usually something Mudge does-which are easily enjoyed and understood.

Teaching Ideas

The characters of Henry and Mudge (as well as other minor characters that appear throughout the series) are not particularly well developed. Also, the setting in many of the books stays the same throughout the book. This should make it easier for young readers to follow and enjoy the story. Some italics and capital letters are used for emphasis. Some young readers may need instruction on how to read those words.

Each story can be studied with a closer look at the story elements. All stories have characters, a setting, a plot, movement through time, and a change that's central to the plot and/or the characters. Readers may think about how much time goes by in each of the three stories. It's also thought-provoking to reread the stories looking to see if each one has a single turning point.

There are many other *Henry and Mudge* books that retain most of the same characters and introduce new ones, while maintaining the same level of vocabulary and content as the first few books. In book or partnership discussions, readers may compare and discuss ways in which the books are similar and different, how the author's voice is consistent from book to book, and whether the characters, settings and plots have changed or remained the same. For example, a teacher may say, "I notice that in the story called 'The Snow Glory', Henry starts to feel angry when Mudge eats the flower. But when he looks at Mudge with his soft brown eyes and his big head, he just feels full of love for him. Henry felt the same way in the first book, *Henry and Mudge*, after Mudge came back from being lost."

Book Connections

Henry and Mudge in Puddle Trouble is part of a large series of books about the same characters. Some other titles include: *Henry and Mudge Under the Yellow Moon*, *Henry and Mudge in the Green Time*, *Henry and Mudge and the Happy Cat*, *Henry and Mudge and the Careful Cousin*, and *Henry and Mudge and the Forever Sea*. Other books that are near the same level in vocabulary, content and theme are the *Little Bear* books by Else Holmelund Minarik and, at a slightly more advanced level, the *Oliver Pig* books by Jean Van Leeuwen.

Genre
Emergent Literacy Book

A Field Guide to the Classroom Library, Lucy Calkins and the Teachers College Reading and Writing Project, Heinemann, ©2002 Teachers College, Columbia University; http://www.heinemann.com/fieldguides

Teaching Uses
Independent Reading; Interpretation; Language Conventions; Partnerships;
Author Study

A Field Guide to the Classroom Library, Lucy Calkins and the Teachers College Reading and Writing Project, Heinemann, ©2002 Teachers College, Columbia University; http://www.heinemann.com/fieldguides

Henry and Mudge: The First Book
Cynthia Rylant

Book Summary

Henry is an only child who is searching for companionship. He asks his parents for a brother, but his parents say no. He tells them that he wants to move because there are no children on his street, and again his parents refuse. Henry then asks his parents for a dog and they finally consent. Henry searches for just the right pet, and he finds Mudge, who grows into a 180-pound dog who drools a lot.

Henry and Mudge do everything together. Mudge loves everything about Henry. Everywhere Henry goes, Mudge follows. But one day, while Henry is in school, Mudge wanders off and gets lost. Henry realizes Mudge is missing and calls for him over and over. At last, Mudge hears Henry and comes running. From that day on, Mudge never goes anywhere without Henry.

Basic Book Information

Henry and Mudge: The First Book is 40 pages long with lively pictures on every page. The chapters can stand alone, making it easier for young readers to hold onto the plot. Cynthia Rylant is the award-winning author of *When I Was Young in the Mountains*, *The Relatives Came* and *Missing May*. Most sentences in this book are short and simple, but occasionally the sentences are somewhat long and descriptive for this level.

This series focuses on the relationship between Henry and Mudge and their adventures together. The whole series does not have to be read in order, but this book makes a good entry point because it describes how the pair originated. Books dealing with Annie, Henry's cousin, should be read in order because a story line develops over the course of the three Annie books. Many of the books in this series have short stories connected by a theme such as winter, moving, or a birthday.

Noteworthy Features

Through the adventures of Henry and Mudge, we learn a lot about who the characters are and how they are changing. Henry's parents are mentioned in each book, but they are not as well developed as their son. Therefore, it is easy for young readers to carry the character of Henry in their minds as they read through each of the books because he stands out compared to the other, human characters. Dialogue is referenced and used sparingly, making this series a very accessible context in which to introduce kids to the challenges of reading dialogue. While reading in this series, children can think about why writers use dialogue and how it should be read.

Series
Henry and Mudge books

Illustrator
Sucie Stevenson

Publisher
Aladdin Paperbacks, 1996

ISBN
0689810059

TC Level
6

A Field Guide to the Classroom Library, Lucy Calkins and the Teachers College Reading and Writing Project, Heinemann, ©2002 Teachers College, Columbia University; http://www.heinemann.com/fieldguides

Teaching Ideas

In this book, as well as the others in this series, the dilemmas Henry and Mudge encounter are typical situations faced by many kids. The drama in *Henry and Mudge* books is not wild adventures with pirates or robbers. Instead, the plotline here revolves around loneliness, anxiety and losing a pet. Young readers generally have no problems relating to these stories and talking about the books. This makes these books a suitable forum for teaching readers the value of personally connecting to the stories they read. It is important to stress that the goal is not simply to say, "I'm the same way," but to see how one's life experience helps one *really* understand the book. Students can talk about times they have felt worried or alone, how lucky Henry is to get a dog, how Henry feels when Mudge gets lost, how Mudge probably feels when he is lost and how Mudge changes Henry's life.

Some other ideas for Post-its and/or discussion include times when Henry is happy and sad in the story, things that Henry likes or dislikes, readers' favorite parts, and parts where students have a personal connection to the story.

Teachers can use this book to teach a strategy lesson on character. They might introduce this lesson by saying, "Today we're going to try to do some deep thinking about the characters in *Henry and Mudge*. We're going to look at how what a character *does* can tell us what a character is *like*. Let me tell you what I mean. Yesterday on the playground, I noticed Audrey share her swing with Amanda even though Audrey wanted nothing more than to be on the swing all by herself. What might that tell us about what kind of person Audrey is?" After students give answers such as 'kind,' 'nice' or 'generous,' teachers can continue: "Now one of the problems with the book *Henry and Mudge* is that we're *not* told Henry is kind or Mudge is nice. Instead, we have to do the same thing we did with Audrey: look at what they do and let that tell us what they're like. So with that in mind, let's see if we can do the same work with *Henry and Mudge*. Who has an example of something Henry or Mudge does that can tell us more about who they are?"

Teachers can also use the text to alert students to be on the lookout for how some words show the passage of time. An example is in the sentence, "Henry *used to* walk to school alone." Rylant also marks the progression of time by Mudge's growth. Many young readers are confused by the collection of ever-larger collars that suggests Mudge's incremental growth; months whirl by in the space of a page. This may be difficult for kids to notice and understand, and would serve as a great mini-lesson.

The last two chapters, in which Mudge gets lost, may prove difficult for some readers, particularly in distinguishing between fantasy and reality. Henry dreams about Mudge still being apart from him when in fact they are back together.

Book Connections

The *Henry and Mudge* series is similar in difficulty to the *Little Bear* series by Else Holmelund Minarik, and the *Poppleton* and *Mr. Putter and Tabby* series, both by Cynthia Rylant. However, the characters in Cynthia Rylant's books become increasingly complex, with *Henry and Mudge* the easiest, *Mr.*

A Field Guide to the Classroom Library, Lucy Calkins and the Teachers College Reading and Writing Project, Heinemann, ©2002 Teachers College, Columbia University; http://www.heinemann.com/fieldguides

Putter and Tabby more challenging, and the *Poppleton* series most challenging of all. The *Henry and Mudge* series is harder than *Tidy Titch* by Pat Hutchins, *Noisy Nora* by Rosemary Wells, and *Stanley* by Syd Hoff. *Frog and Toad* by Arnold Lobel would be a good follow-up series.

Genre
Short Chapter Book

Teaching Uses
Language Conventions; Character Study; Small Group Strategy Instruction; Independent Reading

A Field Guide to the Classroom Library, Lucy Calkins and the Teachers College Reading and Writing Project, Heinemann, ©2002 Teachers College, Columbia University; http://www.heinemann.com/fieldguides

Hey World, Here I Am!
Jean Little

Book Summary

Hey World, Here I Am! is, for the most part, a collection of entries in the voice of the main character, Kate. All capture the angst as well as the joys of growing up. Many students can relate to these charming, precise observations of life.

Basic Book Information

The character Kate Bloomfield appeared also in Little's books *Look Through My Window* and *Kate*. Instead of a story, in this book, Jean Little has written a collection of entries. Of the 47 entries in this book, 37 are poems and 10 are vignettes. A short author's note explains the origin of Kate. *Hey World, Here I Am!* is an ALA Notable Book.

Noteworthy Features

A table of contents lists the poems and vignettes. Some of the poems are written in free verse. A short biography, at the end of the book, mentions to readers that Little is legally blind, an astounding fact in light of the imagery found in these poems. For example, in "Not enough Emilys," Little writes of "the sparkling world of shining sunlight."

Teaching Ideas

Teachers might want to use some examples of Jean Little's poems to illustrate that not all poetry rhymes.

Teachers can also show students how they can use the vignettes in the book as models for their own writing. Groups can discuss how Jean Little has crafted a piece such as "Mrs. Entwhistle" by using techniques such as crisp dialogue ("'On your feet!' Mrs. Entwhistle shrieked") or characters' thoughts ("Taking my seat, I felt a bit taller myself") or action ("I shoved my hands out of sight") or precise verb choice ("I scowled at her"). They can discuss what Kate wants to tell and how Little conveys what Kate wants. Excerpts from *Hey World, Here I Am!* can be reproduced on transparencies and used for multiple purposes during mini-lessons for the writing workshop.

Book Connections

Students might enjoy reading Little's other two books in which Kate appears as a character, *Look Through My Window* and *Kate*. Sharon Creech's *Love That Dog* is a more challenging book in which a story is told largely through a series of connected poems.

A Field Guide to the Classroom Library, Lucy Calkins and the Teachers College Reading and Writing Project, Heinemann, ©2002 Teachers College, Columbia University; http://www.heinemann.com/fieldguides

Series
Kate books

Illustrator
Sue Truesdell

Publisher
Harper Collins, 1986

ISBN
006440384X

TC Level
11

Genre
Memoir; Short Chapter Book; Poetry

Teaching Uses
Teaching Writing; Partnerships; Read Aloud; Small Group Strategy
Instruction

How a House Is Built

Gail Gibbons

Book Summary

How a House Is Built provides a chronological narration of the process of constructing a home, from the architect's drafting table to the laying of the foundation to the finishing touches of the landscapers.

Basic Book Information

This nonfiction picture book is 30 pages long. The bottom of each page contains roughly two sentences of text below a large illustration. Most of the illustrations are labeled with the names of the machines, tools or jobs that the workers are carrying out. The font of the labels is a little smaller than the mid-size font of the text itself, but not so small as to intimidate. There is no index, table of contents, or subheading structure. At the end of the book, there is a final page entitled "Simple Shelters of the Past." It depicts eight homes, with a sentence describing each one.

Noteworthy Features

Merely glancing at its rudimentary colors and smiling construction workers makes *How a House Is Built* at first seem slightly less sophisticated than its text actually is. It does not provide a glossary or any direct definitions of the technical terms, so readers must rely on the illustrations and context of the words to clarify most meanings. Having prior knowledge will help readers tremendously as they try to figure out the definitions from context. For instance, *septic tank* and *septic system* are not explained directly.

The final page looks at "Simple Structures of the Past." Some students and teachers may take issue with this page, as many of these structures are still in use around the world. The word "simple" may also be misleading. For example, building an igloo requires many fewer people than building a large, two-story house, but it also requires specialized skills and experience that very few people have.

Students might also notice that none of the dwellings in the book appears to contain multi-family units, the kind in which the majority of children in cities reside. Students who question this text may become interested in finding out how building apartment buildings is different than building one-family homes.

Teaching Ideas

This is an excellent book for readers who are interested in construction or heavy machinery. The text makes it relatively easy to take notes, so this may be a good book for a beginning note-taker.

Because most pages contain few sentences, *How a House Is Built* gives

Illustrator
Gail Gibbons

Publisher
Holiday House, 1990

ISBN
0823412326

TC Level
8; 9

readers short, isolated bursts of text in which to practice using context clues. During a whole-class strategy lesson or teacher-student conferences, students might be prompted to look at a sentence such as, "The mason is almost finished building the chimney." Many students will not know what a mason is, but they can work on strategies to figure it out. Are all of the people in the illustration masons? Which is labeled "mason"? What is that figure doing? What materials is he using? Many students may not conclude that masonry involves general work with stones, but that it has to do with building chimneys.

Because no other examples of masonry exist in the book, this conclusion is logical. It is important to remember that readers who learn to use context clues effectively sometimes begin with limited definitions. However, because they read carefully and glean information as they go, they revise their definitions with every book that they read, forming increasingly accurate and complete ideas about new words they encounter.

Some students may think that books such as this one are compilations of facts, loose gatherings of information. It helps to confer with readers so they see that lists are arranged according to logic. In this book, the logic is sequential. However, the information *could* have been presented in a different order. It could have first listed the easy things about building a house, and then listed the hard things.

Alternatively, it could have listed the tasks that require many builders, and then the tasks one builder could do on his or her own. During teacher-student conferences, it is interesting to note what readers think a book's structure is. Understanding structure helps many children make meaning of what they read. Students may note that the first four pages of the book provide general information about houses, while the rest of it moves chronologically. Observing how they deal with this structural shift may tell teachers a bit about how children understand nonfiction at this level.

Book Connections

Gail Gibbons has written dozens of careful, nonfiction picture books. Gibbons' *From Seed to Plant* follows a similar chronological structure, and her *Tool Book* relates thematically to *How a House Is Built*. Byron Barton's *Building a House* offers students more reading on this topic.

Genre
Nonfiction; Picture Book

Teaching Uses
Independent Reading; Partnerships; Content Area Study; Reading and Writing Nonfiction; Critique

A Field Guide to the Classroom Library, Lucy Calkins and the Teachers College Reading and Writing Project, Heinemann, ©2002 Teachers College, Columbia University; http://www.heinemann.com/fieldguides

I'm in Charge of Celebrations

Byrd Baylor

Book Summary

The narrator tells us about some of the 108 celebrations she has created for herself in the desert of the southwestern United States. After she takes part in an extraordinary natural event, such as observing a green cloud shaped like a parrot or walking along a trail close to a coyote, she records the occasion in her notebook and decides on a fitting way to celebrate the anniversary in the future. She laughs when people ask her if she is lonely in the desert, because she has become so familiar with the desert and the creatures that inhabit it.

Basic Book Information

Two-page spreads of text and illustrations comprise this 26-page picture book. Each double-page spread contains two or three columns of text, with columns holding from one to five words. Streaks of color from the sparse illustrations angle around the text. Byrd Baylor is the author of four Caldecott Honor books, including three illustrated by Peter Parnall.

Noteworthy Features

Short lines and stanzas give *I'm in Charge of Celebrations* the feel of a poem. With words such as "you" and "Friend," the narrator addresses readers directly. Though her voice is simple and colloquial, her language occasionally becomes lyrical. For example, when describing the gyrations of whirlwinds she has seen, the narrator uses a series of line breaks and the repeated word *and* to convey a sense of a twisting that picks up speed like a whirlwind itself: ". . . moving / up from the flats, / swirling / and swaying / and falling / and turning, / picking up sticks / and sand / and feathers / and dry tumbleweeds."

The book is arranged so that each celebration begins on a different page, much like the books that contain a compilation of poems about the holidays in a calendar year.

Many readers will not be familiar with the desert landscape in this book. Some will imagine that a desert is nothing but sand, and be surprised that the text names so many plants and animals that thrive in this habitat. Many will not know what a yucca is, and some might not know what a cactus is. In general, the least familiar words in the book are not likely to interfere with basic comprehension, though teachers can remind children of strategies to get the gist of unknown words.

Teaching Ideas

I'm in Charge of Celebrations serves the writing workshop not only as a

Illustrator
Peter Parnall

Publisher
Simon and Schuster, 1986

ISBN
0689806205

TC Level
7

model of good writing, but also as a model of writers' habits. In the story, the narrator keeps a notebook. She tells what she writes down and why. Students can look at how the narrator uses her notebook and get ideas for working with their own writers' notebook. Teachers might encourage children to notice the natural world-even the ants crawling through cracks in the playground blacktop-to see if they can find something to write about and celebrate.

Before reading *I'm in Charge of Celebrations*, teachers may begin by reading a different book about the everyday events that children experience (e.g., Sandra Cisneros' *Hairs /Pelitos*). Teachers might ask, "How do you suppose this author got the idea to write a whole book about this? I bet that because she's a writer, she really notices the littlest things. I could write a book about my hands. I've got this green magic marker on my thumb from this morning when we were working on our science studies, and I've got a scar on my finger from when I fell off my bike when I was six. I'm noticing that there are a lot of stories, right in my hand." Soon the class might imagine stories from daily life they could put down on paper.

The illustrations of the book, with their broad swaths of unusual colors, often do not immediately attract children's attention, though they do invite questions. Why is the rabbit portrayed in the middle of a circle? Why is the tail of the falling star touching the narrator and going all around her?

Book Connections

Byrd Baylor and Peter Parnall's Caldecott Honor books are *The Desert Is Theirs*; *Hawk, I'm Your Brother*; and *The Way to Start a Day.* Eve Merriam's *The Wise Woman and Her Secret* and Norma Farber's books of poems are good companion texts.

Genre
Picture Book

Teaching Uses
Teaching Writing; Read Aloud; Independent Reading

A Field Guide to the Classroom Library, Lucy Calkins and the Teachers College Reading and Writing Project, Heinemann, ©2002 Teachers College, Columbia University; http://www.heinemann.com/fieldguides

Jamaica and Brianna
Juanita Havill

Book Summary

Jamaica does not want to wear her brother's old gray hand-me-down boots to go to school. On the way to school, Brianna teases Jamaica about her "boy boots." Jamaica makes a hole in the old boots bigger so that her mother will have to buy her a new pair. As Jamaica searches for new footwear, she comes across boots that are like her friend Brianna's, but, worried that she will be accused of copycatting, Jamaica settles on cowboy boots. Brianna insults the new boots and Jamaica retaliates by calling Brianna's boots ugly. At the end of the book, Jamaica finds gentle words that allow Brianna to feel good about her own boots and the girls become friends again.

Basic Book Information

This 26-page picture book is carefully written, and illustrated by expressive watercolors. Facing pages tend to go together, some containing text with no illustrations, some containing illustrations with no text, and others containing both text and illustrations. This is the third Jamaica book, following *Jamaica's Find* and *Jamaica Tag-Along*. Juanita Havill earned the Ezra Jack Keats New Writer Award for her *Jamaica's Find*.

Noteworthy Features

Much of the story of *Jamaica and Brianna* is conveyed through dialogue. The speaker of this dialogue is not always referenced.

The text itself has been placed to fit around the illustrations. As such, words are not laid out in any consistent place on the page. The illustrations, however, support the text carefully. The characters' expressive faces and posture can help children understand the emotions the text on each page describes.

Teaching Ideas

The book will give children the chance to speak to others about the ways in which they go about choosing words to express their feelings. From this, children can work on choosing words to express how they feel when they write. Children can use the book to think about what they do when they are building friendships, how they know they have hurt someone's feelings and how to fix the situation if they do hurt someone's feelings. Children may want to show this by role-playing through art or writing a short story. Children can also use the book to begin looking at what it means to be a copycat, and learning to appreciate and value their personal styles and selves. The realistic situation provides ample opportunities for text-to-self connections.

Series
Jamaica series

Illustrator
Anne Sibley O'Brien

Publisher
Houghton Mifflin
Company, 1993

ISBN
0395779391

TC Level
5

A Field Guide to the Classroom Library, Lucy Calkins and the Teachers College Reading and Writing Project, Heinemann, ©2002 Teachers College, Columbia University; http://www.heinemann.com/fieldguides

Jamaica and Brianna can be used for strategy lessons on beginning to infer characters emotions from their words. Why might Jamaica tell her mother that her brother's old boots do not fit her? Why does her mother feel the toe of the boots, and why might she be reluctant to buy new ones? After readers are familiar with the story, they might reread and speculate about why Brianna criticizes both pairs of boots Jamaica wears. The subtle illustrations, such as Jamaica's slight grin in the foreground while her mother glumly touches the hole in Ossie's boots, provide further clues about characters that readers can infer.

Reading *Jamaica and Brianna* also leads to discussions on what may have caused Jamaica to change her mind about liking her boots. Because the book's major theme is feelings, children can cooperatively write on Post-its how Jamaica and Brianna are feeling at the start of the book. They can then match these feelings up with a time in their own lives when they felt this way. Children can also have a group discussion based on one interesting Post-it written by a member of the group.

In the writing workshop, the book can be useful as a guide to writing with dialogue. The book's use of dialogue shows how it can bring the story to life. Children can take a closer look at where the author chose to incorporate dialogue and how dialogue can show feelings instead of having a narrator simply name them.

Book Connections

Juanita Havill has written two other books with the same main character, *Jamaica's Find* and *Jamaica Tag-Along*. Peggy Rathmann's *Ruby the Copycat* also deals with issues around friendship and discovering individual taste. *Chrysanthemum* by Kevin Henkes addresses the major theme presented in *Jamaica and Brianna* and how the characters resolve a problem.

Genre
Picture Book

Teaching Uses
Independent Reading; Teaching Writing; Small Group Strategy Instruction; Interpretation

A Field Guide to the Classroom Library, Lucy Calkins and the Teachers College Reading and Writing Project, Heinemann, ©2002 Teachers College, Columbia University; http://www.heinemann.com/fieldguides

Jamaica's Find
Juanita Havill

Book Summary

Jamaica, while playing alone in the park, comes across a red sock hat and a cuddly, stuffed gray dog. Instead of placing both items in the lost and found at the park house, Jamaica returns only the hat and takes the stuffed animal home. At home, Jamaica shows off her dog to her family, which is not thrilled about having a dirty stuffed dog sitting at the dinner table. Once Jamaica is asked to take it out of the kitchen area, she begins to think about whether she did the right thing by keeping the dog. She overhears her mother mention, "It probably belongs to a girl just like Jamaica." While sitting in her room and talking to her mother, Jamaica feels empathy for the owner and decides that she wants to return the dog to the park house. After bringing back the stuffed dog, Jamaica meets a girl named Kristin, the original owner of the stuffed animal. As Jamaica happily reunites Kristin with her missing dog, the girls exchange smiles and become friends.

Basic Book Information

This picture book is a winner of the 1987 Ezra Jack Keats New Writer Award and a Reading Rainbow Selection. This 32-page picture book has at least one illustration for each pair of facing pages. The text in the book can be found on both sides of the page and superimposed over some pictures. The watercolor illustrations in the book closely represent the written text.

Noteworthy Features

The text itself has been placed to fit around the illustrations. As such, words are not in any consistent place on the page. The illustrations, however, support the text carefully. The characters' expressive faces and postures can help children understand the emotions the text on each page describes.

Teaching Ideas

This book is about honesty, compassion, and making good decisions. Jamaica's moral dilemma of dealing with right and wrong is a thread woven from the beginning to the end of the book. In and outside the classroom, there are many ways in which children can learn from this book.

The book can be a mentor text for children who are trying to write their own personal narratives. Many children retell incidents in their own lives without consciously shaping them as stories. They would benefit from a reminder of the features of narrative, and from examples of successful, cohesive stories.

This book also lends itself to teaching the strategy of prediction. Readers could use prior knowledge and looking at the cover to predict what the story

Series
Jamaica series

Publisher
Houghton Mifflin Company, 1986

ISBN
0590425048

TC Level
5

will be about. Throughout the text, they can predict what will happen next and explain the textual basis for their predictions.

Book Connections

Juanita Havill has written two other books with the same main character, *Jamaica and Brianna* and *Jamaica Tag-Along*. In this text, as well as Rod Clement's *Grandpa's Teeth*, the main characters deal with issues of honesty, making choices and attending to their consciences. *Believing Sophie*, by Hazel Hutchins, and *Fanny's Dream*, by Caralyn Buehner, both address the major themes presented in *Jamaica's Find* and show how characters resolve similar problems.

Genre
Picture Book

Teaching Uses
Independent Reading; Teaching Writing; Character Study; Critique

A Field Guide to the Classroom Library, Lucy Calkins and the Teachers College Reading and Writing Project, Heinemann, ©2002 Teachers College, Columbia University; http://www.heinemann.com/fieldguides

Little Bear

Else Holmelund Minarik

Book Summary

Little Bear and Mother Bear are the main characters in four different stories. In the first story, "What Will Little Bear Wear?" Little Bear adds one article of winter clothing at a time so he can go outside and play in the snow. In the end, he discovers, with the aid of his mother's gentle guidance, that his own "fur coat" is best. In "Birthday Soup," Little Bear, believing his mother has forgotten his birthday, decides to go ahead and invite his friends to a birthday party. Each invited friend brings an ingredient for his birthday soup. In the end, his mother arrives with a birthday cake, assuring him that she never will forget his birthday. In "Little Bear Goes to the Moon," Little Bear, deciding he is going to try to fly to the moon, dons his "new space helmet," climbs to the top of a little tree and jumps to "the moon." Imagining he is on the moon, he returns home to his mother and pretends to be a little bear from the moon, as she plays along with him. In the end, he tires of his game and decides to become the real Little Bear once again. In "Little Bear's Wish," Little Bear and Mother Bear are having a bedtime discussion about all of Little Bear's wishes, including sitting on a cloud, going to China, and meeting a princess. When Mother Bear gently tells him that these wishes are impossible he ultimately decides to wish for his mother to ask, "Would you like to hear a story?" Mother Bear proceeds to recount all preceding stories from the book, as Little Bear comments on each. In the end of the story (and the book), Little Bear is tucked in and they say good night to one another.

Basic Book Information

In this book, like in most little chapter books, there is a table of contents that lists the small stories contained in the book. Each story is about 12 pages long. The number of sentences on a page and the length of the sentences vary throughout the book. There are many short, repetitive simple sentences as well as more complicated, lengthier sentences. Maurice Sendak has beautifully illustrated the majority of the pages. This book was first published in 1957, and it launched HarperCollins' series of I Can Read books.

Little Bear is the first of five books by Else Holmelund Minarik featuring the character for whom the series is named. As a pioneer in early chapter books for young children, this series has several features that have become staples in subsequent early chapter books:

Two or three main characters - more can be confusing

Easily distinguished characters: young and old, male and female, distinct personalities

String of small, self-contained predictable episodes centered around everyday, ordinary life events, with few leaps in time or space

Series

Little Bear books

Illustrator

Maurice Sendak

Publisher

Harper Collins, 1957

ISBN

0064440044

TC Level

6

Several short chapters that are sometimes self-contained stories

Print that rarely takes up more than half of a page, leaving room for illustrations

Noteworthy Features

Little Bear is simply yet beautifully written. Else Holmelund Minarik does a terrific job of capturing the voice of Little Bear. It is interesting to note that although Little Bear is called only Little Bear throughout the story, without a "he" or "she" pronoun reference, most readers assume the character is a boy.

The more complex vocabulary can usually be gleaned from context, although a reader could benefit from conversations about a few content-specific words, such as *Viking*. Many of the stories have some humorous sections. The humor is straightforward and easily understood.

Teaching Ideas

For millions of youngsters, *Little Bear* has been an entry into chapter books. Because the book is separated into four stories that are listed in a table of contents, it provides readers natural stopping points. Readers at this level can probably read each chapter in a single sitting. Teachers may use each story (or, in the case of beginning readers, a part of each story) to instruct readers in how to set goals (using a bookmark, Post-It, etc.) for how much they hope to read at each sitting.

At this point in students' reading development, teachers can begin to coach children to try out some more sophisticated reading strategies. For example, teachers can help children understand that often a book will contain a few more challenging pages or passages and that skilled readers are watching out for these "uphill" sections. We may reread these sections, and we sometimes give ourselves a retelling test, trying to retell a part of the story to check if we get it. Readers at this level may want to Post-It passages in the book that really make them think about the story. Readers may also use a Post-It to mark places where they may want to come back and re-read.

Little Bear can also be used to do a character study. The main characters, particularly Little Bear and his mother, have noticeable characteristics repeated in later books in the series. A reader could compare a character to him or herself or could simply discuss what he or she notices and wonders about the character.

Once a teacher supports these conversations and book studies within one series, children can transfer the same line of questioning to any series they are reading, or will soon read. Little Bear's thoughts, wishes and play really mirror those of many young readers. The relationship between Little Bear and his mother is also beautifully rendered. Mother Bear is a constant, loving presence, even as Little Bear makes mistakes, acts foolishly or strikes out independently.

Book Connections

In this series, four books follow this one: *A Kiss for Little Bear, Father Bear Comes Home, Little Bear's Friend* and *Little Bear's Visit*. Often readers who've enjoyed the *Little Bear* books turn next to Arnold Lobel's *Frog and*

A Field Guide to the Classroom Library, Lucy Calkins and the Teachers College Reading and Writing Project, Heinemann, ©2002 Teachers College, Columbia University; http://www.heinemann.com/fieldguides

Toad books.

Genre
Short Chapter Book

Teaching Uses
Independent Reading; Small Group Strategy Instruction; Character Study

A Field Guide to the Classroom Library, Lucy Calkins and the Teachers College Reading and Writing Project, Heinemann, ©2002 Teachers College, Columbia University; http://www.heinemann.com/fieldguides

Magic Tree House: Dinosaurs Before Dark

Mary Pope Osborne

Book Summary

Annie and Jack are sister and brother. In this book, they discover a magic tree house in their backyard that takes them to the time and land of dinosaurs. Annie is very adventurous and always wants to keep exploring, but Jack keeps trying to convince her not to go. Both of them end up going to the place of the dinosaurs because Jack opens a book in the magic tree house about dinosaurs and says, "I wish I could see a Pteranadon for real." Before they know it, they have traveled to the land and time of dinosaurs.

At first, they do not realize where they have traveled. They compare what is outside the tree house window to what they see in their book. Then they decide to go and explore this new land and its creatures. Annie just walks right up to the dinosaurs and touches them. With each dinosaur, Annie tries to be friends while Jack writes notes in his notebook. The last animal they meet is a Tyrannosaurus rex. Frightened, they start to run away. The Pteranadon follows, sweeps them up, and flies them away from the T. rex. They are flown back to the tree house and return home.

Basic Book Information

Dinosaurs Before Dark is a 68-page-long chapter book. There are pictures on every third or fourth page that depict the setting and characters. There are ten chapters that represent changes in scene and have descriptive titles to support the reader.

Dinosaurs Before Dark is the first in the *Magic Tree House* series. It is important to note the order of this series of books, as its storylines continue sequentially. In books one through four, Jack and Annie discover Morgan le Fey, the mysterious owner of the magic tree house. In books five through eight, Jack and Annie are linked together by their mission to help free Morgan le Fey from a spell. In nine through twelve, Jack and Annie solve four ancient riddles. In books thirteen through sixteen the tow of them are Master Librarians. Books seventeen through twenty are linked together by the two characters being given four gifts to help free a dog from a spell.

Noteworthy Features

Most sentences in *Dinosaurs Before Dark* are short and simple, with dialogue throughout. The dialogue in this book is very simple and is mostly between

Series
Magic Tree House

Illustrator
Sal Murdocca

Publisher
Random House, 1992

ISBN
0679824111

TC Level
8

A Field Guide to the Classroom Library, Lucy Calkins and the Teachers College Reading and Writing Project, Heinemann, ©2002 Teachers College, Columbia University; http://www.heinemann.com/fieldguides

Annie and Jack, and one other central character that guides them through the new land. The speaker is always identified clearly so that students are not confused.

This series is ideal for readers who have just recently become accustomed to longer chapter books, because it is an exciting adventure every time. The high drama in *Magic Tree House* books pushes children to read on without stopping. In addition, the places that the characters visit are very interesting and hold readers' attention.

Sources of difficulty lie in isolated, content-specific vocabulary words, such as *Pteranadon* or *Tyrannosaurus Rex*. However, because the world of dinosaurs is so captivating and familiar to kids, it helps draw them in by connecting the story to what they already know about this high-interest topic.

Teaching Ideas

This book is a good book to be read by partners because students can easily keep each on track in an understanding of the plot. Children can be encouraged to read these books silently on their own, but to do so in ways that will allow them to be able to retell the books to each other. During partnership shares, two children who have, for example, read *Dinosaurs Before Dark* will meet for five minutes to retell the story to each other. At first teachers could encourage children to do this while skimming the text. Later, the retellings should consolidate the story into a summary, and include all the elements of a story.

These books are well suited to a range of strategy lessons. All of these can grow out of observing readers with these books and noticing the sources of difficulty they encounter. One challenge in this book will be the specialized vocabulary of dinosaurs, and teachers may want to suggest that readers note if a book focuses on a topic - dinosaurs, soccer, cooking - and realize in advance that the difficult words in a book may be content-specific words related to those themes. "If it is a book on dinosaurs and you encounter a word you've never seen before, you might think, 'Could this be a word about dinosaurs?'"

Book Connections

The *Magic Tree House* series is similar in difficulty to the *Ginger Brown* series by Shannon Dennis Wyeth and the *Marvin Redpost* series by Louis Sachar. The *Magic Tree House* series is harder than *Pee Wee Scouts* by Judy Delton and the *Junie B. Jones* series by Barbara Park. Once readers have had success with the *Magic Tree House* series they may wish to read *The Hit-Away Kid* by Matt Christopher or *The Adventures of the Bailey School Kids* series.

Genre
Short Chapter Book

A Field Guide to the Classroom Library, Lucy Calkins and the Teachers College Reading and Writing Project, Heinemann, ©2002 Teachers College, Columbia University; http://www.heinemann.com/fieldguides

Teaching Uses
Independent Reading; Partnerships; Small Group Strategy Instruction

Marvin Redpost, Class President

Louis Sachar

Book Summary

In this book, the President of the United States makes a surprise visit to Marvin's school on the very day that everyone has dressed up for "Hole Day," when everyone wears clothes with holes in them. Each child in the class prepares a question to ask the President. Marvin asks, "Is there something we should be doing now if we want to be President someday?" The President tells the TV cameras to take a good look at Marvin and says, "You may be looking at a future President." Marvin forgets in all the excitement that he is supposed to go shoe shopping. His family is very angry with him and they do not listen to him tell about his experience at school. They certainly are surprised, however, when they see Marvin and the President on the evening news.

Basic Book Information

This book has 67 pages, with chapters that run from five to nine pages in length. There are no chapter titles. Louis Sachar is also known for his *Wayside School* series and his novel, *Holes*, which won the 1999 Newbery Medal.

Currently, this series has seven books, all of which star Marvin and are told through a third person narrator. The books do not need to be read in sequence. For the readers to get hooked, the first book, *Kidnapped at Birth?*, should not be read first - it tends to be more difficult than the rest of the series because of its references to royalty and to medical lab testing. The other books contain storylines that can sustain the reader because the themes are easier to relate to and understand, especially *Why Pick on Me?* and *Is He a Girl?* The *Marvin Redpost* series can introduce a reader to Sachar's style and humor by way of shorter chapters and less sophisticated plot structure.

Noteworthy Features

This story is very exciting and easily sustains most readers. The characters are consistent throughout the series and so are easy to understand. The print size is medium, as is the spacing between the words and lines. The sentence structure is simple and the pictures aid in defining the plot and supporting the actions of the characters. This is the only book in the series that directly states (on page 11) where Marvin's family lives: "Maryland - less than 20 miles from Washington"

Though the story is interesting, sometimes the reader can become so consumed with the plot that details are missed and important clues are lost. The "President" storyline is so strong that readers can forget Marvin is supposed to go shoe shopping. Many readers miss the big clue on page 57,

Series
Marvin Redpost books

Illustrator
Amy Wummer

Publisher
Scholastic, 1999

ISBN
067988999X

TC Level
8

"His feet were trying to tell him something."

Teaching Ideas

Marvin is an attractive character for children, and he can make a good focus
for a character study. Students can put Post-its on places that reveal
Marvin's traits. They could also talk about the lessons Marvin is learning,
the different predicaments in which he finds himself and whether they, the
readers, would want to be friends with him. Studying his character across
the series would be one way to extend this character study. To get children
in the habit of providing evidence, teachers might encourage them to cite
places in the text that support their assertions about what Marvin is like.
Teachers can also ask if readers see Marvin act out of character, or change
over time.

   Because the basic plot is accessible, students can concentrate on finding
the many subtle points that might otherwise be missed. This book gives a
good opportunity for teachers to encourage students to ask, "What else is
going on here?" For example, both Marvin's teacher and the school principal
act flustered and nervous. A teacher might ask, "How is Marvin's teacher
acting? Why might she act that way?" Most students pick up on the idea of
developing hunches about why characters act the way they do, even if the
author does not explicitly say, by looking at what is happening around the
characters.

Book Connections

This series is similar in difficulty to the *Flower Girls* series and the *Ballet
Slippers* series. It will be helpful if readers have had prior success with such
series as *Junie B. Jones* and *Adam Joshua* before starting with *Marvin
Redpost*. The *Amber Brown* series and the *Aldo* series make good next steps
after *Marvin Redpost*.

Genre
Short Chapter Book

Teaching Uses
Independent Reading; Character Study; Interpretation

A Field Guide to the Classroom Library, Lucy Calkins and the Teachers College Reading and Writing Project, Heinemann, ©2002 Teachers
College, Columbia University; http://www.heinemann.com/fieldguides

Miss Nelson is Missing!

Harry Allard

Book Summary

The sweet teacher, Miss Nelson, has a class that is misbehaving terribly. The next day Miss Swamp, an ugly teacher in an ugly black dress, shows up instead of Miss Nelson, orders the children around and gives them loads of homework. They don't even get a story read to them. The children miss Miss Nelson and go looking for her, but near her house they only see Miss Swamp. When Miss Nelson finally comes back the children don't misbehave at all. Back at home, Miss Nelson closes her ugly black dress into the closet and swears never to tell.

Basic Book Information

This 32-page book has at least one illustration on almost every page. Pages that contains text hold roughly three sentences each. Other titles in the Miss Nelson series include *Miss Nelson is Back* and *Miss Nelson has a Field Day*. James Marshall and Harry Allard have collaborated on many titles besides these, *The Stupids Step Out*, *I Will Not Go to Market Today*, and *The Tutti-Frutti Case*.

Noteworthy Features

Miss Nelson Is Missing! offers many supports for readers. Vocabulary is fairly simple. The pictures, too, provide support, in that they correspond very closely to the words they illustrate.

They provide a better match to the words than is usual in picture books, to the point that even without the words, a reader browsing the pictures could build a relatively accurate outline of the plot for him or herself

Many children catch on to the fact that Miss Nelson is Miss Swamp before the characters in the story catch on, which can be very empowering. It makes readers feel smart to have caught on to the joke or the trick in the story.

Teaching Ideas

Because this is a book which tends to catch on in a classroom, so that lots of children in the room read it within the space of a few weeks, many children come to the book already knowing a summary of the plot, or at least knowing that Miss Nelson and Miss Swamp are the same person. Clearly, this makes it a lot easier to read. In fact, it can make reading it almost like rereading it. This feature of the book makes it an excellent choice for teachers ready to emphasize and build on the social aspect of reading.

In teacher-student conferences, one good way to tell how well students understand this book is to listen for where they think Miss Nelson has gone.

Series
Miss Nelson books

Illustrator
James Marshall

Publisher
Houghton Mifflin Company, 1977

ISBN
0590118773

TC Level
7

Children who actually believe that Miss Nelson has left for Mars or been eaten by sharks - two of the scenarios that the kids in the story imagine as a fate for Miss Nelson -are confused, and either need to read easier books for a while or discuss *Miss Nelson is Missing!* with a partner in order to make more sense of it. Helping readers who are struggling with this book work through it is valuable because of its social power in the classroom.

Miss Nelson is Missing! raises many questions children can discuss. Some partnerships will talk about why the kids in the class behave badly and why, in general, nice people are often exploited. Some readers may talk about the ethics of Miss Nelson lying to her class.

Some teachers use this book as a read aloud to start discussions they feel the class needs to have before having a substitute teacher in the classroom.

Book Connections

Students who like *Miss Nelson is Missing!* may wish to read the other books in this series, *Miss Nelson is Back* and *Miss Nelson has a Field Day*. Those who enjoy guessing what has happened to Miss Nelson may wish to take on some of the chapter book mysteries at this level, such as the *Nate the Great* series.

Genre
Picture Book

Teaching Uses
Critique; Independent Reading; Partnerships

A Field Guide to the Classroom Library, Lucy Calkins and the Teachers College Reading and Writing Project, Heinemann, ©2002 Teachers College, Columbia University; http://www.heinemann.com/fieldguides

Mr. Putter and Tabby Bake the Cake

Cynthia Rylant

Book Summary

Mr. Putter and Tabby Bake the Cake is a part of a series chronicling the adventures of Mr. Putter, an elderly man, and his cat, Tabby. Mr. Putter decides to make his neighbor Mrs. Teaberry a Christmas cake and give it to her as a Christmas present. Mr. Putter cannot understand how anyone, including Mrs. Teaberry, could like fruitcake, so he decides to make a "light and airy cake" instead. The fact that Mr. Putter does not know how to bake a cake does not prevent him from trying. After many hilarious attempts, Mr. Putter bakes Mrs. Teaberry a wonderfully light and airy Christmas cake. Fortunately for Mr. Putter, Mrs. Teaberry shares the light and airy Christmas cake with him.

Basic Book Information

This 38-page book is divided into four chapters. The chapter titles give hints about what will happen in each chapter. This book makes use of colorful illustrations, with at least one per page. Cynthia Rylant is the acclaimed author of a wide range of children's books, including the *Mr. Putter and Tabby*, *Henry and Mudge* and *Poppleton* series.

Noteworthy Features

Rylant employs repetition effectively to help propel the story and give young readers plenty of information about what is going on in the text. The predictable pattern also allows the reader to guess what will happen next. The illustrations are key to this book, since they match the text very closely and can provide a less experienced reader with more support, while more advanced readers can check the illustrations against their comprehension of the text.

Teaching Ideas

This book is about Mr. Putter and his struggle to create the perfect Christmas present for Mrs. Teaberry. The fact that he does not know how to bake a cake and does not have the necessary baking equipment does not stop him, as he is determined to make something nice for his good friend. The theme of perseverance and friendship is central to the story.

Mr. Putter and Tabby Bake the Cake could be used to introduce children to the basics of story structure. This book provides a simple springboard for discussing characters, plot, setting, movement through time, and change, all of which create story structure. The study of a character like Mr. Putter would be a good start. Students can talk with partners about Mr. Putter and what type of character each student feels Mr. Putter is, and what parts of the

Series
Mr. Putter and Tabby books

Illustrator
Arthur Howard

Publisher
Harcourt Brace & Company, 1994

ISBN
0152002146

TC Level
6

text have given them those ideas. Conversations can also focus on other aspects of story structure.

Book Connections

Since this is a part of a series, readers may enjoy following further exploits of Mr. Putter, Tabby, Mrs. Teaberry, and Zeke. Other books in the series include *Mr. Putter and Tabby Walk the Dog, Mr. Putter and Tabby Paint the Porch, Mr. Putter and Tabby Fly the Plane, Mr. Putter and Tabby Pour the Tea* and *Mr. Putter and Tabby Pick the Pears.* The *Henry and Mudge* series is just slightly more challenging than *Mr. Putter and Tabby*. Another book that highlights how persistence can lead to success is *Make Way for Ducklings* by Robert McCloskey.

Genre
Short Chapter Book

Teaching Uses
Independent Reading; Character Study; Partnerships

Muggie Maggie

Beverly Cleary

Book Summary

Maggie Schultz has just started the third grade and within a week the class will begin cursive writing. When Maggie announces this with a gusty sigh to her parents at the dinner table, they laugh. As the rest of the class is trying hard to write, Maggie draws squiggly lines on her paper. Her teacher, Mrs. Leeper, informs Maggie's parents, the principal, and the other teachers in the school of her desire not to learn. Maggie becomes "the girl who won't do cursive." The one exercise she tries-signing her name in cursive-turns out to read "Muggie Schultz" so the other kids on the playground begin to call her "Muggie Maggie." Mrs. Leeper comes up with a plan to inspire Maggie to learn cursive. She asks Maggie to deliver notes around the school. Maggie soon figures out that these notes, which are written in cursive, are about *her*. She resolves to learn cursive in order to find out what Mrs. Leeper is writing.

Basic Book Information

This 70-page book is divided into 8 chapters ranging from 6 to 10 pages in length. There are full-page illustrations throughout the book, but they often do not match the text until a page or two later. Actual cursive writing appears in many of the chapters which helps the reader experience exactly what Maggie is going through, especially if they are new to cursive writing themselves.

Noteworthy Features

Many children can easily relate to Maggie. She has decided that she does not want to learn cursive and nobody can make her change her mind. Even when Maggie begins to want to learn how to read and write cursive, she does not want to tell anyone because she is too proud to admit she's been foolish. She wonders if others think she really cannot do cursive even if she tries, and she wonders what people will think of her when she finally can do cursive.

The cursive writing in the text helps to add to the authenticity of the plot line. Not only does Cleary describe a girl who will not learn cursive, but she also presents examples of how and why. If readers can understand cursive, they can understand notes such as "When is this girl ever going to decide to write cursive?" that are printed in a handwritten font; students who do not know cursive may find themselves spurred to learn, as Maggie is, by feeling left out of something. Readers who understand cursive find themselves in the unusual position of knowing more than the main character.

Publisher
Avon Books, 1990

ISBN
0380710870

TC Level
9

Teaching Ideas

One activity students could do is a character study of Maggie. In partnerships, they could come up with a list of adjectives that describe Maggie. As always, it is crucial for students to support their ideas with textual evidence. They should give specific examples, and can call each other's attention to the pages where they have found their evidence by quoting passages.

Readers will probably want to discuss times they have decided they could not do something even before they tried. Such text-to-self connections should ultimately refer back to the book itself, or back to the student's life, with a new understanding. Students should use their own experiences to help them understand Maggie's.

Book Connections

Any one of Cleary's numerous titles could be used as a follow-up to this one. The *Ramona* or *Henry Huggins* series books offer similar humorous plot lines about the trials and tribulations of growing up.

Genre
Short Chapter Book

Teaching Uses
Independent Reading

A Field Guide to the Classroom Library, Lucy Calkins and the Teachers College Reading and Writing Project, Heinemann, ©2002 Teachers College, Columbia University; http://www.heinemann.com/fieldguides

My Name Is María Isabel

Alma Flor Ada

Book Summary

The first chapter opens with María Isabel eating breakfast and drinking coffee before school. The reader is not told anything about where she is from or why she is nervous about going to school. Slowly it is revealed that she is going to a new school, although it is two months into the school year. Her mother, father and brother Antonio are introduced in the first chapter through dialogue. At the end of Chapter1, María falls and skins her knee; the day is off to a rocky start.

María's family has arrived in New York from Puerto Rico two years earlier. This year, the family has moved to a new neighborhood and she must start school in a new place. In Chapter3, María remembers her old bilingual school where she took classes in both languages. As we find out in Chapter2, she is quite nervous, not only because she is new, but because she must learn English as well.

Throughout the story, there are many sub-plots that readers will need to follow closely. María finds out that there are two Marías in the class and the teacher decides to call her "Mary." She is uncomfortable with this name and does not know how to share this with the teacher. We find out the importance of her name as she describes its history.

Another plot line is that María is dealing with making new friends, struggling to fit in and to participate in the winter festival. She is also learning how to stand up for herself. María reads *Charlotte's Web* and thinks about her life and that of Charlotte and Wilbur. María gets inspiration from the adventures these characters have together and from their caring relationship.

Basic Book Information

My Name is María Isabel has 10 chapters, each about 6 pages long. There is one full-page picture in each chapter to support the text. Alma Flor Ada has worked on more than one hundred books, many of them in Spanish.

Noteworthy Features

The text uses a medium print size and the words and lines appear close together on the page. The sentence structure throughout the book tends to be simple. However, there are many instances of more complex sentences sprinkled throughout the chapters.

The chapters in this book follow each other chronologically. Time is organized by holidays such as Thanksgiving and the December holidays. Each chapter title suggests its major idea. There are many references to the past. The title leads the reader to believe that María will be telling the story. This is not the case; the story is actually told through a third-person

Illustrator
K. Dyble Thompson

Publisher
Aladdin, 1995

ISBN
068980217X

narrator.

Teaching Ideas

At the end of a read aloud, students can turn to each other and talk about María's character. The story focuses on María's journey as she learns how to retain both her language and culture, while also integrating herself into her new experiences and finally becoming comfortable in her new school. Students may also connect María's experiences in school to their own. Many of her fears and her triumphs are universal, and students can understand her better by thinking of their own experience-and perhaps understand their own experiences better by thinking of hers.

When looking more closely at this book, readers may want to pay attention to the cultural setting. The book is about setting, an overlooked element in many stories. Children often read stories and focus on what happens, and perhaps the characters, but rarely the setting of a book. For this reason, teachers might ask children to listen to this book while thinking about how the author makes *place* come alive. What happens in children's minds as they read or hear these words? These prompts could, of course, lead a teacher to demonstrate the way a student can visualize a setting while reading or listening to a book: "Today, please pay special attention to the setting of the story. I'm going to stop after a while and ask you to talk in partners about what you're envisioning."

Book Connections

Good books to read before this would be *The Magic Shell* by Nicholasa Mohr, *Lavender* by Karen Hesse, and the *Flower Girls* series by Kathleen Leverich. Books on the same level as this are the *Amber Brown* series, *Sable* by Karen Hesse and the *Stories that Julian Tells* by Ann Cameron.

Genre
Chapter Book

Teaching Uses
Read Aloud; Independent Reading

A Field Guide to the Classroom Library, Lucy Calkins and the Teachers College Reading and Writing Project, Heinemann, ©2002 Teachers College, Columbia University; http://www.heinemann.com/fieldguides

Nate the Great and Me: The Case of the Fleeing Fang

Marjorie Weinman Sharmat

Book Summary

Nate the Great, a self-proclaimed "detective," tries to solve the case of his friend Annie's missing dog. With help from his dog and his friends, Nate successfully solves the case. Nate thinks about the information; notices people, places and things; looks for facts and clues; asks questions and takes things apart in order to solve the case. After following a misleading clue about a mysterious lady wearing fluffy bunny shoes, Nate discovers that the missing dog, Fang, has been following newly learned tricks in backwards order. Nate realizes that Fang must be waiting in the park for Annie. Fang is found and there is a celebration for Nate at the end of the story.

Basic Book Information

Nate the Great and Me: The Case of the Fleeing Fang has 50 pages with six chapters. The text begins on page seven. The majority of the book is colorfully illustrated. There are additional sections at the end of the book that include a detective certificate for the reader that is "signed" by Nate the Great; a page written in secret code, with directions on how to read it and the actual secret code on the facing page; three recipes for meals that Nate the Great loves to eat; and a page with the answer to a riddle asked on the dedication page of the book.

Nate the Great detective stories have been a highly popular series for 25 years. The characters in this book are the same characters as in all the books in the series. The nature of the "case" and the way in which it is "solved" by Nate are also consistent with the other books in the series.

Noteworthy Features

Throughout the text, notes written directly to readers appear. These notes are set off from the regular text by a bold, seemingly handwritten font and narrow margins. These notes are like readers' Post-Its embedded within the text itself. They offer advice on how to read this mystery and mysteries in general, posing metacognitive questions and suggestions for comprehension.

The six chapters in *Nate the Great and Me: The Case of the Fleeing Fang* have titles that explain something that comes up in the chapter and are meant to intrigue readers. The story contains several flashbacks. The flashbacks throughout the story serve as explanatory commentary, told by one of the main characters. These often set the scene for the case. Although these literary devices may be fun and interesting for the more sophisticated

Series
Nate the Great books

Illustrator
Marc Simont

Publisher
Dell Yearling, 1988

ISBN
0440413818

TC Level
7

reader, they can be very confusing to the early chapter book reader of this series. In addition, much of the book is written in Nate's dryly humorous voice. Again, for the early chapter book reader, this kind of humor may be confusing, or may simply go unnoticed. Even more sophisticated readers often fail to realize that in this book, like all of the books in the *Nate the Great* series, Nate does not really do a very good job at all of solving mysteries. Still, readers love the humor on some level, even if they do not fully understand the subtleties.

There are two handwritten, cursive notes within illustrations. These may be difficult for second-grade readers who in many cases have not yet studied cursive writing.

Teaching Ideas

Although the characters, story format, setting, and mystery are the same as in the other books in the *Nate the Great* series, this one seems somewhat more challenging and sophisticated. In this book, there is more text per page, the story is longer, the mystery itself is more complicated, and the added elements mentioned above (change of voice, wry humor, etc.) are noticeably more difficult than the preceding books in the series. If used as part of a study of the *Nate the Great* series, this would be a good book with which to end. If used in isolation, it would be more appropriate for a reader who has some knowledge of the genre and solid fluency at this level.

Independent readers should actually pause to address the bold asides in the text's second font, which appears first on page 12. These notes encourage excellent reading behaviors, such as rereading ("Did you notice that Fang wasn't there?"), determining which information is relevant ("Are dog rhymes and feather-dusting clues? I don't know yet") and visualization ("...draw a picture of a huge, fangy dog running away from two tiny poodles"). The book also encourages scrutiny, also a good skill for readers. For example, it promises that the answer to the missing six-letter word on the dedication page is "somewhere in this book," and points out the role of illustrations in supporting text by stating, "We might have a clue in this picture." Readers who stop to consider each of Nate's asides will practice good reading skills, especially around the genre of mystery.

Books from the *Nate the Great* series are probably most apt to be studied as examples of mystery. When children embark on early chapter books, most of what they will read are mystery stories. It makes a lot of sense, then, to work with children around the features of this genre. Readers will thus want to pay special attention to chapters three and four, in which Nate the Great calls attention to the idea of a "red herring." This staple of mystery writing is designed to throw off readers with clues that lead nowhere. During teacher-student conferences, students may want to strategize ways to detect false leads, and recall some red herrings they remember from other books they have read.

Book Connections

There are many other books in this series. Most of them are slightly easier than this one. Some titles include *Nate the Great, Nate the Great and the Lost List, Nate the Great Goes Undercover,* and *Nate the Great and the Sticky Case.*

A Field Guide to the Classroom Library, Lucy Calkins and the Teachers College Reading and Writing Project, Heinemann, ©2002 Teachers College, Columbia University; http://www.heinemann.com/fieldguides

This series tends to be more challenging than the *Young Cam Jansen* series, but easier than the regular *Cam Jansen* series, both by David A. Adler. *The A to Z Mysteries* series by Ron Roy are also more challenging.

Genre
Short Chapter Book; Mystery

Teaching Uses
Independent Reading; Small Group Strategy Instruction; Partnerships

A Field Guide to the Classroom Library, Lucy Calkins and the Teachers College Reading and Writing Project, Heinemann, ©2002 Teachers College, Columbia University; http://www.heinemann.com/fieldguides

Oliver

Syd Hoff

Book Summary

Oliver, an elephant, travels with ten other elephants across the sea to work in a circus. When they arrive, the circus man claims he ordered only ten elephants, so Oliver continues looking for work. He tries a zoo, but it already has enough elephants. He tries - and fails -to be a family pet. He tries to ride people like a horse but that doesn't work out either. Then he plays with children in a playground, showing he can be a dancing elephant. The circus parade comes down the street but no one notices. They are all watching Oliver dance. The circus man realizes he can use Oliver in the circus after all. Oliver goes off to the circus but promises never to forget the children.

Basic Book Information

This is a short chapter book, though it doesn't technically have chapters. It is somewhat longer than many others on this level.

Noteworthy Features

This narrative is told in the third person with simply structured sentences. The passage of time is implied, rather than indicated through transitional phrases that would make it more explicit. Some simple inferences are required - the taxi driver tells Oliver "you need a moving van," implying that he is too big for the taxi. When the children say, "Don't forget us," Oliver says, "Of course not, elephants never forget. And even a rhinoceros would remember the fun we had." This is meant to be a joke but some readers may not understand. Vocabulary is simple with a few words, such as *type* or *weigh*, which may be unfamiliar to some readers. The story contains a good deal of dialogue, which is referenced, though the speaker is sometimes identified at the end, and sometimes in the middle of the dialogue, rather than at the beginning.

Teaching Ideas

A teacher will want to look over the books in his or her classroom, anticipating the challenges they may pose for readers and planning ways to translate these challenges into learning opportunities. As children begin to read longer books like *Oliver*, one of the challenges for them is to avoid "tunnel vision." Sometimes at this transitional stage, readers crawl through books with their noses close to the print, saying each word in its turn but not accumulating the words into sentences, let alone into a coherent story. Children will have learned about the importance of chunking letters into rhymes in shared reading and word work. They're likely to know that it's easier to read *r-i-n-g* if one sees *ing* as a unit. The ability to do so "on the run" while reading will improve children's fluency, allowing them to focus their attention on making meaning.

It's helpful for children to know that when they read a book like this, they can also chunk bigger portions of the text, noticing how some of the pages go together as a unit. A teacher could set it up for children to do this sort of chunking by introducing the book by saying, "This is *almost* a chapter book. If it *did* have chapters, I think pages 7-14 would be Chapter One and it would be named 'Oliver's Problem.' You could read to learn about his problem. A lot of stories tell you the problem right up front, and this is one of them. Then, the next chapter might be pages 15-40, and it would be named 'Oliver Keeps Trying.' The next big chunk would be Chapter 3, pages 41-64, and it might be called, 'Things Get Better.'" Instead of *telling* these divisions to a reader, a teacher might ask children to read with a Post-It and that idea in mind saying, "If *you* were to divide this story into chunks like chapters, how would they go? Mark what seems like the beginning of a new chapter with your Post-it and be ready to explain your thinking."

To help young readers stay in this, or any other book, longer for the purpose of deepening their comprehension, teachers could support children in asking questions about the text. After modeling with read alouds, he or she might invite readers to jot their own questions on Post-Its as they read and come together with a partner before or after reading to talk over their questions. In *Oliver*, for example, students may question why most people in the book don't appear surprised to see Oliver walking around on the street. Or, they might notice that Oliver is the only *named* character in the book - everyone else is "the lady" or "the man." What could be the reason the author did this? Or that the girls and women in this book all wear skirts or dresses. Is this true in Hoff's other books?

Book Connections

Other Syd Hoff books include *Sammy the Seal*.

Genre
Short Chapter Book

Teaching Uses
Independent Reading; Interpretation; Small Group Strategy Instruction

A Field Guide to the Classroom Library, Lucy Calkins and the Teachers College Reading and Writing Project, Heinemann, ©2002 Teachers College, Columbia University; http://www.heinemann.com/fieldguides

Pedro's Journal: A Voyage with Christopher Columbus

Pam Conrad

FIELD GUIDE

D

Illustrator
Peter Koeppen

Publisher
Scholastic, 1991

ISBN
0590462067

TC Level
9

Book Summary

Pedro's Journal tells the story of Christopher Columbus' voyage to the Americas from the point of view of a ship's boy traveling with him in the *Santa María*. Pedro does not have knowledge "of maps or charts or distant journeys." He is called to transcribe Columbus' formal log, and to sketch some of what he sees. He dedicates his journal, a parcel of letters and drawings to his dear mother, "who has lost so much and who I pray will not lose me as well. . . . "

Basic Book Information

This book has 80 pages, divided into 35 diary entries from August 3rd, 1492 to February 14, 1493. The illustrations look like pencil sketches. Some entries are preceded by italicized verses that are almost prayers. The story is told in the first-person narrative, from Pedro's point of view. Other books by the author are *My Daniel*, *The Tub People*, *Stonewords*, *Prairie Visions: The Life and Times of Solomon Butcher* and *"Prairie Songs."* *Prairie Songs* won the 1986 International Reading Association's Children's Book Award.

Noteworthy Features

There are places in the book that nudge us as readers to pause in order to appreciate the language: "This was much like a farmer opening the gate to let in a plague of grasshoppers," or "The air was thick with mutiny and betrayal. . . ."

Teaching Ideas

In the author's note at the end of the book, Conrad claims *Pedro's Journal* is fiction, and that she has not written it to teach history. Students who have not read this genre before may not understand the difference between historical fiction and history. In conferring with them, teachers should make sure readers understand this distinction. Also, there may be information that children do not understand if they lack background knowledge. Readers should monitor for their own comprehension, checking to see what they can figure out from context and what aspects of this history they need help in understanding.

Readers might note the differences between Columbus and Pedro. At first Columbus seems to be kind, noble, gentle and harmless, but later takes slaves, separates families and begins to think he is unstoppable. On the other

A Field Guide to the Classroom Library, Lucy Calkins and the Teachers College Reading and Writing Project, Heinemann, ©2002 Teachers College, Columbia University; http://www.heinemann.com/fieldguides

hand, throughout this journey, Pedro remains steady in his actions. He is the young man who tries to persuade the "plague of grasshoppers" not to destroy the native land.

Book Connections

Other books on this theme that can serve as great read alouds, include *Morning Girl* by Michael Dorris, winner of The Scott O'Dell Award for Historical Fiction, and its Spanish translation, *Tainos*. For independent reading, children may try Peter Roop's *I, Columbus: My Journal, 1492-1493*; *Explorers*; and *Encounter*, a picture book by Jane Yolen. Others can read *Cristobal Colón, Step into Reading with Christopher Columbus*, and *En la Venecia de Marco Polo*. Two titles from their Explorers Collection (Exploradores) are *People From the Past*, and *Travelers and Traders*.

Genre
Biography; Nonfiction; Memoir; Historical Fiction

Teaching Uses
Independent Reading; Content Area Study

Pee Wee Scouts: Cookies and Crutches

Judy Delton

Book Summary

As the title suggests, there are two storylines in *Cookies and Crutches*, the initial book in this series. The first storyline involves baking cookies. At the end of the school day, all the first grade scouts run to the bus that will take them to the house of their troop leader, Mrs. Peters. Mrs. Peters informs them of what they have to do to earn their scout badge: bake cookies by themselves. Everyone is excited, except Roger White, who says, "Baking cookies is for girls!" He calls Sonny, a boy who actually wants to bake cookies, a "sissy." Mrs. Peters convinces them that if you like to eat, then you should like to cook. They end their meeting with a singing of their Pee Wee Scout song, and Roger agrees to bake cookies to earn his badge.

In the second storyline, the conflict between Roger and Sonny flares up again when they go ice skating. When Sonny brings his mother along, Roger again calls Sonny a "sissy." Through the dialogue and events that follow, the competitive nature and relationship of the characters is developed. Molly ends up on crutches because she twists her ankle in her too-tight skates. Sonny's mom turns out to be the best skater of all. In the end, everyone gets a skating badge, except Molly, who gets a Good Patient Badge.

Basic Book Information

Cookies and Crutches is a 69-page chapter book. There are 8 chapters of varying length, from 5 to 12 pages. Black-and-white illustrations occur every few pages. Cookies and Crutches should be read as an introduction to the *Pee Wee Scouts* series, which has thirty different titles. The order in which the series is read does not matter, but the later books become more difficult. Each book has a table of contents listing the chapter titles (there are about 7 chapters per book). It is important for children reading this series to have experienced other books with less dialogue first, such as James Howe's *Pinky and Rex* series.

Noteworthy Features

The titles support the main idea of each chapter. The print size and spacing between words is medium. The spacing is double between many of the paragraphs in a fashion that emphasizes, for readers, that the new paragraph signifies a new thought or event that will take place. Dialogue is usually referenced at the end of the speech, but sometimes in the middle. There is some use of pronouns when the dialogue is referenced.

Series
Pee Wee Scouts

Illustrator
Alan Tiegreen

Publisher
Bantam Doubleday Dell, 1988

ISBN
0440400104

TC Level
8

A Field Guide to the Classroom Library, Lucy Calkins and the Teachers College Reading and Writing Project, Heinemann, ©2002 Teachers College, Columbia University; http://www.heinemann.com/fieldguides

Teaching Ideas

The pictures could support the plot for readers, though they often appear on the page after the action has been described. The facial expressions in the illustrations give the reader insight into the characters' personalities and feelings. A teacher might need to point out to readers that by looking closely at the illustrations in a chapter book we can understand more about the events in each chapter.

If children are reading this text in book clubs, teachers might suggest that members of each group think about different aspects of their texts. The obvious place to begin is with an inquiry into a character. Both with and without teachers, book groups can strategize ways to get to know a character, including looking at what the other characters say about that character; what a character does; how a character changes in a book or across books; how the character thinks and feels and how the relationship between characters changes. Students can develop hunches or theories about a character and put Post-its on parts that support their hunches. They can also put Post-its on parts that show a person acting "out of character." They can become experts on a particular character and talk to the group about what they have found, or use their Post-its to guide discussions.

There are more characters in this series than in other books at this level. Book groups may want to list the characters and hold themselves to the goal of knowing a bit about each character. The characters are developed primarily through dialogue. For example, we learn about Rachel's character and how Molly feels about her through Molly's internal thoughts: "No one in first grade had anything Ultra suede, except Rachel. Rachel's family must have a lot of money, Molly thought. Rachel turned up the collar on her jacket. 'My dad has figure skates too,' said Rachel. 'Black ones.' Black-schmack. Rachel's whole family were probably show-offs." There are a lot of things for a reader to pay attention to in order to understand the characters and their motivation.

It is important for group discussions that students stay close to the text, rather than simply mentioning their own lives, telling personal stories and neglecting the book itself. Students should hold each other accountable to the text by asking questions such as "What's your evidence for that?" or "Where in the book do you see an example of that?" or "What page gave you that idea?"

Book Connections

Cookies and Crutches is similar in difficulty to the *Junie B. Jones* series by Barbara Park, the *Triplet Trouble* series by Debra Dadey and the *Marvin Redpost* series by Louis Sachar. Books to follow this series are *Sweet and Sour Lily* by Sally Warner, the *Magic Tree House* series by Mary Pope Osborne and *The Littles* by John Peterson.

Genre
Short Chapter Book

A Field Guide to the Classroom Library, Lucy Calkins and the Teachers College Reading and Writing Project, Heinemann, ©2002 Teachers College, Columbia University; http://www.heinemann.com/fieldguides

Teaching Uses

Independent Reading; Small Group Strategy Instruction; Partnerships

A Field Guide to the Classroom Library, Lucy Calkins and the Teachers College Reading and Writing Project, Heinemann, ©2002 Teachers College, Columbia University; http://www.heinemann.com/fieldguides

Piggins
Jane Yolen

Book Summary

In this charming mystery, the Reynard family of foxes has a dinner party. The Reynards explain to their guests that they would like to sell the diamond lavaliere Mrs. Reynard is wearing because it has a curse on it. Before their guests can buy it, however, the lights go out, there is a tinkling noise and then a scream. Someone has stolen the lavaliere from around Mrs. Reynard's neck. The party calls in the butler, Piggins, to use his detective powers to solve the case. After discovering and explaining several clues, the lavaliere is found and the culprits apprehended. All is peaceful again, thanks to Piggins.

Basic Book Information

Piggins has 29 pages. All facing pages have at least one large, lavish illustration. This is the first in a series of *Piggins* books, including *Picnic with Piggins* and *Piggins and the Royal Wedding*. Jane Yolen is the celebrated author of a wide range of children's literature, including such titles as *Owl Moon*, *Letting Swift River Go*, and *The Devil's Arithmetic*.

Noteworthy Features

Before the mystery is revealed, readers see a cross-section of the house, showing what each character is doing. The text to match this picture reads almost like stage directions. "UPSTAIRS Mr. and Mrs. Reynard are dressing. . . . IN THE HALL Piggins sets out hats and coats. . . ." Those new to the series may not understand that every part of the picture corresponds to the text's description. The author implies all of these events take place simultaneously, but does not explicitly say so. Readers must figure out how the text works by reading it in conjunction with the illustration.

Close examination of the pictures can help readers understand the clues that Piggins discovers, and their significance. For example, in one illustration, while everyone else has interrupted their meal to search for clues, the culprit disinterestedly sticks a fork in a piece of shrimp-a telling detail that does not appear in the text.

The pictures also help children grasp the elevated vocabulary the book employs. Instead of a diamond "necklace," for instance, Mrs. Reynard wears a diamond "lavaliere." Although the key words are easy enough to figure out from the pictures, there are many specific and uncommon words throughout, and readers could easily slip off the trail of understanding by guessing too many wrong in a row. If children seem to be getting mired in confusing parts, they might just have to put the book aside for a little later in the year; reading ahead to try to get the gist of the story is often a good comprehension strategy, but in this case readers would learn the answer to

A Field Guide to the Classroom Library, Lucy Calkins and the Teachers College Reading and Writing Project, Heinemann, ©2002 Teachers College, Columbia University; http://www.heinemann.com/fieldguides

Series
Piggins books

Illustrator
Jane Dyer

Publisher
Harcourt, Brace & Company, 1987

ISBN
0152616861

TC Level
9

the mystery, perhaps before fully understanding the mystery itself. If this is okay with readers-it may well be if other students in the class have already read it and given away the ending-then no harm will be done by rereading tricky parts or guessing at unusual vocabulary using the broader context of the entire book.

Though the book itself offers no context clues to help readers guess this, they may be interested to learn that *reynard* is the French word for fox.

Teaching Ideas

Reading this book aloud to children offers those who cannot tackle the complicated vocabulary on their own a chance to enjoy this mystery. During a read aloud, students can work on gathering clues from the pictures as they listen to the text. It can be difficult for some children to find their place again in the sizable chunk of descriptive text once they have briefly turned to the picture, and this is an activity they must do again and again in order to compare words to pictures. If they find this too difficult and tiresome, kids may give up looking at the picture, which means they may miss out on some clues and much of the fun of the book. Teachers can help readers by suggesting they keep their finger, bookmark, index card or Post-it right at the place in the text where they have left off to look at the picture. This skill of interrupting oneself while reading to check something and then going back to the reading without missing anything is a very useful skill for children to learn, not only because of the many interruptions life throws at readers, but also because it is precisely the kind of interruption readers face on many standardized reading tests.

Every book in the *Piggins* series involves the same characters. Students might draw on more than one book to gather evidence of a character's personality. Even the minor characters, such as Sara the scullery maid, have certain traits that are brought out in every book. In these books, however, the main thrust is not character development or the internal life of anyone in particular, but the mystery itself. Because of this, a character study serves only to help readers play detective themselves. A character study here helps readers practice gathering evidence to support their opinions and search through text for the details, but is not likely to yield rich discussions about the characters themselves.

Piggins books are all written in the present tense, which is highly unusual for picture books or mysteries. If children notice this on their own, they may want to discuss why the writer made this choice, and the effect it has on the writing. In the writing workshop, this book can model how the present tense lends immediacy and suspense to the mystery; students may wish to write mysteries in this tense as well.

Jane Yolen has written dozens of books for children in dozens of styles, and a random assortment of her books brought together for an author study may leave students befuddled. Perhaps collecting a few *Piggins* books together is the best way to understand more how this author works. In that way, readers can see that the author and illustrator always begin the books the same way. They can see the way the silhouettes are used throughout the pages facing the colored pictures, the phrases that repeat and the sarcasm that evolves throughout the books.

A Field Guide to the Classroom Library, Lucy Calkins and the Teachers College Reading and Writing Project, Heinemann, ©2002 Teachers College, Columbia University; http://www.heinemann.com/fieldguides

Book Connections

Children who like this book may enjoy other mysteries as well. The *A to Z Mysteries* series of chapter books is written at a comparable level. *Encyclopedia Brown* books are slightly more challenging than *Piggins*, but a reader can move to them after these have been well read.

Genre
Picture Book; Mystery

Teaching Uses
Independent Reading

Pinky and Rex and the Bully
James Howe

Book Summary

Kevin, the third-grade bully, calls Pinky a "sissy" because Pinky likes the color from which he gets his nickname. Being bullied embarrasses Pinky. He starts to make some changes in his life, including changing his name to Billy, giving away his stuffed animals, and not playing with his best friend because she's a girl. Finally, Mrs. Morgan, who lives across the street, helps Pinky to realize that he should not change for other people, but that he should do what is right for himself.

Basic Book Information

Pinky and Rex and the Bully has 40 pages. There is at least one picture on each two-page spread, which helps support the text. In addition to the *Pinky and Rex* series, James Howe is the author of *Bunnicula* and its popular *Howliday Inn* sequels, as well as *There's a Monster Under My Bed* and *There's a Dragon in My Sleeping Bag*.

This series shows a realistic friendship between Pinky, a boy, and Rex, a girl. The reader should begin this series with the first book, *Pinky and Rex*. While each book can be read individually, events in the series are cumulative. In order to fully appreciate the strong friendship between Pinky and Rex, the reader should also read *Pinky and Rex and the Spelling Bee*. The character of Mrs. Morgan is originally introduced in the fourth book in the series, *Pinky and Rex and the Mean Old Witch*, and a brief mention of Rex's younger sibling in this book alludes to an earlier book in the series, *Pinky and Rex and the New Baby*.

Noteworthy Features

The chronological storyline of *Pinky and Rex and the Bully* makes it easy for readers to follow. Pictures throughout the book support the plot. The print size is large, but the spacing between the words and lines is small. The volume of text on the page varies. Even though this book at first appears less difficult than other books at this level, the fact that the spacing of the print is smaller and the line spacing is smaller makes for more difficult tracking of the words across the page.

Each chapter is headed by a title that gives the reader a clue to the event in that chapter. The start of each chapter marks the passing of time since the end of the previous chapter, with varying degrees of complexity. Between Chapters 1 and 2, the story skips from the time Mrs. Morgan invites Pinky in

Series
Pinky and Rex books

Illustrator
Melissa Sweet

Publisher
Simon & Schuster, 1996

ISBN
0689808348

TC Level
8

A Field Guide to the Classroom Library, Lucy Calkins and the Teachers College Reading and Writing Project, Heinemann, ©2002 Teachers College, Columbia University; http://www.heinemann.com/fieldguides

for lemonade to the time they are sitting on her back porch drinking it; between Chapters 5 and6, more than a day has passed, and Pinky alludes to taking his stuffed animals back from his sister-an event that occurs, in a sense, offstage, outside of the text provided to readers.

Though the basics of the plot are quite accessible, readers need a high level of inference in order to comprehend this book fully. For example, on the first page, after the third-grade bully pushes Pinky off his bike, Pinky's cheeks are "fever-hot," and readers need to piece together the emotions his flushed cheeks suggest. There is a lot of dialogue in the text as well, but the style of referring to who is speaking -when the narrator actually names the speaker-is inconsistent. Readers must be aware of this. There are several minor characters that the reader needs to hold in their head. In addition, readers often confuse Pinky for the girl character.

Teaching Ideas

This series has been used successfully in a variety of ways. *Pinky and Rex* books can be used in a reading center that focuses on a study of characters. In addition, because this series sparks strong conversations, it works well in read alouds and small group discussions. Pinky's character is especially rich because he defies many stereotypes for boys.

Independent readers who take on the *Pinky and Rex* series are developing strategies to help them tackle longer books. Teachers can confer with readers about monitoring for sense, reading without a "finger pointer," reading without saying aloud the words on the page or any other appropriate strategy that will support the readers in having success with these larger texts.

These books can also help readers practice inferring characters' emotions. Why does Pinky wake up so many times and wonder where he is after he has given away his stuffed animals? What is "the hardest thing [Pinky] would ever have to do in his whole life," (page 24) and what words does he struggle to find on page 26? Why does Mrs. Morgan's speech about painting convince Pinky to change his mind about being called "Billy," and why does he end up giving her a present? Students can learn to ask questions like these of any book they read.

Book Connections

This series is similar in difficulty to the *Little Bill* series by Bill Cosby and the *Cam Jansen* series by David Adler. A reader should first experience success with *Mr. Putter and Tabby* and *Poppleton*, both by Cynthia Rylant, before reading this series. After reading *Pinky and Rex*, Barbara Park's *Junie B. Jones* series makes a good next step, as does Judy Delton's *Pee Wee Scouts* series.

Genre
Short Chapter Book

A Field Guide to the Classroom Library, Lucy Calkins and the Teachers College Reading and Writing Project, Heinemann, ©2002 Teachers College, Columbia University; http://www.heinemann.com/fieldguides

Teaching Uses
Independent Reading; Partnerships; Character Study

Poppleton
Cynthia Rylant

Book Summary

Poppleton is the first book in a series about a pig and his friends. There are three separate, yet connected, stories in the book. In the first story, "Neighbors," Poppleton the pig moves from the city to the country. He thoroughly enjoys his new life, which includes napping in the sunroom, planting in the garden and sharing meals with his new neighbor, Cherry Sue (a goat). When Poppleton begins to tire of eating every meal with Cherry Sue, they discover that they both want to be alone sometimes, but have been afraid to hurt one another's feelings by saying so. After their talk, they become even better friends. In the second story, "Library Day," the reader learns about Poppleton's passion for spending Mondays at the library reading his favorite books. Poppleton follows the same routine, brings the same reading "tools" (such as a tissue, in case there is a sad part in the book he's reading), and buries his head in a good adventure for the day. In the third story, "The Pill," Poppleton cares for his sick friend Fillmore (another goat), who refuses to take his medicine until Poppleton hides it in a piece of Cherry Sue's heavenly cake. Fillmore proceeds to eat the whole cake to "find the pill." When Fillmore says he still needs a whole *other* cake to get his pill down, Poppleton decides to become sick too! The two friends spend the next few days in bed together and "polish off" 27 cakes.

Basic Book Information

Poppleton is the first in a series of books about Poppleton and his friends. The book is 48 pages long and separated into three stories listed in a table of contents. The stories stand alone and can be read separately or as part of a larger story. Every page is illustrated.

This wonderful series does not have to be read in any particular order, but students should read several *Poppleton* books because the characters reveal themselves across the series. Readers will come to know Poppleton so well that they'll find themselves smiling when he returns to old antics we've seen in earlier books.

The *Poppleton* series has a great deal in common with *Frog and Toad* because both series tell of friendships that endure ups and downs, which result from the differences between the friends. The *Poppleton* series should be read after readers have experienced *Henry and Mudge* and *Mr. Putter and Tabby* (also written by Cynthia Rylant), as *Poppleton* is more complex. Over the course of the series we get to know not only Poppleton but also his friends Hudson, Cherry Sue, Marsha, Gus and Fillmore.

Noteworthy Features

The text of *Poppleton* is simply written but hilarious and heart-warming.

Series
Poppleton books

Illustrator
Mark Teague

Publisher
Scholastic, 1997

ISBN
059084783X

TC Level
7

Most of the humor is readily accessible to the early reader, but some of the more subtle humor (e.g., when Poppleton reads, he holds "lip balm for a dry part") may go unnoticed.

Most of the story lines are simple and easily understood. There are some sections, however, in which the young reader will have to infer the motivation behind a character's actions, for motivations are not explicitly written into the text. Young readers may have trouble understanding that Poppleton soaks Cherry Sue with a hose because he is frustrated that she once again wants to eat with him, or that Fillmore refuses to hear in *which* piece of cake his pill is hidden in so that he will have an excuse to eat as much cake as possible.

This book, like the others in the series, is episodic, meaning each chapter stands on its own; young readers need not remember a continuous plot for the entire book. Each chapter has a supportive title. The illustrations support some part of the text on each page. Pages have anywhere from two to five sentences of text. There is dialogue throughout the book, all of which is referenced at the beginning or end of the sentence.

Teaching Ideas

Because this is the first book in a wonderful series, teachers will probably want to do some small group work to support children as they read it, setting the stage for them to read the remaining books more independently. In a book introduction, a teacher might say, "This is a book about Poppleton. Poppleton is a pig who loves naps, gardening, reading books at the library and chocolate cake. He has just moved from the city to the country and is becoming friends with his new neighbors, Cherry Sue and Fillmore. Just like when we make new friends, Poppleton doesn't always know what to say or how to act."

The straightforward humor is a great topic for discussion in read aloud and partnerships. For example, when Poppleton soaks *himself* with the hose to apologize for soaking Cherry Sue, the teacher and students can all have a good laugh and talk about why that's funny. The more subtly humorous parts can be discussed at greater length. For example, a teacher may say, "It's funny, but a little surprising, when Poppleton soaks Cherry Sue with the hose after she invites him over for lunch. Cherry Sue is being nice. Why is Poppleton acting like that? How do we know?" This discussion may inform children trying to write humor, and it may also give them new ways to think and talk about humor in their own, independent reading.

Poppleton presents several opportunities for readers to make some personal connection to the characters. Their experiences are not especially deep, but they do mirror the lives of children enough for some discussion. For example, in the story called "Library Day," Poppleton is totally committed to and invested in his love of books. A teacher may say to young readers, "I know exactly how Poppleton feels when he packs the same things each time he goes to the library. Every time I sit down to read my favorite book, I have my favorite bookmark in my hand and I always drink a cup of tea."

A Field Guide to the Classroom Library, Lucy Calkins and the Teachers College Reading and Writing Project, Heinemann, ©2002 Teachers College, Columbia University; http://www.heinemann.com/fieldguides

Book Connections

Other titles in the Poppleton series include *Poppleton and Friends* and *Poppleton Forever*. Cynthia Rylant's *Henry and Mudge* and *Mr. Putter and Tabby* series are comparably difficult. Arnold Lobel's *Frog and Toad* books touch on similar themes of friendship.

Genre
Short Chapter Book

Teaching Uses
Independent Reading; Character Study; Partnerships; Small Group Strategy Instruction; Critique

A Field Guide to the Classroom Library, Lucy Calkins and the Teachers College Reading and Writing Project, Heinemann, ©2002 Teachers College, Columbia University; http://www.heinemann.com/fieldguides

Poppleton and Friends
Cynthia Rylant

FIELD GUIDE

D E

Book Summary

In the first story in *Poppleton and Friends*, Poppleton the pig has been feeling landlocked, so he decides to go to the beach for a day with his friend Hudson. He wants to sit on the sand, watch the waves and collect shells. Poppleton and Hudson have a great time and tell Cherry Sue all about it.

Poppleton's next problem is that he can't get rid of his dry skin. Cherry Sue tells him to put oil on it, but that doesn't work. He is still as dry as a dandelion. Next Cherry Sue tells him to put honey on his skin. All that does is make him want some biscuits. Will Poppleton ever get rid of his dry skin?

In the third and final story, Poppleton discovers that eating grapefruit is supposed to make you live long. However, Poppleton hates grapefruit. It makes his eyes tear up, his lips turn outside in, and his face turn green. After learning a valuable lesson from Hudson's 100-year-old Uncle Bill, Poppleton throws out all the grapefruit he bought.

About the Series

This wonderful series doesn't have to be read in any particular order, but it is good for students to read many of the books in the series because Poppleton's character reveals itself across the series. Readers will come to know Poppleton so well that they'll find themselves smiling when he returns to old anticsthey've seen in earlier books. "There he goes again," some children say.

The *Poppleton* series has a great deal in common with Arnold Lobel's *Frog and Toad* - both series tell of a friendship that endures ups and downs, which occur because of the differences between the friends. As *Poppleton* is more complex, the *Poppleton* series should be read after readers have experienced *Henry and Mudge* and *Mr. Putter and Tabby,* also written by Cynthia Rylant.

Basic Book Information

Poppleton and Friends is 48 pages long. Most sentences are short and simple, but there are sentences that are long and descriptive.

There are lively pictures on every page, most of which match and enhance the text. This is an episodic chapter book. Because each chapter stands on its own, it is easier for young readers to hold onto the plot over the course of the book. Each chapter has a supportive title as well.

Poppleton is a lovable, warm character who isn't afraid of sharing his feelings and laughing at himself. Over the course of the series, readers also get to know his friends Hudson, Cherry Sue and Fillmore.

Noteworthy Features

There are three main characters that recur in the series: Poppleton, Hudson and Cherry Sue. Other characters are introduced, but names are not usually

Series
Poppleton

Illustrator
Mark Teague

Publisher
Scholastic, 1998

ISBN
0590847880

TC Level
7

given (e.g., the saleslady and the tree doctor). This helps students remember them and hold onto the story better.

There is much more dialogue in this series than in *Henry and Mudge*. However, it is always referenced. The reference is also a little more difficult than in *Henry and Mudge* because pronouns, rather than proper names, are used.

Children will have no problem relating to the feelings exhibited by Poppleton, and how he and his friends help and hurt each other. Some of the situations are rather bizarre-like dry skin and grapefruit-but kids find them funny and point out that Poppleton is not always the smartest pig on the block.

There is some vocabulary that might stump young readers, such as *lint*. Understanding what lint is will help your readers understand that Poppleton is mistaken-he really doesn't have dry skin. Rather it is the lint from the sweater he has been wearing for the past three days.

The humor here can be difficult in spots and many readers find Chapter2, "Dry Skin," particularly hard. For example, Poppleton says, "putting on oil only made me hungry for French fries." Asking why Poppleton is hungry for French fries yields rather interesting responses. It is important to explain why that is funny, and then ask them why Poppleton is hungry for biscuits after he puts on the honey. See if they can make the connection.

Teaching Ideas

Since the dialogue is a bit complex, teachers can make overhead transparencies of these pages and teach kids how the names or pronouns reference the dialogue (e.g., page 42 and 45 versus the embedded references on page 16). It is really important to know who is talking when a pronoun is used.

During the reading, students can look for and make note of: the times when Poppleton is acting smart or silly; the parts that reveal Poppleton's character; the times when Poppleton acts like a pig; the parts that show friendship between Poppleton and Hudson and/or Cherry Sue; and the funny parts.

For discussion, students may wish to talk about: what Poppleton likes to do; the lessons that Poppleton learns; who is a better friend (Hudson or Cherry Sue); whether Cherry Sue is helpful or mean in "Dry Skin"; and if they would be friends with Poppleton.

Teachers may want to encourage students who have read other books by Cynthia Rylant to do an author study and notice aspects of her craft, the characters she creates and the themes that reappear in her work.

Book Connections

Poppleton and Friends is an early chapter book comparable in difficulty to *And I Mean It, Stanley* by Crosby Bonsall, *Owl at Home* by Arnold Lobel and *Minnie and Moo* by Denys Cazet. *Albert the Albatross* by Syd Hoff, *Hattie and the Fox* by Mem Fox and *Noisy Nora* by Rosemary Wells are good precursors to this series. *Arthur's Honey Bear* and the rest of the books in this series by Lillian Hoban would be good follow-ups.

A Field Guide to the Classroom Library, Lucy Calkins and the Teachers College Reading and Writing Project, Heinemann, ©2002 Teachers College, Columbia University; http://www.heinemann.com/fieldguides

Poppleton should be read after readers have experienced other Cynthia Rylant series books such as *Henry and Mudge* and *Mr. Putter and Tabby*, because it is more complex.

Genre
Short Chapter Book

Teaching Uses
Independent Reading

Shoeshine Girl

Clyde Robert Bulla

Book Summary

Ten-year-old Sarah Ida arrives in Palmville to stay with her Aunt Claudia for the summer. Her mother is sick, but her parents also wanted to get her away from a friend who has been shoplifting. Sarah Ida does not want to be in Palmville, and she makes this clear with anger and rudeness. When she pressures a neighbor girl into giving her money, Aunt Claudia confronts Sarah Ida. Angry that she is not given any money to spend during the summer, Sarah Ida rushes out to get a job just to spite Aunt Claudia. This new job and her relationship with her boss change her forever.

Basic Book Information

Shoeshine Girl is 84 pages long. There is a picture in every chapter and some of them give information that is not explicit in the text. Clyde Robert Bulla has written dozens of books in several different genres, including *The Chalk Box Kid* and *The Paint Brush Kid*, which are as emotionally authentic as *Shoeshine Girl*.

Noteworthy Features

The realistic depiction of the changes in Sarah Ida helps readers to recognize familiar human behavior in the story. There is only a single storyline, although some events cause surprising turns. There are few characters: Sarah Ida, her Aunt Claudia, her neighbor Rossi, and Al, the shoeshine stand owner. The whole story takes place in the same location. Time is structured clearly: breaks on the page and asterisks indicate chronological leaps forward.

Teaching Ideas

An introduction to a character is one way a teacher can help readers become involved with this book. *Shoeshine Girl's* most significant challenge is that it requires readers to infer carefully. For instance, readers must understand *why* Sarah Ida is scared to cry when she settles into her new bed at Aunt Claudia's.

Because Sarah Ida 's sullen anger gives way to sensitivity, Shoeshine *Girl* has the emotional complexity to lend itself to character study. Whole-class mini-lessons can model how to look for moments when characters change and why, which students can label with Post-its. During the independent reading that follows such mini-lessons, students reading *Shoeshine Girl* can notice and record the places where Sarah Ida changes, and why. A Post-it might read: "As soon as she called Al's medal a piece of tin, she was sorry. Now Sarah Ida is learning how to care."

Illustrator
Jim Burke

Publisher
Harper Trophy, 1973

ISBN
0064402282

TC Level
9

A Field Guide to the Classroom Library, Lucy Calkins and the Teachers College Reading and Writing Project, Heinemann, ©2002 Teachers College, Columbia University; http://www.heinemann.com/fieldguides

This book can also serve during a reading workshop mini-lesson to practice discerning which characters speak which lines of dialogue. Page 19, for example, is mostly dialogue, but there are only two references to speakers. By studying the page together with an overhead projector, students can notice that it alternates between Aunt Claudia and Sarah Ida. They can follow it if they are careful to note the pattern and ask themselves, "Whose voice is this? Who would say that?"

Clyde Robert Bulla's books span different reading levels. Once a book like *Shoeshine Girl* has been featured in a read aloud or in a class study, an author collection of his books is very popular in the class library.

Book Connections

Shoeshine Girl is comparable in difficulty to the *Amber Brown* series by Paula Danziger and the *Julian* series by Ann Cameron. The *Ramona* series by Beverly Cleary and the *Elisa* series by Johanna Hurwitz would be good follow-ups.

Genre
Short Chapter Book

Teaching Uses
Independent Reading; Read Aloud; Partnerships; Character Study

A Field Guide to the Classroom Library, Lucy Calkins and the Teachers College Reading and Writing Project, Heinemann, ©2002 Teachers College, Columbia University; http://www.heinemann.com/fieldguides

The Absent Author

Ron Roy

Book Summary

Dink, a.k.a., Donald David Duncan, loves mysteries and mystery stories. He writes to his favorite mystery author, Wallis Wallace, and invites him to visit Dink's home in Green Lawn. Remarkably, Wallace agrees-as long as no one kidnaps him along the way. When the big day comes, Wallis Wallace is nowhere to be found. The police think he just missed his plane, but Dink knows better. It's up to Dink and his two best friends, Josh and Ruth Rose, to find Wallace. As the three friends follow leads using their deductive detective skills, they uncover the truth: Wallis Wallace is a woman, *and* she's been planting clues and creating a mystery for them to solve all day long. In the end, Ruth Rose solves the mystery, and Wallis Wallace promises to dedicate her next book to the three pals.

Basic Book Information

The Absent Author is the first book in the *A to Z Mysteries* series, which features one title for each letter in the alphabet. The series itself is part of *Stepping Stone Books*, published by Random House. The recurring main characters in the series are Dink, Ruth Rose and Josh. This book is 87 pages long, with 10 untitled chapters. The chapters average 8 to 12 pages in length and include small black-and-white illustrations that support one small portion of the text.

Noteworthy Features

The author, Ron Roy, does a good job of creating a mystery within a mystery by making the main characters mystery book lovers. As the story unfolds, the author introduces essential mystery book elements such as cliffhangers, mistaken identities and important clues embedded in seemingly trivial details.

There are many minor but important characters that are integrated throughout the story. This may be confusing to readers at this level. The text includes a lot of referenced and non-referenced dialogue, complex sentence structure, frequent and varied use of italics and capital letters as well as some challenging vocabulary.

Teaching Ideas

Most students reading at this level are already familiar with the mystery genre, so *The Absent Author* will help them practice some of the special strategies readers of mysteries use to "crack the case." To do so, students must be mindful of all of the details that do not seem to make sense, as these usually provide clues to the mystery.

Series
A to Z Mysteries

Illustrator
John Steven Gurney

Publisher
Random House, New York, 1997

ISBN
0679881689

TC Level
9

This is also a good book for partner and independent reading for the reader who is beginning to read longer, more detailed and more complexly structured books. Partners can discuss their observations, make predictions, reread to find places where they may have missed a clue, and jot down the numbers of pages on which they find clues.

Teachers may also want to use this book to introduce children to, or have them practice using a kind of formal or informal graphic organizer in their notebooks or on chart paper. This can be used to keep the clues straight, to follow the plot, or to keep track of characters who may or may not be important. Readers can section their notes into boxes that contain the various characters' names and some detail that distinguishes that character's role. Or, readers can chart on a graph the way in which different elements of mystery are introduced into the text.

As readers become more familiar with the mystery genre, they may want to do a comparison across several series and explore ways in which the *A to Z Mysteries* resemble other books in this genre. Or, after reading other books in the same genre, they may come back to the series to reread and compare. They can look for, discuss and write about things that seem universal in all mystery stories. How do the detectives seem alike in their methods? What literary devices do the authors use consistently?

Book Connections

The Absent Author is part of the *A to Z Mysteries* series, which is organized by alphabet. Some of the other titles include *The Bald Bandit* and *The Jaguar's Jewel*. Other mystery series that are similar to this one include the *Magic Tree House* and *The Boxcar Children*.

Genre
Short Chapter Book; Mystery

Teaching Uses
Independent Reading

The Best Christmas Pageant Ever

Barbara Robinson

Book Summary

This uproariously funny story is a splendid read aloud and an equally satisfying book for independent readers. When Mrs. George Armstrong breaks her leg, another mother (whose daughter narrates the story) reluctantly replaces her as the director of the children's Christmas pageant. The pageant has always been a predictable event-the same script, the same costumes, and the same two children playing Mary and Joseph. This time, however, the Herdmans get involved. The six Herdman children (Ralph, Imogene, Leroy, Claude, Ollie, and Gladys) have regularly terrorized kids in school. Now, having heard that desserts are served in Sunday school, they show up at church and decide they want to participate in the pageant.

Fearing Herdman wrath, the other children let the Herdmans take over all the major roles: Mary, Joseph, the three wise men, and the Angel of the Lord. Mrs. Armstrong is appalled, and her criticism angers the woman who has replaced her. She vows to make this the best Christmas pageant ever, complete with the Herdman children. As expected, the Herdmans turn rehearsals upside down, in part because they have no idea what the Christmas story is about. They ask amusing questions (what were the wadded-up clothes Mary wrapped the baby in?) and offer blunt comments (the wise men should tell the innkeeper where to get off and get the baby out of the barn).

At first, Alice Wendleken, the prissy girl who previously has played Mary, finds fault with everything the Herdmans do. But the Herdmans' insistence on using ordinary language to discuss the details of the Christmas story gradually leads other children to see the story in a fresh and meaningful way. After a disastrous (and funny) final rehearsal, the night of the pageant arrives. The Herdmans' unorthodox performance casts a new light on the Christmas holiday and leads to general agreement that this was, indeed, the best Christmas pageant ever.

Basic Book Information

The paperback version of the book is 80 pages long. The story is divided into 7 numbered chapters and includes 7 amusing, black-and-white illustrations. The narrative is structured in past tense and moves forward chronologically, but the narrator seems very close to events, almost as if they were unfolding as she relates them. Although the story involves Christmas, it has appeal for people who do not celebrate Christmas as well as for those who do.

Noteworthy Features

The first-person narrator is a classmate of Imogene Herdman and Alice

A Field Guide to the Classroom Library, Lucy Calkins and the Teachers College Reading and Writing Project, Heinemann, ©2002 Teachers College, Columbia University; http://www.heinemann.com/fieldguides

Illustrator
Judith Gwyn Brown

Publisher
Harper Trophy, 1998

ISBN
0064402754

Wendleken. The narrator appears to be a fifth grader, and the spoken language with which she tells the story is accessible to young readers. Although the narrator's name is never mentioned, her personality comes through strongly in the wry account she offers. For example, as pageant roles are being assigned, she says: "There was one Herdman left over, and one main role left over, and you didn't have to be very smart to figure out that Gladys was going to be the Angel of the Lord." When her mother tells Gladys that the Angel brought the good news to the shepherds, the narrator observes, "Right away all the shepherds began to wiggle around in their seats, figuring that any good news Gladys brought them would come with a smack in the teeth." The concluding episode, when the Herdmans take the Christmas pageant quite seriously, is managed with an effective shift in tone. The sweet ending of the story proves as memorable as the opening.

Teaching Ideas

This book makes a spectacular read aloud, one that can pull the classroom community together in shared laughter. For the book to work magic in a classroom, however, it is important to also honor books that focus on non-Christian holidays. Teachers should be sensitive to any guidelines in their school regarding the use of fiction built around a specific religion.

Expressed in an abstract way, one premise of the book is the fact that the language used to celebrate traditional cultural events is often so formal in tone that it is inaccessible to some, and may even blur historical reality. In Chapters 5 and 6, the Herdmans disrupt pageant rehearsals with questions and comments about the Gospel story. Students can follow the Herdmans' growing understanding of the holiday. How do those explanations change the way children perceive the Gospel story? Teachers can also ask children to share examples of texts read during their own holidays and festivals. Then they can discuss what "ordinary" truths underlie the formal language.

Characterization is central to this book, making it a text with which to do character studies. It is interesting to note that the author includes few details regarding the appearance of the Herdmans or Alice Wendleken. Instead, she brings these characters to life by describing their actions. Independent readers or book clubs may choose to focus on a particular Herdman, and learn about his or her character through what the text states, what the text leads readers to infer, and the response the character evokes from interactions with other characters. During a read aloud, students can turn and talk to partners about the same matters.

Readers might also wish to question the text and consider the author's decisions about point of view. Why did Barbara Robinson make this a first-person story? Who is the narrator? Why is she in a good position to tell the story? Perceptive readers will notice that narrator contributes little to the action-she simply tells what she observes-but the way she presents her observations frequently adds to the humor. For example, she notes that the Herdmans arrived ten minutes late for the first pageant rehearsal, "Sliding into the room like a bunch of outlaws about to shoot up a saloon." Children can look for other examples of colorful comments from the narrator.

A Field Guide to the Classroom Library, Lucy Calkins and the Teachers College Reading and Writing Project, Heinemann, ©2002 Teachers College, Columbia University; http://www.heinemann.com/fieldguides

Book Connections

Another book with a similarly touching and humorous pageant scene is *Ramona and Her Father*, by Beverly Cleary. Barbara Robinson brings the Herdman children-wildness and all-back for the sequel, *The Best School Year Ever*.

Genre
Short Chapter Book

Teaching Uses
Read Aloud; Independent Reading; Character Study

A Field Guide to the Classroom Library, Lucy Calkins and the Teachers College Reading and Writing Project, Heinemann, ©2002 Teachers College, Columbia University; http://www.heinemann.com/fieldguides

The Gardener

Sarah Stewart

FIELD GUIDE

Book Summary

When the Great Depression keeps her parents from earning a living, young Lydia Grace goes from her family's farm to the city to work in her Uncle Jim's bakery. Lydia Grace embarks on a mission to make her sour-faced uncle smile and to make her new home one that she can call her own. As each month passes, Lydia Grace brings obvious physical changes to her environment and even subtler emotional changes to her uncle.

Basic Book Information

A 1998 Caldecott Honor book, *The Gardener* holds 19 double-page spreads of illustrations. Letters from Lydia Grace to her family are situated on the upper corners of twelve pages, surrounded by the text's expressive illustrations.

Noteworthy Features

The pages of *The Gardener* must be read in order, because each letter builds chronologically on the previous one. The letters share consistent features: a greeting to Lydia Grace's family, a salutation, and often a postscript about the results of Lydia Grace's latest attempt to make Uncle Jim smile.

When hearing the book read aloud, young readers pick up on the book's style almost immediately. Children start to see the text's repeated structure at the appropriate places in each letter.

Readers will want to pay close attention to the illustrations. Those illustrations begin before the title page and continue after the copyright information at the back of the book. Unlike many books, the front and end papers do not merely reproduce drawings from the middle, but are part of the narrative itself. In total, there are seven double-page illustrations without text, none of which should be passed over quickly.

The passage of time is marked not only by Lydia Grace's experiences in the city, but also by the life cycle of her garden. The reader sees the growth of flowers from seeds to full bloom.

The sentences in each letter are fairly long with some terms that are specific to making bread and gardening. One way to help these long sentences make sense is to remind children to practice reading with expression. This might take a little practice.

Teaching Ideas

Used during independent reading or whole-class read alouds, *The Gardener* is a great book for the teaching of inference. The essential plot is easy to follow, but subtleties in the text offer students a wealth of information.

Illustrator
David Small

Publisher
Farrar, Straus, and Giroux, 1997

ISBN
0374325170

TC Level
8

A Field Guide to the Classroom Library, Lucy Calkins and the Teachers College Reading and Writing Project, Heinemann, ©2002 Teachers College, Columbia University; http://www.heinemann.com/fieldguides

From Lydia Grace's first letter alone, children can infer the following (and possibly more): Lydia lives with both her parents and grandmother, that the family is struggling financially, that Papa is deeply upset at the prospect of his daughter's leaving, that Lydia Grace behaves responsibly, that Grandma pushes her to excel and that Uncle Jim and Lydia Grace have not seen each other for years-if they have ever seen each other at all.

During a read aloud, students can turn and talk to each other periodically to discuss everything they can infer about Lydia Grace and her relationship to her family. In teacher-student conferences, teachers may want to check to see how much students are picking up by reading between the lines.

The illustrations in this book offer just as many inferential possibilities as the text, so even if teachers read it aloud to a whole class, *The Gardener* should be available for students to hold in their hands. Halos of white encircle many of the key parts of illustrations to help focus readers' attention. These luminous splashes often contrast with the other parts of the illustrations, popping boldly forward from the backgrounds of a bleakly gray train station or the drab, brown city Lydia Grace finds when she first steps out of the taxicab in front of Uncle Jim's bakery. Once they know the story well, students can even flip through the book a few times without reading the text, looking for details that are not in Lydia Grace's letters. On the title page, for instance, children might notice Grandma and Lydia Grace proudly returning with lettuce from their garden, while Mama and Papa look down glumly at what may be Uncle Jim's invitation for Lydia Grace to come to the city.

Students without prior knowledge of the Great Depression may struggle to understand why Lydia Grace has to leave home to work at such a young age, or why Uncle Jim almost smiles when his bakery is nearly full of customers. Children might be helped with a quick introduction to this historical period.

Book Connections

Sarah Stewart and David Small have teamed up previously to produce *The Money Tree* and *The Library*. Martina Selway's *Don't Forget to Write* also uses letters to narrate a story of a girl adjusting to life in a new place, in this case her grandfather's farm.

Genre
Historical Fiction; Picture Book

Teaching Uses
Partnerships; Read Aloud

A Field Guide to the Classroom Library, Lucy Calkins and the Teachers College Reading and Writing Project, Heinemann, ©2002 Teachers College, Columbia University; http://www.heinemann.com/fieldguides

The Great Kapok Tree: A Tale of the Amazon Rain Forest

Lynne Cherry

Book Summary

Two men enter a rain forest. The larger of the two points to an enormous kapok tree, then exits. After the smaller man begins chopping into the tree, he grows tired, sets down his ax and falls asleep. Animals and a Yanomano boy whisper to the man as he sleeps, each pleading another reason not to chop down the kapok tree. The man awakens to find himself surrounded by jungle creatures and the boy. He begins to chop away at the tree again, but stops suddenly and walks out of the rain forest.

Basic Book Information

Though technically fiction, *The Great Kapok Tree* presents all of the information of a nonfiction text on rain forests and ecological preservation. It is about thirty pages long. At the beginning of the book, before the title page, there is a short introduction to the book itself. In that introduction, there is a short explanation of the layers of the rainforest and the density and types of creatures who live there. Immediately after the story is a note from the author to readers encouraging them to preserve the rain forest. The front and end papers of the book show the same map of the world depicting the places where the rainforests have been wiped out. The borders of the map are decorated with illustrations of the beautiful land and air creatures that inhabit the Amazon. Each of these pictures is labeled with the animal's name.

Noteworthy Features

Because the pictures are beautiful and enticing, children may be eager to pick up the book, and may dive into a subject previously unfamiliar to them. The lush and colorful illustrations also serve to further the purpose of the book: to spread appreciation of the beauty of the rainforest. The pictures help convey the meaning of the story. They also help children learn the appearances of the many unfamiliar animals in the story.

There is one paragraph of text on each two-page spread. Much of the vocabulary and sentence structure is fairly straightforward, though some of the content-specific vocabulary, such as "cock-of-the-rock" and "three-toed sloth," may be unfamiliar. Prior knowledge of concepts such as pollination and erosion will help students understand the animals' concerns.

Children who recognize the Spanish "señor" may be surprised by the

Illustrator
Lynne Cherry

Publisher
Harcourt, Brace & Company, 1990

ISBN
015200520

TC Level
10

spelling of the repeated word, "senhor." Teachers can point out ahead of time that the story takes place in Brazil, where Portuguese is spoken. This information is noted in very small print at the front of the book between the dedication and the copyright.

Teaching Ideas

Teachers who like to give readers context before they begin to read an informational writing will certainly want to familiarize readers with the plight of the Amazon rainforest. On the other hand, this book might serve as an introduction to that plight, though it appears to assume that readers already understand the magnitude of the threat. Children thus may not grasp that, when the man chopping in the story stops, that threat still persists. Students may discuss what the man represents metaphorically, especially in light of Cherry's postscript.

Stylized informational texts such as *The Great Kapok Tree* can present facts in a literary and visually compelling way. Students might look at the author's craft in this and other such texts, noting not only the author's word choice, but also the devices the author uses to deliver information, such as giving animals the power of speech so that they can argue the importance of the tree.

Obviously, many teachers use this book to help children learn about conservation and the rainforests. The book is a clear overview of some of the main reasons for conserving the rainforests, and also serves as an introduction to some of the indigenous fauna.

Some readers may have difficulty pulling the facts out from within the fiction. The animals in the story talk, and do not engage in natural animal behaviors, such as fleeing from each other or even eating the man. Readers must simultaneously suspend some disbelief *and* trust that the information in the text is true. How is the reader to know that what the animals whisper in the man's ear is real? This may be something that the teacher explains, or it may be something the reader figures out, perhaps by knowing enough about the rainforest to know that some of what the animals say is true, thereby allowing the reader to guess that the rest of it is also true. It could also be something that a reader hypothesizes and then turns to other sources to verify.

Book Connections

Lynne Cherry's other ecologically-themed book, *A River Ran Wild*, narrates the history of a river, incorporating maps and a time line. There are many other beautifully crafted informational picture books available for children. *Where Once There Was a Wood*, by Denise Fleming, *Welcome to the Green House* and *Welcome to the Ice House*, both by Jane Yolen, deal with ecological issues and make excellent models of the craft of writing.

Genre
Picture Book; Nonfiction

A Field Guide to the Classroom Library, Lucy Calkins and the Teachers College Reading and Writing Project, Heinemann, ©2002 Teachers College, Columbia University; http://www.heinemann.com/fieldguides

Teaching Uses
Reading and Writing Nonfiction; Independent Reading; Content Area
Study; Critique

The Kids of the Polk Street School – The Candy Corn Contest

Patricia Reilly Giff

Book Summary

The Candy Corn Contest is third in the series known as *The Kids of the Polk Street School*. Ms. Rooney tells the class that they will have a contest. Every page read by a student affords that student one guess as to how many candy corns are in a big jar on Ms. Rooney's desk. Whoever guesses correctly will win the jar as a Thanksgiving gift. Richard "Beast" Best is sure he will not get enough guesses to win, for he is such a poor reader that he has already been held over one grade. To make matters worse, Richard is having a sleepover, and does not want his best friend Matthew to come because Matthew wets the bed. Because of this, he starts to feel angry with Matthew, and he intentionally hurts his feelings. Richard wants the candy corn so badly that while the rest of the class is outside, he sneaks three pieces from the jar, only to discover later that Ms. Rooney has already counted them exactly. Richard is tormented by his thievery and tries to figure out a way to change the number written at the bottom of the jar. As he sneaks into the class to do this, his friend Matthew catches him. With Matthew's help, Richard is able to replace the candy corn in the jar. He ends up telling Ms. Rooney the truth, apologizing to Matthew and learning a valuable lesson about honesty and friendship.

Basic Book Information

The Kids of the Polk Street School series includes twelve books, each set in a different month. The main characters in the series are the 13 kids in Ms. Rooney's class. *The Candy Corn Contest* has 76 pages with 11 chapters. The story takes place over several days in November and is generally set in and around Ms. Rooney's classroom at the Polk Street School. There is one black-and-white illustration per chapter. The author, Patricia Reilly Giff, has written many popular books for children and this series in particular is an old favorite of chapter book readers at this level.

Noteworthy Features

Although much of the vocabulary, concepts, and dialogue are relatively straightforward, there are several places in the book where it is a little difficult to follow the actions and dialogue of the characters. This is particularly true in the classroom scenes when the students are talking with Ms. Rooney. Much of the dialogue jumps around, the way it would in a classroom, but this causes it to be a little confusing. In Chapter 3, for example, Ms. Rooney lectures about the Pilgrims, and her words are in

Series
The Kids of the Polk Street School

Illustrator
Blanche Sims

Publisher
Bantam Doubleday, 1984

ISBN
044041072X

TC Level
8

quotation marks. In between her sentences, however, appear Richard's thoughts about the sleepover. Thus, Ms. Rooney's spoken words and Richard's internal monologue interrupt each other on the page. Similarly, on pages 48 and 49, Richard whispers to his friends while a different teacher talks to the whole class, and again, readers must follow two conversations simultaneously.

Teaching Ideas

Often in this series, the main character goes through some kind of change. For example, Richard wants so much for his sleepover party to go well that he risks hurting Matthew's feelings. After Matthew helps Richard, Richard realizes that his friendship with Matthew is more important to him than his sleepover. Richard becomes kinder and more reflective. In a conference or a mini-lesson, teachers may coach readers to use Post-Its and perhaps their reading logs to chart when, how, and why a character has changed. This research allows reading partners to ground their conversations in specific textual references.

Another opportunity for teaching readers at this level is to discuss with children how to predict. The important thing to teach children when they predict is that their predictions must be grounded in textual evidence, which includes prior awareness of how texts in a genre or series tend to develop. If they feel that a group of students needs a lot of support in order to become active, constructive readers of a text like this, teachers might say, "As you are reading today, try to find the places in the story where Richard is feeling bad about cheating or being mean to Matthew. When you find those places, see if you can guess what will happen next." Teachers may suggest and model questions or comments that readers can ask themselves or each other at these points, such as: "I'm getting a funny feeling here that something is going to happen" or, "I wonder why Matthew is pretending that he can't make it to the sleepover now?" or, "I think Richard is feeling bad that he hurt Matthew's feelings because now he is being really helpful to him." These are also great opportunities for the teacher to model how readers actually think as they read. During mini-lessons before independent reading, teachers can demonstrate for readers aloud all the questions, predictions and reactions that readers have as they read - the internal dialogue the reader has with a book; during the sharing session at the end of independent reading, students can do the same with their own questions, predictions and reactions.

Book Connections

There are many titles in *The Kids of the Polk Street School* series including *The Beast in Ms. Rooney's Room, December Secrets, Sunny-Side Up,* and *Lazy Lions, Lucky Lambs.* Other chapter book series that are similar to these are *The Pee Wee Scouts, Mary Marony* and *The Adventures of The Bailey School Kids. The New Kids of the Polk Street School,* which is about Emily Arrow's little sister and her friends, is easier than the regular *Kids of the Polk Street School* series.

A Field Guide to the Classroom Library, Lucy Calkins and the Teachers College Reading and Writing Project, Heinemann, ©2002 Teachers College, Columbia University; http://www.heinemann.com/fieldguides

Genre
Chapter Book

Teaching Uses
Interpretation; Independent Reading; Character Study; Small Group Strategy Instruction

The Mouse and the Motorcycle

Beverly Cleary

Book Summary

"I wouldn't mind a few mice," says Keith, as he and his family check into a run-down hotel on their cross-country road trip. Ralph S. Mouse wouldn't mind a boy staying in room 215, either. After all, kids leave behind crumbs of cookies and candy. In his wildest dreams, though, Ralph has never imagined that the boy would leave out a toy motorcycle that was just the right size for him. The temptation of riding the bike is so great that Ralph decides to take a spin, and ends up falling headfirst into a trashcan. When Keith discovers him, Ralph expects the worst, as his mother has warned him about humans. However, the boy is happy to have found a mouse. So begins a great friendship.

Ralph and Keith speak the same language and work out an agreement about riding the bike. With Keith's permission, Ralph takes trips into the forbidden corridors of the hotel at night. When Ralph's carelessness causes him to lose the bike, he thinks Keith will never forgive him. Keith is angry, but he forgives Ralph, and even continues to deliver room service to the mouse family. When Keith falls sick, Ralph goes to great lengths to find him an aspirin. It is the most daring adventure that Ralph has ever had and proves that he is growing up. Back in Keith's good graces, Ralph is given the bike after the boy leaves the hotel.

Basic Book Information

The *Mouse and the Motorcycle* contains 158 pages divided over 13 chapters. Chapter titles are listed in a table of contents. Small, black-and-white illustrations appear every two or four pages. Beverly Cleary is the acclaimed author of over thirty books, including the *Ramona* series.

Noteworthy Features

The brevity of the chapter lengths will let children who are beginning to read chapter books set attainable goals for themselves. The chapter titles are teasers, like "Adventure in the Night" and "Ralph Takes Command." Such titles spark readers' interest and give them some information about the chapter's subject matter.

Readers will note that in this story (as opposed to Dick King-Smith's books about friendships between English-speaking animals and people), Ralph and Keith can communicate with one another. Cleary explains the phenomenon by saying, "Neither the mouse nor the boy seemed the least bit surprised that they could understand the other. Two creatures who shared a love for motorcycles naturally spoke the same language." Keith's and Ralph's family both speak English as well, but they do not understand one another. Readers who pay attention to detail may find this intriguing.

Illustrator
Louis Darling

Publisher
William Morrow and Company, 1965

ISBN
0380709244

TC Level
9

A Field Guide to the Classroom Library, Lucy Calkins and the Teachers College Reading and Writing Project, Heinemann, ©2002 Teachers College, Columbia University; http://www.heinemann.com/fieldguides

There are not many characters in the story: Ralph and his family, Keith and his family and the hotel staff. *The Mouse and the Motorcycle* is set entirely at the hotel, primarily in room 215. These factors will help young readers keep a handle on the unfolding story without being overwhelmed by too many setting changes or characters. In fact, Ralph S. Mouse's small size makes room 215 seem like an entire universe. He has an adventure underneath the hotel bed with a vacuum cleaner on the attack.

The illustrations help readers get a sense of the scale in the story. For instance, when Ralph drives the motorcycle into the trashcan, readers can see just how enormous the trashcan is in relation to him. The illustrations may help readers get perspective on what the world would look like to a mouse.

Teaching Ideas

There are two main worlds that exist in *The Mouse and the Motorcycle*: the human and the mouse. The book switches often from the perspective of the mice to that of the humans, such as when Keith is sick with a fever and his father goes on a search for an aspirin. After he asks the night clerk, he finds out that the nearest drugstore is closed and he will not be able to get an aspirin till the morning. Ralph then sets out on the same mission. This is a life-threatening endeavor for a mouse, which includes staying out of sight of humans, dodging dogs, and finding a way to carry a large, poisonous pill. Readers in partnerships or individually may want to Post- it sections of the book where the mouse and humans experience the same event in completely different ways.

Ralph and Keith's friendship bridges the gap between the mouse and human worlds. The fact that they understand one another testifies to this. Readers may also note reasons besides their love of motorcycles that help them to speak the same language. For instance, both Keith and Ralph are in the process of growing up and are often in too much of a hurry. When Keith shares a story about hitting a tree with his bike after forgetting to use the hand brakes, the story makes Ralph "feel better. He was not the only one who got into trouble."

As noted before, the fact that Ralph and Keith both speak English and understand one another, yet their families do not, may be a source of confusion for some readers. There are other characters, such as the bellhop, who also understand mice. Readers may want to form theories about what characteristics enable these minor characters to speak with and comprehend mice. Ultimately, *The Mouse and the Motorcycle* contains an element of fantasy. Readers must suspend their disbelief when the boy and mouse speak the same language. Additionally, the way that Ralph runs the motorcycle is by making the noise "Pb-pb-b-b-b." The faster he makes the noise with his mouth the quicker the bike moves across the floor. Readers with great imaginations will delight in the cleverness of such scenes and love the idea of a mouse riding along the corridors of a hotel on a toy bike.

The structure of many of the sentences throughout the book may prove difficult. During the action scenes, many of the sentences are lengthy and are divided with commas. The use of commas in these action-packed scenes creates a feeling of suspense. The list-format of the sentence parallels the flood of thoughts and actions being experienced by Ralph. Teachers can

A Field Guide to the Classroom Library, Lucy Calkins and the Teachers College Reading and Writing Project, Heinemann, ©2002 Teachers College, Columbia University; http://www.heinemann.com/fieldguides

model how the sentences sound when read and explain that the commas, unlike periods, create only a short pause instead of a full stop. In a writing workshop, children may want to emulate this use of commas to create passages where both the characters and the sentences have little time for the full stop of a period.

Book Connections

Beverly Cleary has written numerous chapter book series, which could be grouped together in a classroom library. Readers who enjoy *The Mouse and the Motorcycle* may want to followup with *Runaway Ralph* and *Ralph S. Mouse*. After that, they may be inspired to read another series by Beverly Cleary. Children who enjoy books in which animals take on many human characteristics may enjoy books by Dick King-Smith, including *The Cuckoo Child*, *Pigs Might Fly*, and *Babe*. These books are similar in that they explore animals' perspectives by giving them a voice.

Genre
Chapter Book

Teaching Uses
Small Group Strategy Instruction; Independent Reading

A Field Guide to the Classroom Library, Lucy Calkins and the Teachers College Reading and Writing Project, Heinemann, ©2002 Teachers College, Columbia University; http://www.heinemann.com/fieldguides

The One in the Middle Is the Green Kangaroo

Judy Blume

Book Summary

Freddy Dissel is in the second grade and he is the middle child in his family. Freddy feels like "the peanut butter part of a sandwich, squeezed between Mike and Ellen." Freddy worries that he will always be "a great big middle nothing," so he decides to do something that Mike and Ellen never have - he will try to be in the school play. Even though the play is only for fifth and sixth graders, Ms. Matson decides that Freddy should play a special part: the Green Kangaroo. During the performance, Freddy's nerves settle down as he realizes that his family is in the middle of the audience, but he is up on stage alone. When the play is over, the audience claps enthusiastically. Freddy feels "great being Freddy Dissel."

Basic Book Information

The One in the Middle Is the Green Kangaroo is a 40-page chapter book. The story is continuous, without chapter breaks. Color illustrations appear on every page.

Noteworthy Features

There are some expressions in the story that children may enjoy: "he felt like the peanut butter part of the sandwich" and "his stomach bounced up and down." The text is written simply and there is a special message-finding out that you truly are special.

Teaching Ideas

The theme of wanting to be special or wanting to stand out is one that many readers relate to easily. Often teachers use this book with partnerships and book clubs to encourage "conversation stamina." One way teachers do this is to have students mark places with Post-its where they have strong reactions or insights into Freddy's character. Students then take turns "talking off" each Post-it with the goal of discussing each point as deeply as possible.

Book Connections

This book is similar to the *Cam Jansen* series by David A. Adler. We recommend that the reader first experience success with the *Pinky and Rex* series by James Howe. A good follow-up would be *Freckle Juice*, also by Judy Blume.

Illustrator
Irene Trivas

Publisher
Dell Publishing, 1981

ISBN
0440467314

TC Level
8

Genre
Short Chapter Book

Teaching Uses
Independent Reading; Partnerships; Book Clubs

The Paint Brush Kid

Clyde Robert Bulla

Book Summary

In this sequel to *The Chalk Box Kid*, Gregory and his friends paint an elderly neighbor's home. Gregory paints a mural with pictures from Uncle Pancho's past life in Mexico, including a portrait of what Gregory thinks Uncle Pancho's long-lost son looks like. The story peaks as Uncle Pancho's house is slated to be demolished to make way for a highway, but Gregory's mural saves the house. The reader does not find out if Uncle Pancho's son is ever found.

Basic Book Information

It is helpful to read *The Chalk Box Kid* first, although *The Paint Brush Kid* contains a summary of the first book so that readers can read this sequel with the first book in mind. This 67-page book has chapter titles, listed in a table of contents that signal readers as to the major theme of each. Pictures that complement the story appear in every chapter.

Noteworthy Features

Simple text is the hallmark of this book, making it possible for young readers to feel confident when reading it alone or with a partner. Usually, sentences are short and simple and quotations referenced, though some dialogue is used without references to which character is speaking. The action all takes place in Gregory's neighborhood, and except for some flashbacks, time passes linearly. Although there is no extensive character development, readers may be able to relate to and understand characters and their actions because they seem real.

The Paint Brush Kid has three parallel storylines: Will the house be saved? Will Pancho's grown son see him on TV and come home? Will Gregory be able to like Uncle Max, who takes over Gregory's room in *The Chalk Box Kid* and now just loafs around playing guitar? Some plot elements are introduced suddenly, like the lost son. Readers will need to be alert to the surprises, and to keep plot lines in their heads. Like *The Chalk Box Kid*, this book ends somewhat inconclusively, which may leave readers wanting another book to follow. Some terms, such as *freeway* and *man from the state*, are not explained, and may need to be introduced. Some readers may have trouble with the past perfect tense, as in "He *had given* Gregory the idea for the chalk garden. . .Gregory *had had* no place to plant a garden"[emphasis added]. At least one reader has assumed "had had" was a misprint.

Teaching Ideas

Because this book holds many characters that have little character

Series
The Chalk Box Kid, The Paint Brush Kid

Illustrator
Thomas B. Allen

Publisher
Random House, 1999

ISBN
0679892826

TC Level
8

development, a teacher may wish to introduce this book by bringing up Gregory's achievements in *The Chalk Box Kid*, when he draws a whole garden on the walls of an old building. Teachers might go on to introduce *The Paint Brush Kid* by saying something such as, "In this book, Gregory gets a chance to help his neighbor, Uncle Pancho. Uncle Pancho needs his house painted, not just with color, but also with pictures from the old man's stories about his life in Mexico. Gregory learns a lot about Uncle Pancho, who has a son he is looking for."

In guided reading sessions or teacher-student conferences, teachers could help children identify the three problems that form the three-pronged plot in the book. Students could follow the storylines with charts or by recording the events of each plot line. They could notice the surprises when the plot takes an unexpected turn. For example, on page 21, Uncle Pancho reveals that he has left Mexico to find his son after his wife has taken the son away. This is a new element not foreshadowed earlier.

Students might also list the characters and their traits. For example, on pages 11 and 12, Ivy's mother, Mrs. Brimm, says of Uncle Pancho, "He helps everybody, but does anybody ever help him?" She then gives the children a loaf of home-baked bread to give Uncle Pancho. Students can think about characters by looking at examples of their behavior.

Book Connections

The Paint Brush Kid is similar in difficulty to *Beans on the Roof* by Betsy Byars and the *Jigsaw Jones* mysteries by James Preller. After reading the *Chalk Box Kid*, a reader may turn to *The Polk Street School* series by Patricia Reilly Giff and the *Marvin Redpost* series by Louis Sachar.

Genre
Short Chapter Book

Teaching Uses
Independent Reading; Read Aloud; Partnerships

A Field Guide to the Classroom Library, Lucy Calkins and the Teachers College Reading and Writing Project, Heinemann, ©2002 Teachers College, Columbia University; http://www.heinemann.com/fieldguides

The Reason for a Flower

Ruth Heller

Book Summary

The Reason for a Flower is a great book for introducing botany to children. Scientific words are used throughout the book, including "stamen," "nectar," and "herbivorous." These words are embedded in the pictures so that the reader can figure out their meaning. The lilies show the stamens and anthers, and roots are shown for carrots, beets, and even ginger.

Basic Book Information

The Reason for a Flower is a nonfiction book with 20 two-page, full-color spreads. There is a page in the front, before the title page, that repeats the very end of the book.

Noteworthy Features

Text placement is very inconsistent, though it often helps the reader look closer at the pictures. For instance, the words "ANTHER" and "STAMEN" curl around images of these plant parts, which makes them function simultaneously as part of the main text and as labels. Words with every letter capitalized have accompanying illustrations and definitions. "HER - BIV - O - ROUS" and "CAR - NIV - O - ROUS" are written in syllables in capitals across the page so the reader can say the word. The text is limited and well chosen so readers are not encumbered with wordiness and fancy phrases. The voice of the text is close and friendly.

The text rhymes, but only sporadically, as if the author were writing in free verse that happens to occasionally rhyme. Because the rhyming pattern is irregular, students who rely upon patterns may become confused.

Teaching Ideas

This book is both poetic and informational. Readers need to look closely and read carefully. This is a book that should be read slowly and used for discussion and thinking. *The Reason for a Flower* can also be used to view an alternative structure for conveying information. Not many nonfiction books play with words and their sounds, or have pictures such as the ones contained in this book.

Rhythm and poetic forms can be studied with this book. As the book starts, "This one has become . . . a plum," the student can hear the assonance, or repeated vowel sounds, in *one, become* and *plum*. "From an anther on a stamen to a stigma on a style/ pollen grains must travel and stay a while" shows more familiar end-rhymes. It also shows alliteration (repetition of beginning consonant sounds), with *stamen, stigma,* and *style.* Onsets as well as rimes can be highlighted for playfulness and understanding

A Field Guide to the Classroom Library, Lucy Calkins and the Teachers College Reading and Writing Project, Heinemann, ©2002 Teachers College, Columbia University; http://www.heinemann.com/fieldguides

Illustrator
Ruth Heller

Publisher
Paper Star, 1983

ISBN
0698115597

TC Level
7; 8; 9

of poetic forms.

Book Connections

Ruth Heller has written other books that follow this same style and format, including *Color* and *Animals Born Alive and Well*. Ruth Heller is also known for her "World of Language" series with such books as *Kites Sail High: A Book About Verbs*. Jane Yolen's *Water Music* uses poems as informational text, and her stylized language in *Welcome to the Green House* uses evocative language to tell about the rainforest. Georgia Heard's *Creatures of Earth, Sea and Sky* and Yvonne Winer's *Spiders Spin Webs* also fuse poetry and nonfiction.

Genre
Nonfiction; Picture Book

Teaching Uses
Partnerships; Content Area Study; Reading and Writing Nonfiction

A Field Guide to the Classroom Library, Lucy Calkins and the Teachers College Reading and Writing Project, Heinemann, ©2002 Teachers College, Columbia University; http://www.heinemann.com/fieldguides

The Three Bears

Paul Galdone

Book Summary

This book retells the traditional story of the three bears. Three bears live in the woods: a big one, a middle-sized one and a baby one. Their porridge is too hot to eat, so they go for a walk while it cools. While they are gone, a little girl named Goldilocks goes into their house. She samples all of their porridge and tests all of their chairs, finishing the baby's food and breaking the baby's chair. Then she goes to their beds, and falls asleep in the baby's. The bears come home and discover their bowls of porridge, chairs and beds have been tampered with. They find Goldilocks and wake her up. She flees in terror of the bears, never to be seen by them again.

Basic Book Information

This picture book has about two or three lines of text on every page. The text is positioned beneath the humorous, sketch-style illustrations.

Noteworthy Features

One interesting aspect of this rendition of the classic story is the use of different size type fonts to represent the different bear's voices. The different sizes beg to be read aloud in varying voices. Groups often enjoy, and benefit from, reading the story aloud with different parts played by different group members, including a narrator.

Teaching Ideas

Like Paul Galdone's other well-known folk tales, this one is great to use with struggling readers. The readers know a bit of the story already, so they know what to expect from the text, and may even know some of the repeated phrases by heart. Galdone's folk tales are also perfect for strugglers in that they are fairly simply written, without a lot of adjectives, figurative language and clauses to wade through. They often have repeated activities or repeated phrases, so the text is predictable in that sense, too.

While the stories tend to be easy to read, the topics for discussion can be quite complicated and interesting. This allows children who cannot read on the same level as the rest of the class to participate in the discussion of the story at the same level because they can grasp and refer to the text at the same level as their peers.

One unusual thing about this version of the fairy tale is that in the illustrations of this one, Goldilocks has missing teeth. Kids can read all sorts of things into this. Is she missing teeth because she has lost her baby teeth, or because they are rotten? Is the author trying to tell us that she is not a nice person by making her not look nice? Is that a fair way to judge

Illustrator
Paul Galdone

Publisher
Little, Brown and Company, 1999

ISBN
0395288118

TC Level
6

character?

Once children are trying to figure those questions out, they tend to start to look at Goldilocks' behavior in a new light. How can she enter the house of strangers, eat their food, break their furniture and go to sleep? Why doesn't she try to fix what she has broken, and why doesn't she apologize?

Book Connections

Paul Galdone has also rendered *The Three Billy Goats Gruff*, *The Three Little Pigs* and many other folk tales into simple and fun picture books for kids. Comparing other versions of these stories, especially revisionist versions such as John Scieszka's, like *The True Story of the Three Little Pigs*, can make for great discussions.

Genre
Picture Book; Fairy and Folk Tale

Teaching Uses
Critique; Independent Reading; Character Study; Interpretation

Tooter Pepperday

Jerry Spinelli

Book Summary

Tooter shows her unhappiness about her family's decision to move to Aunt Sally's farm by handcuffing herself to a pipe in the bathroom of their suburban home. At every turn, she fights what adults want her to do. Once at the farm, Tooter tries to mess things up so they will have to leave the farm. Although she is acting defiantly, all of this is quite funny. There are many farm jokes and silly scenes. Near the end of the book, after perhaps nearly a month on the farm, Tooter changes. As she tends to an egg and helps it to incubate, she begins to love life on the farm.

Basic Book Information

Tooter Pepperday has 85 pages with 12 chapters. There is one illustration in each chapter set across from the matching text. *Blue Ribbon Blues* is the sequel to *Tooter Pepperday*. Jerry Spinelli, a favorite of older readers, has also written *Crash, Stargirl, The Library Card* and *Maniac Magee*, winner of the 1991 Newbery Medal.

Noteworthy Features

The humor in *Tooter Pepperday* keeps kids laughing and eager to read more. Many readers delight in the "yucky" aspects of the farm life against which Tooter rages.

The titles of chapters do not foreshadow their content, but are instead designed to intrigue readers. The plot line is straightforward and time moves in a linear fashion, without flashbacks or large jumps ahead.

Some vocabulary might cause problems, but most of it can be inferred from context. Challenging words include words like "desperate," "incubate," "woozy," and "sabotage." There is also some affected speech, which Aunt Sally has adopted from movies so that she sounds more like a farmer. Readers will not need to translate these expressions exactly, and they add a humorous touch to the character of Aunt Sally, who, unlike Tooter, loves everything about farm life and eventually helps Tooter to like it as well. It might be helpful for students to try reading aloud some of Aunt Sally's country talk-and to hear teachers read it-so they can savor the sound of it.

Teaching Ideas

Once children have read most of the book, they will probably notice that Spinelli sets the reader up to contrast the two Tooters: the one who exists before her transformation, and the one who exists after. Readers may (especially with coaching) notice the turning point in Tooter and even locate clues about why she has changed her attitude towards the farm. They

A Field Guide to the Classroom Library, Lucy Calkins and the Teachers College Reading and Writing Project, Heinemann, ©2002 Teachers College, Columbia University; http://www.heinemann.com/fieldguides

Series

Blue Ribbon Blues, Tooter Pepperday

Illustrator

Donna Nelson

Publisher

Random House Stepping Stone, 1995

ISBN

0679847022

TC Level

8

may discuss this with partners. Some children may even decide to make a two-column chart, noticing characteristics of and differences between the old and new. (This is a way to study character that can help readers in any book they read.) These readers will notice Tooter's turning point near the end of the chapter "Two Tooters" because of the many contrasting examples. "The old Tooter would not go near goat's milk. The new Tooter drank chocolate goat's milk for breakfast." The old Tooter, who had resisted the chore of turning the hen's abandoned egg, begins to feel like the egg's "mother," and willingly continues to tend the egg until it hatches.

In some books, readers get to know characters through their actions and dialogue. In this book, there is a third person, omniscient narrator who reports not only what Tooter says and does, but also what she thinks. The narrator even lets readers in on some of Tooter's parents' thoughts. This makes this a great book in which to study character.

Students may choose to put sticky notes on funny parts in the book and to tell their partner or the teacher why they thought those sections were so funny. They might identify their favorite parts and explain why they liked these.

It would also be worthwhile to take a step back from this book and compare Tooter to another character from a different book. For example, Junie B. Jones (in Barbara Park's series of the same name) is also an outrageous, funny and strong main character. Readers could jot down the character traits that both girls share and those they do not. For instance, the over-the-top behavior of both girls and the kind but firm reactions of the adults around them are similar. Junie, however, does not change much from the beginning to the end of a book, while Tooter does.

Book Connections

Children who enjoy this book may want to read its sequel, *Blue Ribbon Blues*. The *Junie B. Jones* and *Marvin Redpost* series offer many more books at this level that have spirited protagonists. The *Amber Brown* series, also built around a strong-willed main character, is a little more challenging.

Genre
Short Chapter Book

Teaching Uses
Independent Reading

A Field Guide to the Classroom Library, Lucy Calkins and the Teachers College Reading and Writing Project, Heinemann, ©2002 Teachers College, Columbia University; http://www.heinemann.com/fieldguides

We Had a Picnic This Sunday Past

Jacqueline Woodson

Book Summary

It is the day of the big family picnic and Teeka and her grandmother are buzzing with excitement. As members of the family arrive in the park, Teeka, the narrator, comments about each person and the food each has brought for the potluck. Teeka obviously enjoys herself, telling readers on the last page, "You should have been there."

Basic Book Information

This 27-page picture book contains bold illustrations on every page. There are roughly two paragraphs of text on one side of every two-page spread. A Coretta Scott King Honor recipient, Jacqueline Woodson has written many novels for older readers, including *I Hadn't Meant to Tell You This* and *If You Come Softly*. Woodson's *The Other Side* is another subtly crafted picture book, though the subject, illustrations and overall tone are far less exuberant than those of *We Had a Picnic This Sunday Past*.

Noteworthy Features

Set on a single afternoon, this story is structured simply and chronologically. Vocabulary should present most students with few challenges. Though many characters enter the park, readers can understand the story while remembering just three: Teeka, Grandma and Cousin Martha, whose arrival and notoriously dry apple pie are anticipated throughout the story.

In spite of these easier elements, *We Had a Picnic This Sunday Past* is fairly complex. Dialogue is set off from the rest of the text not by quotation marks, but by bold print. The speaker of the dialogue is rarely referenced, and sometimes the subject of the dialogue is also hard to discern. For example, some readers may not immediately understand that the "boy" whose baking skills Grandma praises is an adult, Uncle Luther. Reading aloud with inflection is important and helpful for students who are trying to reproduce the cadence of the text.

The figurative language of Teeka's narration also adds a layer of complexity to the story. Phrases such as "a pail of peaches fresh as summer" make her voice poetic. Students at first may not see the humorous word play in asides such as "the most delicious store-bought cake Cousin Martha **never** made" and "Reverend Luke can eat like the devil-strange, since he's such a holy man."

Teaching Ideas

Though technically a work of fiction, *We Had a Picnic This Sunday Past* has

Illustrator
Diane Greenseid

Publisher
Hyperion, 1998

ISBN
0786802421

many of the elements of memoir. It is a first-person narrative that, through images and anecdotes, provides a window into the life of the narrator. Teeka's perspective and observations are central to this story. Used in the writing workshop, this book can serve as a model to which students refer while they write their own memoir. Mini-lessons can look at how Woodson creates Teeka's strong voice, how to show detail instead of telling it, and how to comment subtly on the action instead of just listing what happened next. Enlarging text on an overhead transparency or chart paper can help children see examples during these whole-class mini-lessons.

After students are familiar with the story, they might reread to examine the relationship between Teeka and her grandmother. Children may notice how Teeka's behavior mirrors Grandma's. The two whisper conspiratorially, and Teeka appears to share her grandmother's passion for gossip and judgment. Both of them enjoy bragging. In the illustration on the second page, their arms jut upward at complementary angles, and later they fold their arms and throw back their heads in identically indignant poses.

Negotiating the challenging dialogue is crucial for children's understanding. Some students will be able to imagine the book's natural inflection and to hear in their heads all of the characters' distinct voices. Others may need to hear someone else read it. Teachers who plan to read *We Had a Picnic This Sunday Past* aloud should prepare carefully first. They must plan how they will differentiate Teeka's narrative commentary from dialogue that the characters utter to each other; students may miss one of the key features of the book otherwise. Also, teachers must distinguish the voices of different characters. Slight adjustments in tone, pitch and pace can suggest everything from Auntie Kim's sweetness to Cousin Martha's frenetic energy. As both Teeka and Grandma whisper frequently, teachers should decide in advance when they plan to raise or lower their volume. Finally, teachers should plan to read sensitively. Reading any dialect well requires naturalism, not theatrical exaggeration. Hearing this story read in overblown accents will not enrich it for students, but distract them.

Book Connections

Shortcut, by Donald Crews; *Nana Upstairs & Nana Downstairs*, by Tomie dePaola; and *Home: A Collaboration of Thirty Distinguished Authors and Illustrators of Children's Books to Aid the Homeless*, edited by Michael J. Rosen and Franz Brandenberg, offer strong examples of memoir.

Genre
Memoir; Picture Book

Teaching Uses
Read Aloud; Independent Reading; Partnerships; Teaching Writing

What Makes a Bird a Bird?

May Garelick

Illustrator
Trish Hill

Publisher
Mondo, 1988

ISBN
1572550082

TC Level
10; 11

Book Summary

The question of the title structures this nonfiction text. The book proposes possible answers to questions about what separates birds from other types of animals, and then eliminates each proposed answer. For example, in italics, the text asks, "*Is it a bird because it flies*?" The next twelve pages give examples of flying creatures, such as bats and insects, that are not birds and birds that do not fly. After walking the reader through several of these guesses -singing songs, sporting wings, building nests, and laying eggs -the defining trait, having feathers, is revealed.

Basic Book Information

This nonfiction picture book has 29 pages. Although it is about animals and Mondo publishes it, it does not appear to be part of the Mondo animal nonfiction series. Many of the common characteristics of that series, such as captions, a table of contents and an index, are absent here. Every page contains a full-color illustration, around which text is situated.

Noteworthy Features

This text's organization is unusual. Not many nonfiction books organize their information based on a likely path of thinking by the reader. This book models for readers a way of thinking: asking a broad question, generating hypotheses and then refuting them. For example, after the book points out that chickens and ostriches stick to the ground, the text addresses readers directly: "Can you think of a bird that doesn't fly?" Each hypothesis of what characteristic separates birds from other animals appears in italics.

The text is written in a colloquial sort of style that will be easy for many readers. Challenging vocabulary, such as "oil sac," "brittle" and "molt," appears infrequently.

Teaching Ideas

As mentioned above, the text leads the reader through a mental version of the scientific method. Teachers can use this book to illustrate the scientific method in thinking.

Some teachers also use this book when giving young writers ideas for organizational structures for their nonfiction writing. Not only is this structure unusual, but the hook at the beginning and the end has been crafted for excellent effect. This, too, provides a strong model for young writers. Learning to anticipate readers' questions and to provide lengthy answers full of supporting details will serve children well in any genre in which they write.

Book Connections

May Garelick's *Where Does the Butterfly Go When It Rains?* and *Who Likes It Hot?* also rely on questions to structure informational texts. Nancy Winslow Parker and Joan Richards Wright's *Bugs*; Margery Facklam's *Creepy, Crawly Caterpillars*; and Etta Kaner's *Animal Defenses: How Animals Protect Themselves* are additional, animal-themed nonfiction books at this level.

Genre

Nonfiction; Picture Book; Mystery

Teaching Uses

Content Area Study; Partnerships; Read Aloud; Reading and Writing Nonfiction

A Field Guide to the Classroom Library, Lucy Calkins and the Teachers College Reading and Writing Project, Heinemann, ©2002 Teachers College, Columbia University; http://www.heinemann.com/fieldguides

Why Don't Haircuts Hurt?

Melvin Berger; Gilda Berger

Book Summary

This text provides an accessible introduction to many different processes, parts, and functions in and of the human body. It answers a series of questions, including everything from "Which muscles do you control?" to "What causes stomach rumbles?"

Basic Book Information

This nonfiction picture book has 48 pages. There is a table of contents and a small key to metric abbreviations on the same page as the Library of Congress data. An introduction and three large sections of questions and answers follow. A large, red font marks the start of new sections. An index lists page numbers for the topics covered. Beneath the index are a few sentences about the authors and illustrator.

Noteworthy Features

Why Don't Haircuts Hurt? is written in a question-and-answer format, with three or four questions answered in short paragraphs on every double page spread. The font of the questions is large and blue, while the font of the answers is small and black. Despite its small size, the font of the answers is easy to read, and the small amount of text for each answer makes it less intimidating than it might otherwise be.

The pictures in the book are realistic, colorful, and scientific. The illustrations aim to make body processes more clear. Many of the pictures have several labeled parts (with the labels in small, unobtrusive font); others show body functions as a whole.

The first words directly after a question rarely form complete sentences, although these words are followed by a period. Because the book uses this structure, a reader cannot browse through the book, reading the answers without the questions. Because each question and answer is written as a whole, children can easily read only bits and pieces of the text, and still get a lot of information.

Overall, the book is more a string of questions than a cohesive text. New sub-topics are introduced without much warning. Further, the sequence of questions does not follow here an immediately apparent logic. For instance, "What gives hair its color?" and "How is skin color like hair color?" are separated by the question, "How fast does hair grow on your head?" Questions, therefore, do not always build on each other, which may confuse some readers.

Illustrator
Karen Barnes

Publisher
Scholastic, 1998

ISBN
0590130862

TC Level
9; 10; 11

Teaching Ideas

The authors' note at the start of the book, itself in the question-and-answer form, asks: "Why read a question-and-answer book?" The Bergers tell readers that their natural curiosity may "lead to *more questions* calling for *more answers*." Following questions that yield more questions may be the most useful way to read this book. Some readers come to it after they have a specific question about the human body, and then read through the relevant section of the book looking for their question. While this makes a good opportunity to teach the value of an index, chances are the exact question will not be written in this book. If children realize this, they may come to the book with less specific expectations, and may get more out of it. Readers can also be instructed to read sections that are related to their question to see if any information is given that helps them.

Why Don't Haircuts Hurt? can be used in a science reading center. The style of questions models important thinking students can apply in their own work in science. Asking "How much...?" "What makes...?" and "How does...?" helps students frame their own investigations. Such questions also serve students when they read nonfiction texts in all disciplines, helping them look for and pick out critical information that they wish to know.

Children can use the question-and-answer format in their own nonfiction writing. *Why Don't Haircuts Hurt?* can thus serve as an example in the writing workshop.

Book Connections

Melvin and Gilda Berger have written more than a dozen question-and-answer books on a wide range of subjects, including *Do Stars Have Points?* and *Do Whales Have Bellybuttons?*

Genre
Nonfiction; Picture Book

Teaching Uses
Content Area Study; Reading and Writing Nonfiction; Partnerships

A Field Guide to the Classroom Library, Lucy Calkins and the Teachers College Reading and Writing Project, Heinemann, ©2002 Teachers College, Columbia University; http://www.heinemann.com/fieldguides

You Can't Eat Your Chicken Pox, Amber Brown

Paula Danziger

Book Summary

Amber is going to London with Aunt Pam and to France to see her Dad, who is separated from her mother. While packing, she learns that her mother is dating a new man. Amber has been wishing that her parents would get back together. This wish, mixed with her desire to be free from the worry and conflict that this creates, is a major theme of the books in this series. While Amber is in London, she gets chicken pox. Her father comes to see her and tells her he will move back to New York. The book ends with letters to her teacher and her mother expressing her feelings about the divorce.

Basic Book Information

There are currently six books in the *Amber Brown* series. The books get longer and more complex as Amber ages, and the later books sometimes allude to events in earlier books. The author reintroduces characters and past events in each new book so that it's not absolutely necessary for readers to read them in sequence.

This book has 101 pages, with chapters of 8 or 9 pages in length. There are no chapter titles or table of contents. Cartoon-like illustrations appear every few pages. Handwritten letters and doodles occasionally blend in with the standard typeface of the text. Paula Danziger is the award-winning author of many books, including *The Cat Ate My Gymsuit*, *The Pistachio Prescription*, and *Can You Sue Your Parents for Malpractice?* The character of Amber was inspired by Danziger's niece, Carrie.

Noteworthy Features

The author uses spoken language patterns to write dialogue, and they involve some broken sentences and phrases. The author also uses British terms such as *flat, lift, queue, pounds* and *pence*.

The plot in *You Can't Eat Your Chicken Pox, Amber Brown* is believable and realistic. Students can hold the story in their minds. As with all the books in this series, Amber has a strong narrative voice. Readers do, however, need to be aware of some jarring shifts in the setting. For example, the third chapter takes place on an airplane and the fourth suddenly begins with unpacking in England; the text does not explicitly state that Amber has gotten off the plane, left the airport and found her way to her destination in London. Dialogue in this book is frequently embedded in paragraphs of text, which makes it hard to discern and distinguish the speaker. Sarcasm

Series
Amber Brown books

Illustrator
Tony Ross

Publisher
Scholastic, 1996

ISBN
0590502077

TC Level
9

and language play may also confuse some readers.

Teaching Ideas

The *Amber Brown* series provides a good opportunity for students to engage in a character study. Amber has a strong and defined personality; her humor and incisive commentary provide much for children to discuss. Students can discuss her character in partnerships, in book clubs, or after whole-class read alouds. Because Amber's character ages and develops over the course of the series, comparing earlier books in the series to later ones can prove especially fruitful.

Because other story elements are not complex, *You Can't Eat Your Chicken Pox, Amber Brown* would also be a good book to use for strategy lessons designed to teach readers how to read dialogue that is not cited or referenced. If, during conferences, teachers notice that students are struggling to follow stretches of dialogue in which the narrator does not say who is speaking, they can work with students on developing strategies to determine which character is speaking. The dialogue here can also be copied onto an overhead transparency to use during mini-lessons on sorting out unreferenced dialogue.

Book Connections

Students may wish to read other books in this series by Paula Danziger, including *Amber Brown Forever*, which is slightly more challenging. Ann Cameron's *Julian* series, Clyde Robert Bulla's *Shoeshine Girl* and Jerry Spinelli's *Tooter Pepperday* offer more realistic fiction for readers at this level.

Genre
Short Chapter Book

Teaching Uses
Independent Reading; Character Study; Small Group Strategy Instruction

A Field Guide to the Classroom Library, Lucy Calkins and the Teachers College Reading and Writing Project, Heinemann, ©2002 Teachers College, Columbia University; http://www.heinemann.com/fieldguides

Young Cam Jansen and the Ice Skate Mystery

David A. Adler

Book Summary

As in the other Young Cam Jansen books, chapter one explains how Jennifer Jansen earns her nickname, Cam, because of her good memory. Other characters are introduced, and there is a test where Cam proves her memory prowess. Cam goes ice skating with her friend Eric and his father. Eric wants to be responsible, and asks to hold the key to the locker. After skating for a while, Eric thinks he's lost the key. Cam uses her amazing memory to figure out the location of the lost key. In chapter five, Cam reveals how the key ended up in her pocket.

Basic Book Information

Young Cam Jansen books have a medium size print with comfortable spacing between the lines and the words. The illustrations lend support to the text and include important details. The reader can see what is happening, notice important clues, and gain insight into the thinking going on in Cam's head. The story is composed of simple sentences, most of which end at the end of the line.

Noteworthy Features

There is one major plot for readers to follow - finding the key. Of all the Young Cams, which are somewhat easier than the books in the regular Cam Jansen series, this is the easiest to follow and could make a good place for a reader new to the series to start. The characters are straightforward and include Cam, Eric and his father. The chapter titles are supportive and aid the reader in predicting what will happen (e.g., "Let's Skate" and "Crash"). Readers will need to pay attention to both text and pictures to get the full story. The vocabulary is mostly familiar with an occasional exception (e.g., *lockers* may be unfamiliar to some readers).

Teaching Ideas

A teacher may want to preview the story for an individual or a group of readers in a way that gets them started doing what mystery readers mainly do, which is to act as if they, too, are the crime solvers looking for clues. Conferences with the teacher or book talks between partners might focus on what was learned about how we read mysteries. We'll want them to notice important features, including the fact that readers tend to learn at the very beginning such important elements as the identity of the crime-solver,

Series
Young Cam Jansen books

Illustrator
Susanna Natti

Publisher
Puffin (Easy to Read), 1998

ISBN
0141300124

TC Level
6

whether he or she has a sidekick, and what the mystery will be. In coaching young readers to notice such characteristic features of a particular kind of text - in this case a mystery - we set them up to approach their next experience with that kind of text in a more informed way - with a sense of, "I have some ideas about how mysteries go..." We can also help them realize in a general way that proficient readers are always making subtle adjustments in their approach, depending on the type of text as well as their purpose as a reader. If the whole class is studying the genre of mystery, the share at the end of independent reading time provides a good opportunity to collect ideas and observations from across the class and to discuss strategies that helped them read more effectively.

The *Young Cam Jansen* books are great for retelling work because there is similar sequencing in all of them. Typically, objects are mysteriously lost and Cam finds them. Many chapter books at this level are episodic, with each chapter almost a story unto itself - this one is not. It therefore provides some additional challenges, which are likely to require some teaching and discussion. In a conference, teachers can coach partners to stop to retell and talk about one chapter before beginning another, and to talk about how one chapter connects to the previous chapter. Teachers can use the experiences of those reading the Young Cams as material for planning mini-lessons that anticipate upcoming needs of other readers in the class as they, too, transition out of episodic chapter books and into those structured in this cumulative way.

When students are reading independently, they can put Post-its on clues they accumulate along the way. Post-Its can be marked with a "C" for clue, and the reader can jot these clues in his/her reading notebook. After a few chapters, the reader can reread the clues and try to solve the mystery.

In writing workshop, a teacher might have a mini-lesson on the layout of these chapter books. As an introduction to this mini-lesson, a teacher might say, "Yesterday we talked a little about revising our pieces. I noticed some of you were unsure of how to do this, so I thought we'd look at how this author plans the layout of his pieces. Looking more closely at the chapters in his books, I noticed that each chapter is about a specific moment or event in the story. That makes me think that when the author planned out his book, he thought about the story in parts or chunks, and what parts seemed to go together. One way I can imagine he might have done this would have been to read through the draft of his piece and circle all the parts that talk only about one chunk of the story - like getting to the party. We're going to try that today. Please read through your writing draft and circle the parts that seem to go together. If you have different sections use different colors to circle the sections that go together."

Book Connections

Young Cam Jansen and the Ice Skate Mystery is similar to *Amanda Pig*, written by Jean Van Leeuwen. Another *Young Cam Jansen* book included in this library is *Young Cam Jansen and the Dinosaur Game*. Good books to read before this are the *Nate the Great* series written by Marjorie Weinman Sharmat. The *Young Cam Jansen* books provide a great transition to the regular *Cam Jansen* series, as well as to the *Marvin Redpost* books written by Louis Sachar.

Genre
Short Chapter Book; Mystery

Teaching Uses
Independent Reading; Small Group Strategy Instruction; Teaching Writing

Index